The Missing Links

Formation and Decay of Economic Networks

James E. Rauch
editor

Russell Sage Foundation
New York

The Russell Sage Foundation

The Russell Sage Foundation, one of the oldest of America's general purpose foundations, was established in 1907 by Mrs. Margaret Olivia Sage for "the improvement of social and living conditions in the United States." The Foundation seeks to fulfill this mandate by fostering the development and dissemination of knowledge about the country's political, social, and economic problems. While the Foundation endeavors to assure the accuracy and objectivity of each book it publishes, the conclusions and interpretations in Russell Sage Foundation publications are those of the authors and not of the Foundation, its Trustees, or its staff. Publication by Russell Sage, therefore, does not imply Foundation endorsement.

Library of Congress Cataloging-in-Publication Data

The missing links : formation and decay of economic networks /
James E. Rauch, editor.
    p.   cm.
Includes bibliographical references and index.
ISBN 978-0-87154-709-5 (alk. paper)
1. Business networks.   2. Social networks.   3. Economics—Sociological
aspects.   4. Sociology—Economic aspects.   I. Rauch, James E.
HD69.S8M577 2007
302.4—dc22

                                                        2007008667

Text design by Suzanne Nichols.

RUSSELL SAGE FOUNDATION
112 East 64th Street, New York, New York 10021
10   9   8   7   6   5   4   3   2   1

CONTENTS

ABOUT THE AUTHORS

JAMES E. RAUCH is professor of economics at the University of California, San Diego, and research associate at the National Bureau of Economic Research.

RONALD S. BURT is the Hobart W. Williams Professor of Sociology and Strategy at the University of Chicago Graduate School of Business.

MATTHEW O. JACKSON is professor of economics at Stanford University and director of the Stanford Institute for Theoretical Economics.

RACHEL KRANTON is professor of economics at the University of Maryland.

BILL MCEVILY is an associate professor of strategic management at the Rotman School of Management, University of Toronto.

DEBORAH MINEHART is associate professor of economics at the University of Maryland.

KAIVAN MUNSHI is professor of economics at Brown University.

JOEL M. PODOLNY is the Dean and William S. Beinecke Professor of Management at the Yale School of Management.

RAY REAGANS is an associate professor of organizational behavior and theory at the Tepper School of Business, Carnegie Mellon University.

MARK ROSENZWEIG is the Frank Altschul Professor of Economics at Yale University.

TOBY STUART is the Charles Edward Wilson Professor of Business Administration at Harvard Business School.

JOEL WATSON is professor and chairperson of economics at the University of California, San Diego.

EZRA W. ZUCKERMAN is associate professor of strategic management and economic sociology at the Massachusetts Institute of Technology's Sloan School of Management.

To all of those who have used their networks on our behalves.

ACKNOWLEDGMENTS

This book is the culmination of the project of the Working Group on the Formation and Decay of Economic Networks, which met six times during the years 2002 to 2005 at the Russell Sage Foundation headquarters in New York City. Members of the group were Ronald S. Burt, Rachel E. Kranton, Kaivan Munshi, James E. Rauch, Toby E. Stuart, and Ezra W. Zuckerman. We are very grateful to the Russell Sage Foundation for its financial support of these workshops and to the many other social scientists, too numerous to list, who participated in these meetings and whose contributions and scholarship greatly enrich all of the chapters in this book.

Chapter 1

Introduction: On the Formation and Decay of Interdisciplinary Boundaries

Joel M. Podolny and James E. Rauch

Networks of personal connections are ubiquitous in economic life. Thirty to 60 percent of all new employment relations are estimated to be the result of personal ties (Bewley 1999). Networks are used extensively to raise capital, both by households (for example, through rotating savings and credit associations [Besley, Coate, and Loury 1993]) and by entrepreneurs (for example, through syndicates of venture capital firms [Sorenson and Stuart 2001]). Networks structure the diffusion of new technology among businesses, ranging from village farmers in less-developed countries (Bandiera and Rasul 2006) to manufacturers in Silicon Valley (Saxenian 1999). International trade and investments flow along paths determined by small networks of former employees of corporations such as IBM or giant networks such as that of overseas Chinese (Rauch 2001). The members of these economic networks find them valuable because they create or substitute for trust and because they provide "thick" information regarding business opportunities.

Given that networks are important social and economic phenomena, inquiry into the formation and decay of networks becomes important for at least two reasons. First, understanding network formation and decay is crucial to drawing out policy implications of research showing the impact of economic networks: once the value of these networks has been demonstrated, we would like to know whether and how to help them form or to prevent their decay. What policies can help ethnic business networks that promote entrepreneurship to form among groups where such networks are weak or absent? Is intervention justified to retard the decay of networks that help match workers to employment opportunities? Second, we need to understand the process of network formation and decay in order to handle the problem of endogeneity, which often plagues estimates of the impacts of economic networks. For example, technology may diffuse more rapidly between members of a network than among nonmembers; but at the same time, people who use the same technology have a greater incentive to talk to each other and build relationships. Without understanding how networks formed or broke up in the first place, the causal effect of networks on technological diffusion cannot be correctly identified and the impact of networks cannot be accurately estimated.

The fact that these questions deserve to be answered does not by itself imply that the answers will be enhanced by an interdisciplinary dialogue between economists and sociologists. Though economists and sociologists have addressed themselves to the issue of network formation and decay, they have worked from very different premises.

The Economics and Sociology Approaches to Network Formation and Decay

In the past, the economic conceptions of networks seemed to remove much of the stuff of networks that sociologists found interesting and important. Economic conceptions of networks seemed more often than not to abstract from structural properties such as centrality, density, structural equivalence, and role equivalence—structural properties that arguably had been the central concern of the sociological perspective on networks from the mid-seventies to the mid-nineties. Moreover, in those instances in which economists did find the pattern of network ties to be of interest (Jackson and Watts 2002), the theoretical treatment of structure required assumptions that made their approach too abstract for empirical research. This is evident from chapter 2 in this volume, Matthew O. Jackson's survey of the economics literature on network formation. Economic conceptions of networks also seemed to treat an actor's links within a network as something apart from the actor's self, a fact that seemed increasingly to trouble sociologists from the mid-1990s on, as they came to conceptualize networks as constituent elements of identity. Because the sociologists believed that networks informed and shaped preferences, they thought it made little sense to treat networks as a form of capital that is analytically separate from an actor and thus something in which an actor chooses to make or not make investments.

The sociological conception of networks troubled economists insofar as it did not lend itself to equilibrium conceptions of markets or economic organization. So a sociologist might posit that one particular pattern of ties is more valuable than another, but the sociologist could not explain why one actor has the more valuable pattern and the other does not. Does the actor with the more valuable network pattern have qualities that the other actor with the less valuable pattern does not? If so, then network patterns are simply epiphenomenal, reducible to some innate characteristics of the actors. This concern is highlighted in chapter 4, Toby Stuart's survey of the sociological literature on network formation. If not, then there seems a dissatisfying indeterminateness about the actual pattern of ties that exists. Sociologists would point to chance and path dependence as alternative explanations for the pattern of ties. However, for most economists, these explanations hardly constitute a theory: chance is not a theory, but a null, and the idea that the pattern of ties at time t + 1 is a determined by the pattern of ties at time t simply avoids the question of what determines the initial pattern of ties.

This book offers a new convergence between economists' and sociologists' approaches to the study of networks. In order to lay out the features of this convergence, it will be helpful to think about a theory of network formation and decay as consisting of three phases or aspects. The first is the initial state, what one might call the "state of nature," that exists at the start of the process of network formation and decay. The second is the mechanism underlying the change in the pattern of network ties. The third is the developed state, the state of the network after the mechanism has operated on what exists in the "state of nature."

Traditionally, sociologists and economists differed in the ways in which they conceptualized each of these aspects. Economists tended to conceptualize the "state of nature" as consisting of independent, atomized actors who would make decisions regarding with whom they should or should not form links. Such imagery has a strong affinity with that in other areas of economic research, such as the literature on labor markets, where atomistic individuals and firms make decisions that result in matches. Sociologists, by contrast, have tended to regard the notion of atomized actors as an analytical fiction that facilitates modeling but obscures the fact that one never can find individuals who exist outside a web of social relations. Individuals are born into a set of relations, and although their actual ties may change over time, sociologists posit that the self is never analytically separate from the ties connecting it to others. Mark S. Granovetter (1985) articulated such a position in his manifesto-like article on the "embeddedness" of economic action, but the basic idea has theoretical roots going back to the classic theorists such as Emile Durkheim (1947) and Georg Simmel (1964).[1]

These different images of the state of nature lent themselves to different explanatory mechanisms of tie formation and decay. The economic imagery lent itself to functional agent-based mechanisms. To the extent that ex ante conditions are characterized by atomized actors with given interests, information, assets, and property rights, the explanation for what links do and do not form is ultimately rooted in the distribution of interest, information, assets, and property rights. The relational contracting literature provided numerous examples of work that is indicative of these agent-based explanations (see, for example, Williamson 1991; Baker, Gibbons, and Murphy 1999; McMillan and Woodruff 1999). Put crudely, in the beginning there are actors and broad environmental conditions; ties then arise, and to understand which actors are tied and which are not, one needs to focus only on the characteristics of the individual actors.

Unlike economists, sociologists did not look to the characteristics of actors to understand the formation and dissolution of ties; rather, they looked to the preexisting pattern of ties as the fundamental determinant of subsequent tie formation. To understand who will form links with an actor at a given time period, one first needs to understand with whom that actor already has links—in effect, one must know the actor's position in the network. Ranjay Gulati's (1995) work on alliance formation provided a particularly straightforward illustration of a positional mechanism. In his work, the likelihood that two firms will form an alliance is determined primarily by the extent to which those two firms have ties to the same other firms. These ties to common others represent a form of reputational control that fosters cooperation. Other illustrations of a positional logic underlying the pattern of tie formation were Olav Sorenson and Toby E. Stuart's (2001) examination of the geographical dispersion of venture capital syndicates and David Robinson and Stuart's (forthcoming) examination of the pattern of equity relations between pharmaceutical and biotechnology firms. In both of these studies, an actor's position in the network at a particular time is the clearest determinant of the links that will or will not form at a later time.

These different posited mechanisms underlying the changing pattern of ties in turn gave rise to different "end," or "developed," states. In the economic models, the end, or developed, state was an equilibrium state; absent a change in environmental conditions or a change in the characteristics of the actors in the model, there would be no change in the pattern of ties. An economic model would be incomplete if it failed to specify an end state in which no actor had the incentive and ability to remove existing links or form new ones.

Sociological accounts of network formation and decay generally imply no such equilibrium; sociologists seek to understand how networks unfold over time without worrying about whether the unfolding is converging on a stable state. Because sociologists generally have not been concerned about specifying the conditions for a stable end state, it is probably more accurate to say that sociologists are interested in network change and evolution, rather than in network formation. The word "formation" implies the coming into being of a stable pattern—something is formed; the word is thus arguably more compatible with the way that economists have traditionally looked at networks than with sociologists' view. Table 1.1 summarizes the interdisciplinary differences that we have just discussed.

For sociologists, the bottom-line message from economists is the

Table 1.1   A Comparison of Sociological and Economic Perspectives

	Sociology	Economics
State of Nature (t − 1)	Linked nodes	Independent nodes
Mechanism	Positional	Agent-based
Developed State (t)	Linked nodes	Equilibrium configuration
Framing of Network Change	Evolution	Formation

Source: Authors' compilation.

need to take into account agent heterogeneity and self-selection when evaluating network effects on agent performance. For economists, the bottom-line message from sociologists is the need to take into account the ways in which "embeddedness" and past interactions constrain or guide current formation and decay of network links. The new convergence mentioned previously between economists and sociologists' approaches results from both groups' responses to these bottom-line messages from the other discipline, and is reflected in chapters 6 to 8 in this volume. By combining the sociology and economics approaches to network formation and decay, both groups can obtain more theoretically satisfying accounts of network evolution (formation and decay) and more reliable methods of econometrically identifying network effects. Economists, with their concern for evaluating the efficiency of model outcomes, can discover new levers for policy intervention.

The advances in our understanding of formation and decay of economic networks made possible by interdisciplinary dialogue may be of relevance to the vast "social interactions" literature, much of which is implicitly concerned with noneconomic networks. Traditionally, this research has ignored network structure and confined analysis to average behavior in a neighborhood or peer group, or to other summary statistics such as the percentages of individuals who choose certain actions (Durlauf and Cohen-Cole 2004; Brock and Durlauf 2006). However, more recently this literature has begun to consider detailed network structures, using techniques similar to those used by sociologists, such as asking individuals for their contact lists (see Echenique, Fryer, and Kaufman 2006). To get a sense for how these insights could be useful to recent social-interactions research, consider a study of the impact of having friends who smoke on the incidence of teenage smoking. A researcher concerned with endogeneity (smokers congregate where smoking is legal and form friendships) could use assignment to the same elementary school classroom (past interaction) as an instrument for current friendships.

The Strategy of this Book

This volume begins with surveys of the economics and sociology literatures on network formation and decay in order to flesh out these skeletal descriptions of the two approaches. Each survey is followed by an original, paradigmatic illustration of that approach. These chapters are examples of best practice that show off the virtues of each approach to network formation and decay. The book concludes with three chapters that attempt to merge the economics and sociology approaches and thereby address the key shortcomings of the respective literatures. In order to facilitate interdisciplinary understanding, technical detail is kept to a minimum in all chapters.

Matthew Jackson begins his survey of the economics literature (chapter 2) by describing the historical roots of the economics approach to network formation and decay. These led up to Jackson's seminal 1996 article, with Asher Wolinsky, "A Strategic Model of Social and Economic Networks," in which they introduced the key concept of "pairwise stability." A network is pairwise stable if it satisfies two conditions. The first condition is that if a link between two agents is absent then it cannot be that both agents would benefit by adding that link. The second condition is that if a link between two agents is present, then it cannot be that either agent would benefit from deleting that link. Jackson then shows by example that "efficient" networks that maximize the sum of payoffs to all the agents need not be pairwise stable, and that pairwise stable networks need not be efficient. The reason is that when choosing whether to form or maintain links, an agent in a network does not take into account his impact on relationships between other pairs of agents who are connected indirectly through him. The importance, in the economics approach, of both the complete freedom of choice regarding formation and decay (deletion) of network links and the concern with efficiency (social welfare) are in sharp contrast to the features of the sociology approach.

Jackson goes on to describe the numerous applications of the economics approach. It can be applied to analyzing networks with different substantive content of the agents and links, such as collaborations between firms, trading alliances between countries, and sharing of information between employees and job seekers; and to explaining different patterns of the links themselves, such as high local clustering and short distances between any two randomly selected agents (the "small world" phenomenon). All of these applications remain at the level of theory, however. Chapter 2 concludes with a comparison of economists' choice-based approach to network formation and decay with the chance-based approach favored by natural scientists.

In chapter 3, Rachel Kranton and Deborah Minehart analyze the formation of industrial supply relationships by constructing a model of strategic network formation that is similar to most models in the economics literature. Each member of a group of identical manufacturers decides whether to form links to each supplier in a similarly undifferentiated group. These decisions result in a "buyer-supplier" network. To analyze which network structures will form, Kranton and Minehart first solve for the profits of the manufacturers, given the existing network structures, then work backward to ascertain what ties the manufacturers will form, given the profits they anticipate. The key tradeoff is between the advantages of forming links to suppliers who are well connected and forming links to an exclusive set of suppliers. A manufacturer might have less incentive to link to a supplier who has many other customers, for the manufacturer would anticipate paying that supplier a high price. On the other hand, suppliers who anticipate charging and getting high prices also have a greater incentive to make quality-enhancing investments. Without an analysis of the buyer-supplier network *in toto*, this tradeoff would not become evident.

Kranton and Minehart find that when the suppliers' investments are cheap, every manufacturer wants to form one large network with excess capacity—one with more than enough suppliers to meet demand from all the manufacturers. The manufacturers can then pay a low price. In contrast, when suppliers' investments are expensive, every manufacturer wants to form a smaller network without excess capacity. Each network should have the minimum number of manufacturers necessary to raise the price enough to cover the cost of the quality-enhancing investments by the suppliers. In other words, even when networks are capacity-constrained, manufacturers prefer to share suppliers rather than maintain exclusive supply networks.

In chapter 4, Toby E. Stuart offers a detailed assessment of the sociology literature on the formation of economic networks, with particular emphasis on "horizontal networks" among organizations in a given industry or field. Stuart first reviews some of the theoretical accounts for why networks should matter in markets. Because contracts cannot remove all of the transactional risk in markets, networks become important in promoting market-based relationships. Stuart then distinguishes the mechanisms whereby networks enable market exchange when contractual mechanisms are insufficient. First, networks are conduits—or "pipes"—for the diffusion of information about numerous potential exchange partners. Second, in addition to being conduits for information, the pattern of ties can be an indicator of otherwise unobservable differences in the competence of potential exchange partners. Third, to the degree that brokers emerge in the pattern of exchange relations, these brokers can bridge otherwise disconnected exchange partners. Fourth, networks encourage market exchanges by promoting a sense of obligation among potential exchange partners. Finally, networks contribute to market exchanges by serving as a reputational control mechanism, discouraging dishonest behavior.

After reviewing the five mechanisms by which networks promote exchange—information diffusion, attributions of competence, brokerage, obligations, and sanctions—Stuart discusses sociological accounts for the origins of networks in markets. He distinguishes three mechanisms: trust, reciprocity, and homophily. A network tie forms between two individuals A & B when A expects that B will act in a way that is consistent with A's interests and B expects that A will act in a way that is consistent with B's interests. A network link also forms between individuals to the degree that each feels the need to give back to the other as a response to what each has received in the past. Finally, a network tie forms among individuals to the degree that the two are alike. Stuart briefly compares these sociological explanations of the origins of networks in markets with economic explanations.

Stuart criticizes sociological treatments of network effects that simply assume the exogeneity of networks without providing proof of it. He contends that sociologists must take seriously the possibility that an actor's network position is simply the spurious manifestation of some nonpositional attribute. Even if the nonpositional attribute is more difficult to empirically identify, it is incumbent on sociologists to rule out the potential spuriousness. Such an argument can be understood as an acknowledgment if not internalization of the fact that agent-based mechanisms could be determinative of the network patterns and their resulting effects.

In chapter 5, Ronald S. Burt looks at the relationship between network stability and reputation stability. Burt argues that if reputational differences are grounded in stable differences in human capital, then one would not expect differences in reputational stability to be correlated with differences in networks. However, drawing on his own theory of structural holes as well as the work of other sociologists who have written on the topic of social capital, Burt argues that differences in reputational stability will be affected by the "relational embedding" around an actor. Relational embedding refers to the extent to which a focal actor is surrounded by others who are themselves connected to one another. In effect, Burt looks at the social closure in the network around the focal actor; he focuses on both the level of closure among those to whom the focal actor is directly connected and the level of closure among those who are one step removed—that is, the level of closure involving friends of friends.

In a study of reputational stability and networks among bankers and analysts in a financial-service firm in the late 1990s, Burt finds that greater closure is associated with more reputational stability. Burt then looks at the effect of closure on the quality of affect and the longevity of relationships. He concludes that closure has a positive impact on both affect and longevity, but the effect of closure on the continuity of a relationship declines with the relationship's age. As the relationship gets older, the strength of the relationship becomes more important than closure in determining the likelihood that the relationship will last.

The analysis in this chapter exemplifies some of the defining characteristics of the traditional sociological approach. The initial state or state of nature is an embedded state that in this case is characterized by the amount of closure around an individual. This degree of closure becomes a fundamental mechanism for understanding the stability of relations. To the degree that a relationship remains stable, that relation becomes a force of closure acting on other dyads in the network. Also, as with much of the traditional sociological work, it is hard to rule out the possibility that network closure and reputational instability are both affected by underlying differences in actors. Suppose, for example, that some actors are more entrepreneurial, taking on new risks and new challenges; others are less so. One might expect the more entrepreneurial individuals to have both less stable networks and also more unstable reputations.

Chapter 6 is the first of three chapters that attempt to merge the economics and sociology approaches to economic-network formation and decay. Ray E. Reagans, Ezra Zuckerman, and Bill McEvily move beyond a critique of the sociology literature and develop a strategy for teasing apart positional determinants of performance from individual determinants of performance. They argue that one can exploit the multilevel nature of group-performance data to separate out the positional determinants of performance from individual-level determinants. If individuals in a population participate in multiple groups, then it is possible to disentangle individual-level determinants of a group's performance from the positional determinants that arise out of the group's collective network of relations. The performance history of the groups with which an individual is associated forms a proxy for the individual's skill, and controlling for the skill of all the individuals on a team, it is possible to assess how the group's network explains the remaining variation in performance. The group's current network is measured on the basis of their past interactions with one another and with members of other groups. This strategy is adopted to minimize concern about reverse causality from group performance to network structure, but here it is more important to note that it reflects the sociological belief that networks are "sticky," so that past interaction guides current interaction.

In the conclusion of chapter 6, Reagans, Zuckerman, and McEvily note some limitations of this approach. It does not deal with all concerns that one might have about trying to distinguish whether position or person is ultimately the more fundamental determinant of networks and their consequences, but it does provide an approach for a joint consideration of the mechanisms that have traditionally not been jointly considered by economists or sociologists.

Whereas chapter 6 represents sociologists' acknowledgment of agent-based mechanisms underlying networks and their effects, chapter 7, by Kaivan Munshi and Mark Rosenzweig, and chapter 8, by James E. Rauch and Joel Watson, represent economic models in which the state of nature is characterized by a positional structure. Chapter 7 is an empirical examination of the decay of traditional networks in India. The network in which the authors are interested is the "jati," the term for a local subcaste. Exit from the subcaste is operationalized either as marrying outside the jati or migrating from the geographic locale of the jati. Munshi and Rosenzweig find that English-language schooling and relative wealth are positively related to the likelihood of exit. English schooling provides access to white-collar jobs, whereas the caste-based networks are concentrated in blue-collar jobs. Greater relative wealth makes an individual less likely to use the jati for "insurance" in the event of personal hardship over some time period. The state of nature, in which individuals are part of the jati network, is thus a highly structured one reflecting the embeddedness of economic actors in webs of social ties; individuals occupy distinct positions, and agent-based mechanisms then explain the change in the structure.

Munshi and Rosenzweig find that some urban caste-based networks that help members find blue-collar jobs are decaying as globalization increases the attractiveness of English-language schooling and hence exit from these networks. However, the rural caste-based networks that provide insurance are not decaying, despite the increase in wealth inequality generated by the phase of technological progress called the Green Revolution. Technological progress made farming much more attractive to land-owning families, causing the wealthier households to be less likely to migrate—that is, exit their networks. A deeper understanding of the process of network evolution is required to predict the impact of economic growth on these networks. Note that network decay as described in this chapter, unlike in the examples in chapter 5, entails not just disappearance of links but diminution of the capacity of the entire network to serve its members.

Chapter 8, by Rauch and Watson, is a theoretical piece, with the objective of deepening understanding of how various policies affect the formation of networks. Specifically, Rauch and Watson posit a model economy with a network structure of firm-centered clusters and cross-firm bridges. They then investigate how policies affect the equilibrium proportion of clusters and bridges in the model economy. Rational agents choose their networks, but they choose them within the context of an existing network structure in which all the agents are situated. This existing network structure is in turn generated by past interaction.

Rauch and Watson find that agents have inadequate incentives to form cross-firm bridges. Enforcement of restrictive employment contracts such as noncompete or nonsolicitation covenants makes firm-centered clusters less attractive and thereby encourages the alternative, bridges. Bridges are also associated with exchange across communities. The lack of adequate incentives to form bridges therefore leads to excessive exchange within a community or "border effects" that are too large. It follows that, looking across communities such as American states, those that more strongly enforce restrictive employment covenants could be expected to have smaller border effects.

Though the Rauch and Watson model provides new insights for policy, it is a "steady state" model that lacks the dynamics needed to make it useful for econometric identification of network effects. We would like to see evolution from exogenous initial conditions to an equilibrium network structure, so that the initial conditions can provide instruments for network position when evaluating the impact of position on performance.

Conclusion

This brief review of the chapters of this volume should make clear the nature of the disciplinary convergence between economics and sociology around the subject of the formation and decay of economic networks. First, to use the term that Granovetter popularized (1985), sociologists and economists are presuming an embedded context when they study network formation and decay. Second, both sociologists and economists are increasingly turning their attention to studying agent-based mechanisms for networks and their effects. Sociologists attend to such mechanisms because they wish to control for them in an effort to more convincingly demonstrate the relevance of positional mechanisms. Nevertheless, the interdisciplinary attention to agent-based mechanisms, like the interdisciplinary presumption of an embedded context, seems to be ensuring a more productive dialogue between economists and sociologists as they investigate networks and their effects. The last three chapters in this volume thus constitute evidence of real network formation across disciplinary boundaries.

Notes

1. One of the founding figures of the field of organizational behavior, James March, offered a pithy articulation of the sociological view when he once commented, "It is not obvious that in the beginning, God created individuals. Rather, God may have created groups, communities, or some other such basic units, and individuals may have simply been parts of those units in the same way that we think of a cell as being part of a body."

References

Baker, George P., Robert S. Gibbons, and Kevin J. Murphy. 1999. "Informal Authority in Organizations." *Journal of Law, Economics, and Organization* 15(1): 56-73.

Bandiera, Oriana, and Imran Rasul. 2006. "Social Networks and Technology Adoption in Northern Mozambique." *Economic Journal* 116(514): 869–902.

Besley, Timothy, Stephen Coate, and Glenn Loury. 1993. "The Economics of Rotating Savings and Credit Associations." *American Economic Review* 83(4): 792–810.

Bewley, Truman F. 1999. *Why Wages Don't Fall During a Recession*. Cambridge, Mass.: Harvard University Press.

Brock, William, and Steven Durlauf. 2006. "Multinomial Choice with Social Interactions." In *The Economy as an Evolving Complex System III*, edited by Lawrence Blume and Steven Durlauf. New York: Oxford University Press.

Durkheim, Emile. 1947. *The Division of Labor in Society*. New York: Free Press.

Durlauf, Steven, and Ethan Cohen-Cole. 2004. "Social Interactions Models." In *Encyclopedia of Social Measurement*, edited by Kimberly Lempf-Leonard. San Diego, Calif.: Academic Press.

Echenique, Federico, Roland G. Fryer, Jr., and Alex Kaufman. 2006. "Is School Segregation Good or Bad?" *American Economic Review* 96(2): 265–69.

Granovetter, Mark S. 1985. "Economic Action and Social Structure: The Problem of Embeddedness." *American Journal of Sociology* 91(3): 481–510.

Gulati, Ranjay. 1995. "Social Structure and Alliance Formation Patterns: A Longitudinal Analysis." *Administrative Science Quarterly* 38(4): 619–52.

Jackson, Matthew O., and Alison Watts. 2002. "The Evolution of Social and Economic Networks." *Journal of Economic Theory* 106(2): 265–95.

Jackson, Matthew, and Asher Wolinsky. 1996. "A Strategic Model of Social and Economic Networks." *Journal of Economic Theory* 71(1): 44–74.

McMillan, John, and Christopher Woodruff. 1999. "Inter-Firm Relations and Informal Credit in Vietnam." *Quarterly Journal of Economics* 114(4): 1285–1320.

Rauch, James E. 2001. "Business and Social Networks in International Trade." *Journal of Economic Literature* 39(4): 1177–1203.

Robinson, David, and Toby E. Stuart. Forthcoming. "Financial Contracting in Biotech Strategic Alliances." *Journal of Law and Economics*.

Saxenian, AnnaLee. 1999. *Silicon Valley's New Immigrant Entrepreneurs*. San Francisco, Calif.: Public Policy Institute of California.

Simmel, Georg. 1964. *The Sociology of Georg Simmel*. Translated by Kurt H. Wolff. New York: Free Press.

Sorenson, Olav, and Toby E. Stuart. 2001. "Syndication Networks and the Spatial Distribution of Venture Capital Investments." *American Journal of Sociology* 106(6): 1546–88.

Williamson, Oliver E. 1991. "Comparative Economic Organization: The Analysis of Discrete Structural Alternatives." *Administrative Science Quarterly* 36(2): 269–96.

Part I

The Economics Approach

Chapter 2

The Study of Social Networks in Economics

Matthew O. Jackson

As Joel Podolny and James Rauch point out in chapter 1 of this volume, "On the Formation and Decay of Interdisciplinary Boundaries," social networks are endemic to economic interactions. The rise of what might be called "social economics" comes very much from the realization by economists that there are many economic interactions where the social context is not a second-order consideration, but is actually a primary driver of behaviors and outcomes. Obvious examples range from the primary role of social networks for people looking for jobs to their influence on decisions of which products to buy, how much education to pursue, and whether or not to undertake criminal activity.

Although the widespread realization of the importance of the embeddedness of economic activity in social settings has been fundamental to sociologists for some time, and quite eloquently exposited by Mark Granovetter (1974/1995), it was largely ignored by economists until the last decade. The recent interest comes from many economic models having been pushed to their limits, and the consequent discovery that social circumstances can help explain observed economic phenomena (for example, persistent wage inequality) in ways that narrower economic models cannot. I draw a parallel to the recent rise of interest in "behavioral economics," which comes from the realization that a deeper exploration of the psychological underpinnings of human behavior can help enrich the modeling of economic decision makers. Similarly, the recent rise of interest in social economics comes from a realization that a deeper exploration of the social underpinnings of human behavior can enrich the modeling of economic interactions. This is important to understand because it actually results in a distinction with regard to the interest in social networks in economics. Much of the interest comes from a social economics perspective, where social context provides an enriching of economic models, but the ultimate interest is in understanding the allocation of scarce resources. However, as exposure to the literature on social networks has grown, so has the interest in understanding social structure independent of its effect on economic behavior. Both of these motivations lead to bridges with sociology, but with differences in the interface and the extent to which sociologists are part of the intended audience of the studies.

In this chapter I provide an overview of the economics literature on economic and social networks. The plan is to examine the evolution of that literature, and in doing so to provide an idea of the approaches that have been taken and the perspective from which networks have been analyzed. Given the objectives of this volume, I am not attempting to provide a detailed description of what has been asked and answered by the literature,[1] but rather to examine what economists might hope to gain from the analysis and how their paradigm has influenced their approach and the questions that they have tended to ask, and to cite some examples of the research. The discussion does not require any familiarity with the economics literature.

Some Background on Perspective

Let me emphasize the obvious from the outset: much of the economic study of interactions in a social context lies within a "rational choice" framework. So as not to get side-tracked on a discussion of what is embodied in the notion of rationality, let me be a bit more specific. One of the basic presumptions that underlies much of the economic modeling of network formation is the view that the individuals involved in networks choose whom to interact with.[2] Individuals are assumed to form or maintain relationships that they find beneficial, and avoid or remove themselves from relationships that are not beneficial. This is sometimes captured through equilibrium notions of network formation, but is also modeled through various dynamics, as well as agent-based models where certain heuristics are specified that govern behavior. This choice perspective traces the structure and the properties of networks back to the costs and benefits that they bestow upon their participants. This does not always presume that the individuals are fully rational or cognizant of their potential options, or even that they are "individuals" rather than groups or organizations. But, most important, on some level the analyses generally embody the idea that networks where there are substantial gains from forming new relationships or terminating old ones will be more ephemeral than networks where no such gains exist. What to conclude beyond this is open to more debate.

Along with this point of view comes an interest in the welfare implications of the interaction for the society in question. This interest can be understood from two directions. First, once one begins by working with decisionmaking actors who somehow weigh costs against benefits, one is clearly led to the question of how well the system performs. Costs and benefits need to be carefully spelled out, and so there is a natural metric with which to evaluate the impact of a social network or changes in a social network. Second, since some of the interest in social surroundings comes from the fact that models that ignore those surroundings are unable to explain some observed phenomena, such as persistence in inequality among different groups in terms of their employment or wages, one is led back to the issue of why the phenomena are important to begin with. The interest in these issues often emerges from some fairness criteria or from an overall efficiency perspective, where there is a question of whether or not a market is operating as efficiently as it should or could. When markets are viewed in a social context, it can change the ways one predicts resources will be allocated. This then leads back to some welfarist evaluation of the network and the behaviors that emerge.

Another aspect of economists' thinking is worth emphasizing. Their interest tends to go beyond describing what is to explaining why things are the way they are. This may also seem to be an obvious point, but differences in researchers' perspectives on this issue are often a basic source of misunderstanding and miscommunication. This interest in the "why" naturally leads to some abstraction away from the full detail of a setting, which can lead to the omission of important factors. At the same time, the tendency toward abstract modeling can help provide insights into why certain regularities might appear in social and economic networks. For instance, later I will discuss how some fundamental economic reasoning can help explain "small-world" network phenomena.

With this background perspective in mind, let me now turn to an overview of the literature.

An Overview of the Incorporation of Networks into Economics

Although the explosion in networks studies in economics has largely taken place in the last decade, there was much earlier research where social networks were central in economic studies.[3] Some of the earliest studies, by Charles A. Myers and George P. Shultz (1951) and Albert Rees and Shultz (1971), involved the documentation of the importance of social networks as means of obtaining jobs; these served as important precursors to Mark Granovetter's (1973, 1974/1995) seminal work. The interest in social networks in the context of labor markets continued, and two further papers of note were important early bridges between the sociology literature and the economics literature. These were studies, by Scott Boorman (1975) and James Montgomery (1991), that examined the strength of weak ties in labor contact networks, where individuals make explicit choices about the strong and weak ties that they maintain with an eye to the impact this has on their employment and wages. These studies helped enrich the study of the strength of weak ties by examining the explicit trade-offs between them from a given person's perspective and also provided new insights into employment and wages. These studies already exhibit the choice-based approach discussed earlier.

Another place where the importance of network externalities

was quite evident was in product-adoption decisions. One cannot view the decisions of individuals in isolation in many product choices, such as those concerning software or technology-based products where some sort of standards are needed, or where individuals care about the compatibility of their product choices with those of others.

The term "network externality" embodies such relationships. Here there can be effects where groups of consumers lock in on an inferior technology simply because it is pervasive, even when it is clear that some other technology is superior. This results in interesting dynamics in a product's market over time and also in the ways in which firms try to sell such products. Important work on this was done by Michael Katz and Carl Shapiro (see Katz and Shapiro 1994 and Economides 1996 for surveys). Although this work involved studies where social pressures were critical, the attention was mainly on situations where individuals cared about population averages in activities and so the specifics of a social network never entered into the picture in a meaningful way.[4]

This has changed recently, with a renaissance in the diffusion literature, where explicit social network structures are included (I mention some references at the end of this chapter).

Cooperative-Game Theory

An early example of the explicit modeling of network structures, with some perspective on their influence on economic outcomes came through the cooperative-game theory literature. Although the modeling approach is quite abstract, cooperative games are meant to capture a variety of productive enterprises where the cooperation among individuals is fruitful. Into this setting, Roger Myerson (1977) introduced graph structures, with a premise that groups can only cooperate to the extent that they are path-connected, meaning that they can communicate. People who can communicate can cooperate, and generally, in cooperative-game settings, cooperation leads to higher production or utility than separate efforts. Myerson's interest was not in modeling social networks per se but in characterizing a cooperative-game-theoretic solution concept (the Shapley value) without directly imposing a technical condition that was common before that (an additivity axiom). Imposing conditions on how cooperation depended on the communication graph in place and how players were rewarded for their cooperation, Myerson produced a new prediction of how the value should be split among the members of a society, which is now referred to as the Myerson value. A number of studies of cooperative games have followed up on this work (for example, see the overview by Slikker and van den Nouweland 2001).[5] A more direct precursor to the recent modeling of network formation emerged when Robert Aumann and Roger Myerson (1988) examined a three-player example where players could propose to open a communication link with one another. In this setting players anticipate the effect that communication has on cooperative opportunities, and thus ultimately on the value that they will obtain, and then propose links with this in mind.

Modeling the Costs and Benefits of Network Formation

Although the cooperative-games literature found interesting implications of communication structures, the strategic (or game-theoretic) modeling of strategic network formation took off when networks became the basic social structure governing interactions rather than an extension to a cooperative game.

This first appeared in work by Matthew Jackson and Asher Wolinsky (1996). In their modeling, the network of relationships among individuals leads to a productive, or utility, value. That is, costs and benefits to individuals are specified as a function of what the network looks like. Then viewing the individuals as self-interested parties who form and sever links in order to maximize their eventual benefits (net of the cost of creating or maintaining links), one can make predictions about which networks will form.

Outlining this approach is useful, as it typifies much of the recent literature from the economics perspective. The networks of relationships are represented by a graph, for instance, captured via an $n \times n$ matrix, g, where n is the number of individuals in question. In many applications, the entries of the matrix take on a value 1 if the two individuals are linked and a value zero if they are not. If this is a network of friendships, it would be nondirected so that it is a symmetric matrix ($g_{ij} = 1$ if and only if $g_{ji} = 1$), but in other situations where relationships indicate things such as trust, the links could be directed.

The important aspect is that there is some utility or productive value that is realized as a function of the network. That is, there is a function $u_i(g)$ that indicates the value or utility (benefits net of costs) that accrues to individual i if the network of relationships in the society is described by g. If this is a network of buyers and sellers, this would be the profits that would be anticipated based on the trades that would occur if the network were g. If this is a network of alliances among countries, this would be the anticipated welfare of each country as a function of the alliances in place. If this is a network of friendships, this might be some proxy for the happiness or well-being of each individual as a function of the relationships in the society. If this is a network of job contacts, this might be the future expected earnings of an individual as a function of who knows whom.

With such a utility function in hand, we then see the two ingredients of the approach underlying much of the economic discussion of network formation.

The payoffs to each individual underlie the incentives to form or sever links, and they also provide the basis for a welfare evaluation.

Let us start with the welfare considerations. If a network leads to higher payoffs for all individuals in a society, then there is an obvious sense in which it improves welfare. This is a standard notion known as Pareto dominance (named after Vilfredo Pareto, who introduced the idea in the late nineteenth century). We can also ask for a stronger notion of efficiency, namely, that a network maximize the total payoffs to the individuals in a society. This idea has its roots in utilitarianism and is more controversial than Pareto efficiency, but is very useful in network contexts as it can often be used to single out a specific network architecture as maximizing total welfare and is natural in contexts where transfers can be made among individuals, which is the case in many economic applications.

In terms of the choice considerations, the individuals in a society can be modeled as forming or breaking relationships depending on whether the links improve or hurt the individuals' overall utility or payoff. The notion of pairwise stability, introduced by Jackson and

Wolinsky (1996), is a simple way of embodying this principle. A network is pairwise stable if:[6]

- A link between two individuals is absent from the network then it cannot be that both individuals would benefit from adding the link (with at least one benefiting strictly).

- A link between two individuals is present in a network then it cannot be that either individual would strictly benefit from deleting that link.

This concept captures the discretion of individuals in the links they are involved with, and the response of individuals to the costs and benefits they see from network relationships.

This notion is appropriate when it takes consent to form a relationship, as in many applications, but it is just one way of modeling which networks one expects to form. There are many alternatives to this notion that have been explored in the literature, but they basically keep with the same principles of discretion in forming links and the response to incentives. What has been varied is how much discretion people have and how rational they are in responding to incentives.

For example, one can allow individuals to consider changing multiple relationships at a time rather than just considering one relationship at a time (see, for example, Gilles and Sarangi forthcoming). One can also allow groups to coordinate their changes in relationships (for instance, seceding from a network and forming new relationships; see Dutta and Mutuswami 1997; Jackson and van den Nouweland 2005). In the case where relationships are directed, it may be that consent is not needed so that agents can unilaterally form new relationships (for example, Bala and Goyal 2000). One can also model this as a dynamic process where agents potentially make mistakes over time and the network gradually evolves (for example, Jackson and Watts 2002). There are potential variations based on whether or not agents anticipate the further changes that will occur in the network (see, for example, Page, Wooders, and Kamat 2005; Dutta, Ghosal, and Ray 2005; Mauleon and Vannetelbosch 2004; and Herings, Mauleon, and Vannetelbosch 2004).

An example helps illustrate the approach and some of the types of questions that have been asked. Consider a very stylized model of the value of relationships, which was one of the examples from Jackson and Wolinsky (1996), called the connections model.

Here, relationships convey both direct and indirect benefits. The direct benefits are based on the interaction between two individuals, for instance, the exchange of favors or information, while the indirect benefits come from the access to friends of friends. In the connections model, a given individual gets a benefit of δ from each direct relationship that he or she has. The individual also gets a benefit of δ^2 for each other individual who has a minimum path length of 2 to the individual. This is the value of the friend of a friend. When δ is less than 1, the value of a friend of a friend is less than the value of a friend. The individual gets a value of δ^3 for individuals at a distance of 3, and so forth. Maintaining relationships is also costly in terms of time and effort, and so each direct relationship results in some cost to maintain, c.

Figure 2.1 gives the utility payoffs under the connections model for a particular network of relationships among five individuals.

To get a feeling for the concepts, we can ask whether or not this network is pairwise stable. For instance, it has to be that $\delta > c$ in order for 3 to be willing to maintain the link with 5. If $\delta < c$, this network would not be pairwise stable. It would also have to be that $\delta^3 > (\delta^2 - c)$ in order for 1 and 5 not to want to form a link. More generally it is not hard to deduce properties that pairwise stable networks will need to have as a function of the benefits (captured through the parameter δ) and the costs (captured through the parameter c).

We can also characterize the networks that are efficient in this model. There are only three simple architectures that can be efficient: if c is low enough relative to δ, then the unique efficient network is a complete network (every individual is directly linked to every other individual). The idea here is that direct relationships are more valuable than indirect ones, so if the cost of a relationship is small enough, then it is preferable to have all potential relationships be direct relationships. If, instead, the cost is very high relative to the benefits, then we see the opposite extreme where the empty net-

Figure 2.1   Payoffs in the Connections Model

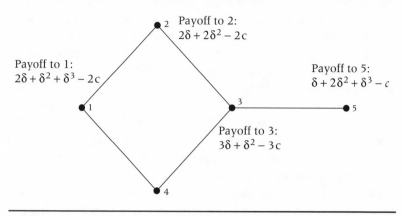

Payoff to 2:
$2\delta + 2\delta^2 - 2c$

Payoff to 1:
$2\delta + \delta^2 + \delta^3 - 2c$

Payoff to 5:
$\delta + 2\delta^2 + \delta^3 - c$

Payoff to 3:
$3\delta + \delta^2 - 3c$

Source: Author's compilation.

work will be the only efficient network, as costs simply outweigh whatever potential benefits there may be. The interesting case is the middle range of costs relative to benefits. In that range, it turns out that there is a unique efficient architecture (efficient in that it maximizes the total society utility), which is a "star" network. So, the efficient network structure is to have a single individual who is connected to each other individual, but where the other individuals are only connected to this center individual. A strong intuition underlies why this configuration is the efficient one. It connects all members of society and does so with a minimal number of links. Also, it does so in a way that makes sure that every individual is at a distance of at most two from every other individual. Unless the cost is so low that two indirectly connected individuals would gain by shortening the distance between them (in which case we would fall in the range of costs where the complete network is efficient), there is no way to improve the total utility of the society by altering the network.

A Tension Between Individual Incentives and Societal Welfare

The connections model illustrates another fundamental point: that there can be a disparity between the networks that are efficient and those that are formed at the discretion of individuals. For example, in the "star" model, the center of a star bears a large cost of maintaining many relationships. The center thus provides a service to the society in providing many indirect relationships between other pairs of individuals. If the center of the star is not compensated somehow for maintaining these relationships (for example, in a case where $c > \delta$), it can turn out that the star is not pairwise stable even though it is the unique strongly efficient configuration. Without some sort of extension of the model where other agents can help compensate the center, there will be an inefficiency in the networks that will form. Whether or not the center can be properly compensated depends on how easy it is for the other individuals to transfer benefits to the center. If this is a trading situation, then monetary transfers might be possible, while in other situations it might be that the center ends up gaining some power or status that translates into a higher utility.[7] The connections model provides the raw benefits and costs, and then any reallocation or transfer of values needs to be modeled in order to understand whether some sort of transfer can help lead efficient networks to be pairwise stable.

One might expect that if agents are free to make promises or transfers of goods, favors, or services to each other, that could help reconcile individual incentives with societal objectives and thus lead to the emergence of efficient networks. The basic idea is that the efficient network results in the highest level of total resources or utility, so if these are appropriately redistributed, then everyone should be better off than they would be in an inefficient network. In some situations, one can envision a government stepping in and using taxes or subsidies to help promote an efficient network to emerge. We see such interventions in a variety of settings, such as government subsidies to foster collaborations in research and development activities, especially when firms could gain from forming relationships along R & D dimensions but might be reluctant to do so if competing along other dimensions. This has been an active area of research, because of the importance of this question and the strong intuition that some sorts of transfers or redistributions should be helpful.

It turns out that even a fully benevolent government that intervenes only in the form of taxing and subsidizing individuals and relationships in order to try to promote the formation of the efficient network cannot always provide the right incentives. Jackson and Wolinsky (1996) showed that there were some very basic situations where in order to lead self-interested individuals to form an efficient network, one either has to treat identical individuals (those who sit in structurally equivalent positions) very differently, or one has to make transfers away from groups that are producing benefits and give it to individuals who are not contributing at all to the productive value. Thus, there are some very simple settings where the only networks that are pairwise stable are inefficient ones, unless there is some intervention that involves transfers that are inherently unfair in one way or another. Bhaskar Dutta and Suresh Mutuswami (1997) showed that this unfairness could be avoided on certain networks and only imposed on others, and could be done in a way such that the individuals are treated fairly provided they end up forming the efficient network and are treated unfairly only when they do not. Sergio Currarini and Massimo Morelli (2000; Mutuswami and Winter 2002; and Bloch and Jackson 2007) have also shown that if individuals are able to make certain promises to compensate each other for relationships when those relationships are formed, efficient networks can emerge in a fairly wide class of settings.

This tension between stability and efficiency arises from the fact that the externalities in network settings can be quite involved, given that individuals are affected not only by who their neighbors are but also by who their neighbors' neighbors are, and so forth. Individual incentives to form or maintain relationships in such a setting can be at basic odds with overall societal welfare. Overcoming this conflict can require strong forms of intervention.

This tension between individual incentives and overall societal efficiency has been further investigated in the context of various specific applications. For example, Rachel Kranton and Deborah Minehart (2001) examined the formation of networks between buyers and sellers. In their model, buyers each want a good and sellers each have a good for sale. The buyers differ in how much they value a unit of the good. In a fully centralized market, one could hold an auction and the good would end up being sold to the buyers who value it most, and societal welfare would be maximized.

However, for a variety of reasons centralized markets are more the exception than the norm. Generally, buyers will form relationships with certain sellers and then tend to trade mainly with them—for example, see Brian Uzzi's (1996) study of the garment industry or Gerard Weisbuch, Alan Kirman, and Dorothea Herreiner's (2000) description of the Marseille fish market. It may be costly for a buyer to form a relationship with a given seller; for instance, in setting up credit, conforming to the seller's inventory and other systems, arranging for delivery, and so forth. In terms of getting a good price, buyers would prefer to have less competition from other buyers and at the same time to be in touch with a large number of sellers who would then compete for a sale. Analogously, sellers would like to be connected to many buyers who would compete for a purchase, but be in competition with a small number of other sellers. The optimal configuration given costs to relationships will involve having some buyers connected to more than one seller and vice versa, to make sure that goods end up in the hands of the buyers who happen to value them the most in any given instance, but will have fewer relationships as they become more costly. It is not obvious whether or not the buyers and sellers will have the right incentives to form the correct number of relationships, and the right ones, from an overall societal efficiency perspective. Kranton and Minehart show that if buyers bear the full cost of forming relationships with sellers, the efficient network will be pairwise stable. It also turns out that if sellers bear a nontrivial cost of forming relationships with buyers, this efficiency result can fail, as shown in Jackson (2003). Buyers turn out to have incentives to form relationships that align with society's objectives, whereas sellers do not. The buyers end up getting their marginal value compared to the next-highest valued buyer and so internalize the welfare effect, whereas sellers simply wish to see as high a price as possible.[8]

Buyer-and-seller models constitute an example of a setting where the tension between individual incentives to form relationships and overall societal welfare has been explored. There are also studies of networks of collaboration among firms (see Bloch 2004 for a recent survey), the formation of job contact networks (Calvó-Armengol 2004), international trading alliances among countries (Furusawa and Konishi 2005), information networks (Rogers 2006), and risk-sharing networks (Bloch, Genicot, and Ray 2005; Bramoullé and Kranton 2005b), to mention just a few areas.

The Explanatory Power of an Economic Approach

Up to this point I have emphasized the modeling approaches taken by economists studying network formation and some of the questions that naturally come up in tandem with such an approach. In addition to understanding tensions between individual incentives and societal welfare, this approach can also offer some fundamental insights into why certain regularities in networks should be observed across applications.

A good example of the insights that economic modeling can yield behind why networks exhibit certain features can be found in the "small-worlds" aspects of networks.

Much has been made of the "small-world" nature of networks, starting with the seminal experiments of Stanley Milgram (1967), who found that the chains of acquaintances needed to establish a connection between individuals who might be quite geographically and professionally distant is remarkably low. Duncan Watts and Steven Strogatz (1998; see also Watts 1999) showed that starting with a regular lattice that is highly clustered on a local level, one needs only a small amount of random rewiring of links in order to have a network that exhibits two key features found in many social networks: highly clustered links on a local level and relatively short distances between any two randomly selected nodes. This provides an important insight that a relatively small number of bridging links can dramatically decrease the diameter of a network, but it still leaves us with the question of why social networks tend to exhibit these features. It answers the how, but not the why. Insights from the economic perspective complement the Watts and Strogatz approach and offer instead of a process that will exhibit such features, an explanation of why people would tend to form networks with such features. Ideas related to this have been examined in a series of papers where there is some heterogeneity in costs (Johnson and Gilles 2000; Carayol and Roux 2003; Jackson and Rogers 2005; Hojman and Szeidl 2006; Galeotti et al. 2005). The basic idea is that high clustering emerges between individuals who have low costs of forming relationships. These low costs of forming relationships arise because people are close geographically or are clustered because of their profession or other characteristics. Although the costs to relationships at greater distances can be quite high, due again either to geographic or some other characteristics, some such relationships still emerge, since they can be very valuable. Such relationships bring access to distant parts of the network and thus provide information and access that one does not get from local sources. The network diameter that emerges cannot be too large precisely because it is valuable to connect to distant parts of a network. Given high costs across larger distances, we expect fewer distant links, but we expect some such links to form because of the rewards they offer.

This is just one example of how an economic approach offers insights into why networks might emerge that exhibit certain characteristics. Another good example of such research is presented in chapter 3 in this volume, by Kranton and Minehart, concerning supplier networks. By analyzing the incentives to form certain supply relationships, the authors are able to explain why one would see a company dealing only with a small number of suppliers when it might be in their short-term interest to deal with more suppliers in order to get them to compete and offer better prices. The insight is that the long-term investment decisions are shaped by the network of supplier relationships. Again, understanding what the costs and benefits are from various configurations of links helps to sort out why (and under what circumstances) one might see specific sorts of networks emerging.

Beyond the Formation of Networks—Behavior Influenced by Networks

Although this volume focuses on network formation, we are naturally led beyond the formation issue. One of the primitives of many economic models of network formation is the costs and benefits that individuals enjoy as members of various network configurations. To assess what the costs and benefits from different networks, we need some idea of what will occur once a network forms; to do this we need to forecast how behavior and the allocation of resources changes as the network changes. This information, besides providing the groundwork for incentive-based network formation models, also is interesting in its own right. For instance, there are obvious questions as to how social network structures influence decisions to buy products, to become educated, to select a profession, to adopt certain political ideologies, to engage in criminal activity, and other life decisions. The point of introducing networks into the study of economic interactions in the first place is to understand the impact of the social context on economic behavior. Thus, networks provide another natural bridge between studies by sociologists and by economists. The body of research in sociology on how social structure affects behavior is extensive, on both the empirical and theoretical sides, and this area has become an increasingly active research area in economics as the connections between the literatures have grown.

For example, one study of how a network of relationships influences behavior is the work of Coralio Ballester, Antoni Calvó-Armengol, and Yves Zenou (2006), on the incentives of individuals to engage in crime. They build a model based on the premise that the benefits from criminal activity depend on the level to which an individual's friends and neighbors engage in it. There are complementarities both in learning about crime and in cooperating in criminal pursuits, and so the benefits depend on the extent to which friends are involved. There are also competition effects at the level of overall criminal activity in the society, as there may be competition among groups or individuals, and there might also be tighter enforcement as overall criminal activity grows. These two forces, local through the network and global through the overall society, influence each individual's decisions as to whether or not and how intensively to engage in criminal activities. Ballester, Calvó-Armengol, and Zenou use an equilibrium approach to predict criminal activity, where each individual chooses a level of criminal activity in reaction to the choices of his or her neighbors as well as the overall level of criminal activity in the society. Interestingly, notions of centrality related to those of Leo Katz (1953) and Phillip Bonacich (1972) figure prominently in characterization of behavior, and individuals with higher levels of centrality in a network are more influential in affecting other individuals' criminal activity.

Other recent studies of how network structure influences behavior increasingly lead back to ever-richer models of network structure and to the sociology literature. These include models of information gathering and public goods provision (Bramoullé and Kranton (2005a), network structure in labor markets (Calvó-Armengol and Jackson 2004; Ioannides and Datcher-Loury 2004), exchange and markets (Kakade et al. 2005), and communication of information (DeMarzo, Vayanos, and Zwiebel 2003), to name a few. Beyond the analysis of specific situations, there are also more general models based on graphical games (see Kakade, Kearns, and Ortiz 2005) that seek to characterize how network structure relates to individual behaviors.

This literature (for example, Lopez-Pintado 2005; Galeotti et al. 2005; Sundararajan 2005; Jackson and Yariv 2007) makes heavy use of degree distribution information to predict behavior. For example, consider a world where actions are complementary. As an illustration, an individual's benefit from buying some products (such as a given cell-phone plan) increases with the number of friends that the individual has who have bought the same product. In such a world, individuals who are more highly connected are more likely to undertake the behavior. As the distribution of degrees varies, the overall distribution of behaviors in the society changes.

Such studies lead to new insights about tipping points and the diffusion of ideas, technologies, opinions, and behaviors through a society. This is a promising area for research, one that brings together details about social network structure and economic and equilibrium reasoning.

Some Concluding Thoughts: Choice Versus Chance and Heterogeneity in Modeling

One limitation faced by an incentive-based approach to modeling network formation is that many of the models that are analytically tractable end up with some limitations on their range. They can provide broad insights regarding things like incentive-efficiency trade-offs, and they can help explain why one might see small worlds and some other prominent characteristics of observed networks. However, many of the models are quite stark in their detail, and as a result end up with networks that are quite simple emerging as the stable or efficient networks. Networks like stars are quite special, and are rarely observed in real social settings. Although they can be thought of as analogues to hub-and-spoke types of networks, it is clear that the models are not so well suited to trying to match the observed form of many large social networks, where there is a huge amount of heterogeneity in the network structures.

There are two ways to deal with this. One is to work with simulations and agent-based modeling to introduce heterogeneity (see Tesfatsion 1997). Another is to introduce some randomness into the settings. Random network models have provided some simple models that ended up providing insights into some observed networks (for example, Barabási and Albert 1999). Such random models, however, end up being somewhat mechanical and new processes can be needed every time some difference in network structure is observed empirically. Whereas the economic approach leans too heavily on choice, random network models lean too heavily on chance. Reality is clearly a mix of these two, where individuals end up seeing only some opportunities to form relationships. Chance determines which relationships they have an opportunity to form, and then they use discretion to decide which ones they will follow through on.[9] This appears to be potentially a very useful future avenue of research.

Bridges Between Literatures

In closing, I offer some thoughts on the formation of bridges between research on networks in sociology and economics. It is easy to find reason to complain about the lack of attention that one discipline pays to another, as literatures tend to be introspective. The barriers across disciplines in terms of backgrounds, terminology, approach, and perspective can be quite substantial, making it very costly to understand, synthesize, and incorporate research from another discipline. It is often easier simply to discount another discipline's approach as being flawed or uninteresting and to ignore it. However, as the settings and questions that researchers in different disciplines are examining begin to converge naturally, researchers have no choice but to take note of each other and to begin to incorporate key ideas, insights, and methods from each other's disciplines. One example: An important nexus between computer science and economics and game theory has emerged in the last five years or so. Computer scientists have become increasingly interested in protocols for routing, queuing, file sharing, and more generally designing systems where many different actors may be involved at once and may have different objectives. Designing such systems leads to the recognition that the actors respond to incentives and that understanding incentives is critical to designing efficient systems. At the same time, economists have been designing markets and auctions that involve potentially many buyers and/or sellers, and combinations of trades and objects for sale. The computational complexity involved in making such markets work, both for the participants and in terms of the market protocols, has become a serious constraint and needs to be properly understood and accounted for. This has resulted in a very healthy exchange, so that an increasingly seamless and interdisciplinary field of research involving both incentives and limited computation is emerging. A very similar confluence between social economics and economic sociology is taking place, given the numerous settings where economic interactions shape social structure, and where social structure shapes economic interactions. As the subjects of study overlap more and more, researchers from the different disciplines have no choice but to take notice of each other. Here again, the tools and perspectives coming in can be quite complementary. The substantial body of work in sociology tells us (among other things) how and when networks matter, and helps us describe them from a variety of structural perspectives. The economic perspective brings decisionmaking actors and takes incentives as a serious input, and with an eye to efficiency and welfare measures, can yield new insights regarding the formation of networks and the influence that networks have on behavior. We already see studies that draw heavily on both sources, and this trend is likely to continue. This volume would not have existed a decade ago, and it is hoped that it becomes part of a growing dialogue between sociologists and economists.

Notes

1. I have written at more length on this topic elsewhere (see Jackson 2004, 2005, 2006, forthcoming).
2. So with respect to "rational choice," the emphasis is on the word "choice" and not on "rational." Models differ in how they view decision-making—whether agents are myopic, adaptive, Bayesian, forward-looking, and so forth—but they generally build on the notion of economic agents making decisions.
3. The importance of the interplay between economic interactions and social circumstances obviously has a rich history, including whole fields such as Marxian economics. Here, I restrict my attention to studies that explicitly involve networks of relationships.
4. This is also true of a large set of studies in labor economics and the economics of education, where peer effects are considered but where explicit network modeling has only recently emerged.
5. Another branch related to cooperation structures and graphs is found in work by Alan P. Kirman (1983) and Kirman, Claude Oddou, and Shlomo Weber (1986), who, in the context of core convergence in exchange economies, analyze the impact of limiting blocking coalitions to connected groups, where connection is defined relative to a Bernoulli random graph.
6. In more formal terms the definition is as follows. Let $g + ij$ denote the network formed when the link ij is added to a network g, and $g - ij$ denote the network formed when the link ij is deleted from a network g. Then a network g is pairwise stable if: for all ij such that $g_{ij} = 0$, if $u_i(g + ij) > u_i(g)$ then $u_j(g + ij) < u_j(g)$; and for all ij such that $g_{ij} = 1$, $u_i(g) = u_i(g - ij)$ and $u_j(g) = u_j(g - ij)$.
7. The payoffs in the connections model do not always reflect the fact that the center fills a structural hole, in Ronald Burt's (1992) sense. There are alternative specifications of payoffs, even with the same total value as a function of the network, that would be more in line with this. For instance, under the Myerson value the center of the star would enjoy a much higher payoff (see Jackson, forthcoming).
8. Another model of buyer-seller networks, one with a very different bargaining protocol, was developed by Margaridas Corominas-Bosch (2004) and explored in laboratory experiments by Gary Charness, Margaridas Corominas-Bosch, and Guillaume R. Frechette (forthcoming).

Although the details differ, efficiency again depends on who bears the cost of relationships.
9. For example, see the discussion in Jackson and Rogers (2005) and Jackson (forthcoming).

References

Aumann, Robert, and Roger Myerson. 1988. "Endogenous Formation of Links Between Players and Coalitions: An Application of the Shapley Value." In *The Shapley Value*, edited by A. Roth. Cambridge: Cambridge University Press.

Bala, Venkatesh, and Sanjeev Goyal. 2000. "A Non-Cooperative Model of Network Formation." *Econometrica* 68(5): 1181–1230.

Ballester, Coralio, Antoni Calvó-Armengol, and Yves Zenou. 2006. "Who's Who in Networks: Wanted, the Key Player." *Econometrica* 74(5): 1403–17.

Barabási, Albert-Laszlo, and Reka Albert. 1999. "Emergence of Scaling in Random Networks." *Science* 15(286): 509–12.

Bloch, Francis. 2004. "Group and Network Formation in Industrial Organization." In *Group Formation in Economics: Networks, Clubs and Coalitions*, edited by Gabrielle Demange and Myrna Wooders. Cambridge: Cambridge University Press.

Bloch, Francis, and Matthew O. Jackson. 2007. "The Formation of Networks with Transfers Among Players." *Journal of Economic Theory* 133(1): 83–110.

Bloch, Francis, Garance Genicot, and Debraj Ray 2005. "Social Networks and Informal Insurance." Unpublished paper (mimeographed). Washington and New York: Georgetown University, Research Group in Quantitative Economics of Aix-Marseille (GREQAM), and New York University.

Bonacich, Phillip. 1972. "Factoring and Weighting Approaches to Status Scores and Clique Identification." *Journal of Mathematical Sociology* 2(1): 113–20.

Boorman, Scott. 1975. "A Combinatorial Optimization Model for Transmission of Job Information Through Contact Networks." *Bell Journal of Economics* 6(4): 216–49.

Bramoullé, Yves, and Rachel Kranton. 2005a. "A Network Model of Public Goods: Experimentation and Social Learning." Unpublished paper (mimeographed). Baltimore, Md., and Toulouse, France: University of Maryland and University of Toulouse.

———. 2005b. "Risk-Sharing Networks." Unpublished paper (mimeographed). Baltimore, Md., and Toulouse, France: University of Maryland and University of Toulouse.

Burt, Ronald. 1992. "Structural Holes: The Social Structure of Competition." Cambridge, Mass.: Harvard University Press.

Calvó-Armengol, Antoni. 2004. "Job Contact Networks." *Journal of Economic Theory* 115(1): 191–206.

Calvó-Armengol, Antoni, and Matthew O. Jackson. 2004. "The Effects of Social Networks on Employment and Inequality." *American Economic Review* 94(3): 426–54.

Carayol, Nicolas, and Pascale Roux. 2003. "'Collective Innovation' in a Model of Network Formation with Preferential Meeting." Unpublished paper (mimeographed). Strasbourg and Toulouse: Université Louis Pasteur and Université de Toulouse.

Charness, Gary, Margaridas Corominas-Bosch, and Guillaume R. Frechette. Forthcoming. "Bargaining on Networks: An Experiment." *Journal of Economic Theory*.

Corominas-Bosch, Margaridas. 2004. "Bargaining in a Network of Buyers and Sellers." *Journal of Economic Theory* 115(1): 35–77.

Currarini, Sergio, and Massimo Morelli. 2000. "Network Formation with Sequential Demands." *Review of Economic Design* 5(3): 229–50.

DeMarzo, Peter, Dimitri Vayanos, and Jeffrey Zwiebel. 2003. "Persuasion Bias, Social Influence, and Unidimensional Opinions." *Quarterly Journal of Economics* 118(3): 909–68.

Dutta, Bhaskar, and Suresh Mutuswami. 1997. "Stable Networks." *Journal of Economic Theory* 76(2): 322–44.

Dutta, Bhaskar, Sayantan Ghosal, and Debraj Ray. 2005. "Farsighted Network Formation." *Journal of Economic Theory* 122(2): 143–64.

Economides, Nicolas 1996. "The Economics of Networks." *International Journal of Industrial Organization* 16(4): 673–99.

Furusawa, Taiji, and Hideo Konishi. 2005. "Free Trade Networks." *Japanese Economic Review* 56(1): 144–64.

Galeotti, Andrea, Sanjeev Goyal, Matthew O. Jackson, Fernando Vega-Redondo, and Leeat Yariv. 2005. "Network Games." Available online at http://www.stanford.edu/~jacksonm/networkgames.pdf.

Gilles, Robert P., and Sudipta Sarangi. Forthcoming. "Stable Networks and Convex Payoffs." *Review of Economic Design*.

Golub, Benjamin, and Matthew O. Jackson. 2007. "Naive Learning and Influence in Social Networks: Convergence and Wise Crowds." Available at http://www.stanford.edu/$\ sim$jacksonm/naivelearning.pdf.

Granovetter, Mark. 1973. "The Strength of Weak Ties." *American Journal of Sociology* 78(6): 1360–80.

———. 1974/1995. *Getting a Job: A Study of Contacts and Careers.* 2nd ed. Chicago, Ill.: University of Chicago Press.

Herings, P. Jean-Jacques, Ana Mauleon, and Vincent Vannetelbosch. 2004.

"Rationalizability for Social Environments." *Games and Economic Behavior* 49(1): 135–56.

Hojman, Daniel, and Adam Szeidl. 2006. "Endogenous Networks, Social Games and Evolution." *Games and Economic Behavior* 55(1): 112–30.

Ioannides, Yannis M., and Linda Datcher-Loury. 2004. "Job Information Networks, Neighborhood Effects and Inequality." *Journal of Economic Literature* 42(4): 1056–93.

Jackson, Matthew O. 2003. "The Stability and Efficiency of Economic and Social Networks." In *Networks and Groups: Models of Strategic Formation*, edited by B. Dutta and Matthew O. Jackson. Heidelberg: Springer-Verlag.

———. 2004. "A Survey of Models of Network Formation: Stability and Efficiency." In *Group Formation in Economics: Networks, Clubs and Coalitions*, edited by Gabrielle Demange and Myrna Wooders. Cambridge: Cambridge University Press.

———. 2006. "The Economics of Social Networks." In *Proceedings of the Ninth World Congress of the Econometric Society*, edited by Richard Blundell, Whitney Newey, and Torsten Persson. Cambridge: Cambridge University Press.

———. Forthcoming. *Social and Economic Networks*. Princeton, N.J.: Princeton University Press.

Jackson, Matthew O., and Brian W. Rogers. 2005. "The Economics of Small Worlds." *Journal of the European Economic Association* 3(2–3): 617–27.

———. Forthcoming. "Meeting Strangers and Friends of Friends: How Random Are Social Networks?" *American Economic Review*.

Jackson, Matthew O., and Anne van den Nouweland. 2005. "Strongly Stable Networks." *Games and Economic Behavior* 51(2): 420–44.

Jackson, Matthew O., and Alison Watts. 2002. "The Evolution of Social and Economic Networks." *Journal of Economic Theory* 106(2): 265–95.

Jackson, Matthew O., and Asher Wolinsky. 1996. "A Strategic Model of Social and Economic Networks." *Journal of Economic Theory* 71(1): 44–74.

Jackson, Matthew O., and Leeat Yariv. 2007. "The Diffusion of Behavior and Equilibrium Structure on Social Networks." *American Economic Review, Papers and Proceedings* 97(2): 92–98.

Johnson, Cathleen, and Robert P. Gilles. 2000. "Spatial Social Networks." *Review of Economic Design* 5(3): 273–300.

Kakade, Sham M., Michael Kearns, and Luiz E. Ortiz. 2005. "Graphical Economics." Paper presented at 17th Annual Conference on Learning Theory (COLT). Banff, Alberta, Canada, July 1-4).

Kakade, Sham M., Michael Kearns, Luiz E. Ortiz, Robin Pemantle, and Siddharth Suri. 2005. "Economic Properties of Social Networks." In *Advances in Neural Information Processing Systems 17*, edited by

Lawrence K. Saul, Yair Weiss, and Léon Bottou. Cambridge, Mass.: MIT Press.

Katz, Leo. 1953. "A New Status Index Derived from Sociometric Analysis." *Psychometrica* 18(1): 39–43.

Katz, Michael, and Carl Shapiro. 1994. "Systems Competition and Networks Effects." *Journal of Economic Perspectives* 8(2): 93–115.

Kirman, Alan P. 1983. "Communication in Markets: A Suggested Approach." *Economics Letters* 12(2): 1–5.

Kirman, Alan P., Claude Oddou, and Shlomo Weber. 1986. "Stochastic Communication and Coalition Formation." *Econometrica* 54(1): 129–38.

Kranton, Rachel, and Deborah Minehart. 2001. "A Theory of Buyer-Seller Networks." *American Economic Review* 91(3): 485–508.

Lopez-Pintado, Dunia. 2005. "Diffusion and Coordination in Random Networks." Unpublished paper (mimeographed). New York: Columbia University.

Mauleon Ana, and Vincent J. Vannetelbosch. 2004. "Farsightedness and Cautiousness in Coalition Formation." *Theory and Decision* 56(3): 291–324.

Milgram, Stanley. 1967. "The Small-World Problem." *Psychology Today* 1(1): 60–67.

Montgomery, James. 1991. "Social Networks and Labor Market Outcomes." *American Economic Review* 81(5): 1408–18.

Mutuswami, Suresh, and Eyal Winter. 2002. "Subscription Mechanisms for Network Formation." *Journal of Economic Theory* 102(2): 242–64.

Myers, Charles A., and George P. Shultz. 1951. *The Dynamics of a Labor Market*. New York: Prentice-Hall.

Myerson, Roger. 1977. "Graphs and Cooperation in Games." *Mathematics and Operations Research* 2(3): 225–29.

Page, Frank, Myrna Wooders, and Samir Kamat. 2005. "Networks and Farsighted Stability." *Journal of Economic Theory* 120(2): 257–69.

Rees, Albert, and George P. Shultz. 1970. *Workers in an Urban Labor Market*. Chicago, Ill.: University of Chicago Press.

Rogers, Brian W. 2006. "A Strategic Theory of Interdependent Status." Unpublished paper (mimeographed). Pasadena, Calif.: California Institute of Technology.

Slikker, Marko, and Anne van den Nouweland. 2001. *Social and Economic Networks in Cooperative Game Theory*. Norwell, Mass.: Kluwer.

Sundararajan, Arun. 2005. "Local Network Effects and Network Structure." Unpublished paper (mimeographed). New York: New York University, Stern Library.

Tesfatsion, Leigh. 1997. "A Trade Network Game with Endogenous Partner Selection." In *Computational Approaches to Economic Problems*, edited by Berc Rustem, Hans Amman, and Andrew Whinston. Norwell, Mass.: Kluwer.

Uzzi, Brian. 1996. "The Sources and Consequences of Embeddedness for the Economic Performance of Organizations: The Network Effect." *American Sociological Review* 61(4): 674-98.

Watts, Duncan J. 1999. *Small Worlds: The Dynamics of Networks Between Order and Randomness*. Princeton, N.J.: Princeton University Press.

Watts, Duncan J. and Steven Strogatz. 1998. "Collective Dynamics of 'Small-World' Networks." *Nature* 393(6684): 440–42.

Weisbuch, Gerard, Alan Kirman, and Dorothea Herreiner. 2000. "Market Organization." *Economica* 110(463): 411-36.

Chapter 3

The Formation of Industrial-Supply Networks

Rachel Kranton and Deborah Minehart*

In the past two decades, the business press in the United States has been full of reports that manufacturers are reducing their supplier base, but until recently there has been no economic theory that can explain this phenomenon. Indeed, it is a puzzle: Why would a manufacturer ever want to reduce the number of its suppliers? Typical theories of industrial organization—which focus on markets, monopolies, or on hierarchies and single vertically integrated firms—cannot help us here. We need a new theory, a new way to understand the many industries, such as the automobile industry, that involve small numbers of manufacturers and small numbers of suppliers. To study these industries, we need a theory of industrial networks.

This chapter provides such a theory. With it we can understand why manufacturers might want to decrease their supplier base. By committing to buy only from a limited set of firms, the manufacturers commit to pay high prices in the future. Hence, suppliers are guaranteed returns from any investments in new quality-enhancing technology. This outcome fits with the stated goal of such policies: reducing a supplier base can yield greater investments in quality and design improvements.

The analysis yields several new insights into supply relations. We

*The views expressed do not purport to represent the views of the United States Department of Justice.

find that when the sellers' investments are inexpensive, buyers will want to link with many suppliers who are linked to many other buyers; the result looks very much like a market where the supply is able to meet total demand. In contrast, when suppliers' investments are expensive, a few supply networks, each serving a subset of the buyers, are optimal. The supply is limited and often is not sufficient to meet demand. Buyers end up paying a price premium, but they may actually prefer this situation, since sellers have the incentive to make investments. The best outcome, then, can involve several buyers sharing a restricted supply base.

This analysis shows the importance of a network model of firms. We see interactions and outcomes that we could not see with previous theories. First, we see that the interaction between a single buyer and a single supplier depends not only on their own relationship but also on the supplier's connections to other buyers, and vice versa. Second, buyers may prefer to share suppliers rather than maintain exclusive supply networks. Finally, whether or not buyers prefer to share suppliers may depend on suppliers' investment costs.

This chapter also illustrates a typical economic approach to the study of networks. In this volume we see much evidence that individuals' decisions and opportunities are shaped by social and economic networks. A question that immediately leaps to an economist's mind is this: If networks affect individual opportunities and constraints, wouldn't people have incentives to shape their networks? This chapter provides a simple model where agents form network links strategically. The industrial-network example gives a precise business context which guides our modeling. We follow the general game-theoretic methodology to study the formation of networks as that discussed in Matthew Jackson's overview (chapter 2, this volume).[1]

In our model, to produce inputs that are valuable to a buyer, both a buyer and a supplier must first have links. Firms that are not "linked" cannot profitably trade.[2] This feature captures an important process that occurs in many industries. Many manufacturers only buy from suppliers they have "qualified" in advance; "qualified" suppliers meet certain standards and other criteria. Manufacturers must decide how many and which suppliers to "qualify." After qualification, in our model suppliers then decide whether or not to invest in equipment that makes their product more valuable to a buyer. These investments determine the network of possible trading relationships. With this network in place, in the second stage buyers and suppliers bargain over prices and sales of inputs. A firm's bargaining power—its ability to sell or buy a good at an appropriate price—depends on the number and distribution of links and investments. For example, buyers face more competition when there are more buyers linked to the same suppliers. Hence, firms must consider in the first stage how the network structure impacts the prices in the second stage and the incentive to invest in value-enhancing assets.

The critical part of the analysis is to determine how the anticipation of a future bargaining position influences a firm's decision to invest in an asset. That is, firms anticipate how the shape of the network influences their supply and demand, and they may want to change their network links to change their future bargaining position. The manufacturers think about how many links to build to suppliers, given the links of other manufacturers. For example, a manufacturer might have less incentive to link to a supplier who has many other customers. The manufacturer would then anticipate paying that supplier a high price. On the other hand, suppliers who anticipate receiving high prices also have a greater incentive to invest in quality-enhancing investments. Our analysis explores this trade-off—between forming links to well-connected suppliers and forming links to an exclusive set of suppliers.

We ask how manufacturers might shape their networks to ensure that suppliers have sufficient returns on investment in assets. We find that when the sellers' investments are inexpensive, buyers want to form a network with more than enough suppliers to meet total demand. The buyers can then pay a low price. In contrast, when suppliers' investments are expensive, it is optimal to have a few supply networks, each one serving a subset of the buyers. Buyers are willing to limit their bargaining power in return for ensuring that sellers receive a high enough price to cover the cost of the quality-enhancing investments.

The model and the analysis show a new way to view industrial structures. A traditional analysis of industry involves many competitive buyers and many competitive sellers. In the mid-1970s Oliver

Williamson (1975) introduced a new view of industry, one in which industry is characterized by hierarchy, not market relations. In this view, the object of study is the relation between a single manufacturer and its supplier. Sanford Grossman and Oliver Hart (1986) and Hart and John Moore (1988) focus on a related issue. When long-term contracts are incomplete, they ask how two firms would both have the incentives to invest in assets specific to the relationship.

Our work builds on this work and advances a new view of the basis of industrial organization: not the market, nor a hierarchy, but a network. Supply networks are a new topic in the economics literature.[3] Of course, researchers in sociology, organizational behavior, management, and other disciplines have studied this setting for years. In the economics literature on industrial organization, the topic areas that have come closest to the network view of industry have been second-sourcing (see, for example, Demski, Sappington, and Spiller 1987; Farrell and Gallini 1988; and Riordan 1994) and vertical integration (see Horn and Wolinsky 1988; Bolton and Whinston 1993]. In contrast to the vertical-integration literature, we take ownership as fixed. We ask instead how many firms will do business with each other. In contrast to the literature on second-sourcing, we focus on how numbers of firms on both sides of the market affect firms' bargaining power.

In the pages that follow, we first describe a general model of industrial networks, discussing the shape and size of the network that is optimal for buyers and when the time such a network would be an equilibrium of a strategic-network-formation game. In the section entitled "An Example of a Network-Formation Game for Industrial Networks" we provide a specific model of industrial networks. Our bargaining model yields the prices that give the incentive to form network links and make investments in quality-enhancing assets. We show how to find equilibrium networks in this setting.

Industrial Networks: A General Model

In this section we construct a prototype two-stage model of industrial networks. First, buyers choose to link to suppliers and suppliers choose whether or not to make a quality-improving investment.[4]

Second, buyers try to procure inputs from suppliers, and prices and allocations of goods are determined.

Our central concern is sellers' incentives to invest in quality-improving assets. When buyers cannot commit to pay a particular price in a contract, anticipated future prices must give suppliers a high enough return so that they have an incentive to invest. This is the now standard paradigm of incomplete contracting (Grossman and Hart 1986; Hart and Moore 1988). In this paradigm, both the number and distribution of links between buyers and sellers affects the outcome.

First, we study networks that are best for the buyers, given that buyers compete for inputs and suppliers must have incentive to invest in assets. We then discuss when such networks are "equilibrium" networks—that is, they are stable in the sense that no one firm can end up better off, given the actions of other firms.

The First Stage: Qualification of Suppliers, Network Formation, and Supplier Investments

There are a total of B_T buyers who each want to purchase $x = 1$ units of input. There are infinitely many potential suppliers who each have the capacity to produce one unit of the input. In the beginning, as in many industrial settings, buyers simultaneously choose to "qualify" suppliers. Only qualified suppliers can sell to a buyer in the future.[5] We sometimes say that a buyer and its qualified suppliers are "linked." We assume that it is costless for buyers to qualify suppliers. In this case, the only reason a buyer would qualify a limited number of suppliers is to limit his supply network. A smaller supply network shields suppliers from competition and guarantees them a high price and thus gives them an incentive to invest in productive assets.

To gain basic insights from the model, we restrict attention to symmetric qualification decisions, where each buyer in a set of buyers invests in the same set of sellers.[6] A network is a group of buyers and suppliers where all buyers have qualified all the suppliers. Let B and S denote the number of buyers and suppliers, respectively, in a given network. All suppliers in a network are linked to exactly B buyers, and all buyers are linked to exactly S suppliers. That is, the B_T buyers are divided into B_T/B groups (subject to integer constraints). Each group contains *B* buyers and *S* suppliers. The remaining suppliers are inactive. We assume that this structure is observable to all firms.[7]

After observing *B* and *S*, suppliers in a network choose whether or not to invest in quality. The asset costs $0 < \alpha < 1$ each and enables the supplier to produce one unit of high-quality output for any buyer in the network. This cost is independent of *B*, which means that the supplier investments are sharable and not specific. For instance, quality could be new computer-aided design (CAD) equipment that increases the precision of suppliers' product. As discussed above, buyers and suppliers cannot write sales contracts across periods. The buyers must ultimately compete to obtain inputs from suppliers.

The Second Stage: Production and the Terms of Trade

After the network is formed, buyers contact suppliers for desired supply. A buyer places a value $v = 1$ on an input produced by a qualified supplier who has invested α.[8] The value of low-quality output is zero, and there is no value of trade between nonlinked buyers and suppliers.

The terms of trade are determined by bilateral bargaining, and the outcome of this process depends on the number of buyers and suppliers in the network. We will discuss the specific process later in the chapter. At this point, we summarize the bargaining outcome to gain a basic understanding on how changes in the network could affect investments. Let $V_B(S, B)$ denote the present discounted payoffs for a single buyer in a network of *S* suppliers and *B* buyers, and let $V_S(S, B)$ denote the present discounted payoffs for a supplier in the same network. The price should not be lower when there are more buyers, and the price should not be higher when there are more sellers. This will be true in our bargaining process.[9] We therefore specify the following baseline relationships between the number of buyers and suppliers, *B* and *S*, and the payoffs $V_B(S, B)$, and $V_S(S, B)$:

$$\frac{\partial V_B}{\partial S} \geq 0, \frac{\partial V_B}{\partial B} \leq 0 \qquad (3.1a)$$

$$\frac{\partial V_S}{\partial S} \le 0, \frac{\partial V_S}{\partial B} \ge 0 \qquad (3.1b)$$

These relationships allow us to grasp some basic points concerning the payoffs of different-size networks and understand what networks are best for buyers.

A General Description of Network Structures That Are Optimal for Buyers

Suppose that a buyer could choose both the number of suppliers and the number of buyers in his network. In other words, he could choose not only the number of suppliers in his network, but also the number of other buyers linked with these suppliers. A buyer must ensure that suppliers are willing to "participate" in the network—that the sellers' discounted payoffs from ex post bargaining cover the cost of investing in the productive asset. Buyers anticipate the prices that will arise in the future and take them into account when forming networks in the first stage.

We can represent this forward-looking behavior by the following constrained-optimization problem. Buyers maximize their payoffs subject to the constraint that suppliers cover their investment costs

$$\max_{S,B} V_B(S,B) \; s.t. \; V_S(S,B) \ge \alpha, \qquad (3.2)$$

where $V_S(S, B) \ge \alpha$ is the suppliers' "participation constraint." Let the solution to this constrained maximization problem be (S^*, B^*). The symmetry of the buyers' payoff functions implies that all the buyers would prefer to be in a network with structure (S^*, B^*) than in any other symmetric network. We call (S^*, B^*) "buyer-optimal" networks.

How would we solve for such buyer-optimal networks? We must consider simultaneously how changes in the number of buyers and changes in the number of suppliers affect buyers' and suppliers' payoffs. Not only the relative number but also the absolute number of buyers and sellers matters. By the property (3.1a) of $V_B(S, B)$ (that is, V_B is weakly increasing in S and decreasing in B) a buyer's returns would be highest in a network with as many suppliers as possible and as few other buyers as possible. However, such networks are not necessarily feasible. Suppliers must earn at least α. Since, for any B, buyers' payoffs are increasing in S and suppliers' payoffs are decreasing in S, the suppliers' participation constraint will be binding. The participation constraint therefore implicitly defines the maximum number of suppliers for a given number of buyers such that the network is feasible. Let $S^*(B)$ be this number of suppliers: $S^*(B)$ satisfies the equation $V_s(S^*(B), B) = \alpha$.[10]

Thus, the participation constraint pins down the ratio of buyers to suppliers in a buyer-optimal network. We can then ask buyers when buyers prefer small or large networks, where in small networks there is a low buyer-supplier ratio. To answer this we can examine how the objective function $V_B(S^*(B), B)$ changes in B. Buyers prefer large networks when $V_B(S^*(B))$ is increasing in B; thus, when

$$\frac{\partial}{\partial S} V_B(S^*(B), B) \bullet S^{*\prime}(B) + \frac{\partial}{\partial B} V_B(S, B) > 0. \tag{3.3}$$

The first term of equation 3.3 is always nonnegative. From equation 3.1, suppliers' payoffs are increasing in the number of buyers. Therefore, $S^{*\prime}(B) \geq 0$. Since buyers' payoffs are always increasing in the number of suppliers, this effect would lead to larger networks. However, the second term is nonpositive. Buyers' payoffs could be decreasing in the number of buyers because buyers may compete for the limited network supply. When this second term is small enough, then, buyers will be better off in bigger networks. By adding more buyers, the buyers can more easily meet suppliers' participation constraint. This allows buyers to increase the number of suppliers. Although the additional buyers intensify the competition for inputs, the increase in the number of suppliers can more than offset any losses.

In our model, qualification is costless, so the only motivation that buyers have to limit the number of suppliers is to protect the suppliers from competition so that they have an incentive to invest in the quality-improving asset. This is a common explanation of the observed trend toward closer relations between buyers and a limited number of suppliers in industries where quality of inputs is important.[11] We will observe this outcome in our model. For α small enough, the buyer-optimal network will include all the buyers. For larger investment costs, the buyers will want to be in smaller networks.

A General Description of Strategic Network Formation and Equilibrium Networks

Equilibrium networks are characterized by "backward induction." Given the second-stage payoffs from noncooperative bargaining between buyers and suppliers, $V_B(S, B)$, and $V_S(S, B)$, we consider the investment decisions of buyers and suppliers in the first stage. Buyers decide whether or not to establish relations with a set of suppliers, and suppliers decide whether or not to invest in assets. To determine whether a division of firms into networks is an equilibrium outcome, we ask whether each firm is doing the best it can, given all other firms' decisions. If the answer is yes, the division is equilibrium.

For example, suppose buyers have split into two groups of size B' and B''. Associated with each group is a set of sellers who invest in assets S' and S'', respectively. The buyers in network (S', B') earn $V_B(S', B')$, and the sellers earn $V_S(S', B')$. The buyers in network (S'', B'') earn $V_B(S'', B'')$, and the sellers earn $V_S(S'', B'')$. This configuration is an equilibrium outcome if, first, no buyer wants to switch networks or qualify a different set of suppliers and, second, each seller in a network earns weakly more than the investment cost α.[12]

Let us apply these conditions to buyer-optimal networks. Take the population of B^T buyers, and divide it as much as possible into sets of B^* buyers. Label the number of remaining buyers as $\underline{B}$ (where $\underline{B} < B^*$). Let each set of B^* buyers qualify S^* suppliers. Let the $\underline{B}$ buyers qualify $\underline{S}$ suppliers, such that $V_S(\underline{B}, \underline{S}) \geq \alpha$. In order for this configuration to be an equilibrium outcome, first, no buyer would want to qualify a different set of suppliers and, second, qualified sellers would all be willing to invest in assets.

When these conditions are satisfied, there could be many other equilibrium networks.[13] Equilibrium networks that are not optimal for buyers could arise as a result of "coordination failures" in buyers' selections of suppliers. It is also important to note the equilibrium networks are not the networks that could maximize buyers' payoffs if buyers were able to collude on prices. In our strategic setting, buyers compete for sellers' inputs. If buyers could collude and agree upon the prices to pay sellers, they could achieve higher-level of profits.

A Two-Stage Network-Formation Game for Industrial Networks

This presentation is necessarily more technical than that in the preceding section, as the game is an example of the type of model used by economists to study strategic network formation. There is a well-specified protocol: In the first stage, agents choose links. In the second stage, there is a strategic game that determines agents' payoffs in given networks.

The basic assumptions about the agents and the technology are as follows. There are B_T buyers, all of whom want to purchase $x = 1$ units of input. There are infinitely many potential suppliers, all of whom have the capacity to produce one unit of the input. A buyer can purchase from a supplier only if he has previously linked to that supplier. There is zero cost to forming the link. A buyer places a value, 1, on any input purchases from a supplier who has invested α.

Stage 1. Buyers each simultaneously choose links to suppliers. The resulting link structure is common knowledge among all agents. Individual suppliers then simultaneously choose whether or not to invest α. Investment decisions are common knowledge among all agents.

Stage 2. Buyers and suppliers play a bargaining game, described next. This game yields the payoff functions $V_B(S, B)$ and $V_S(S, B)$ we used in the preceding section.

A Bargaining Game for a Buyer-Supplier Network

Suppose buyers desire to purchase inputs over a "product cycle" that lasts two periods: $t = 1$ and $t = 2$. In each period, each buyer has new demand for x units of the input. If a buyer does not find a supplier in the first period or does not conclude an agreement in the first period with a supplier to produce all inputs (x) demanded in the first period, the buyer carries over the unmet demand to the second period. That is, if the buyer purchases only $x - k$ units in period 1, it carries over k units of unmet demand to period 2; its period 2 demand will be $x + k$ units. The discount factor between $t = 1$ and $t = 2$ is $0 < \delta < 1$; that is, profits earned in period 2 are only worth δ times profits earned in period 1. Any orders that are not filled by the second period have no value. This model represents an industry with changing product lines, such as the automobile and computer industries. A new generation of products comes on line at the end of period 2, rendering the old generation obsolete, and manufacturers choose to move all of their production into the new product line.[14]

When a buyer finds a supplier for its inputs and the two firms conclude an agreement, the buyer pays the supplier the proposed amount, and the supplier produces the input for the buyer.[15] If a buyer locates an input supplier in the first period, but they cannot conclude a deal, the buyer can either purchase inputs from a non-qualified supplier in that period (this is worth zero dollars to the buyer) or carry over the order to period 2.

SEQUENTIAL OFFERS   Bargaining proceeds as follows after a buyer and seller meet. Each party has an equal chance of being selected to make an offer first. Whichever party has the right to make the offer names a split of one dollar, which the other side can accept or reject. If the offer is accepted, trade takes place. If the offer is rejected, we move to period 2. Again the parties match. In a second-period match, whichever firm makes the offer will be able to extract full surplus from the other. Since networks consist of a small number of buyers and suppliers, firms will consider how their decision to reject an offer in the first period affects network demand in the second period. If any firm rejects an offer, it will increase demand by one unit.

In this model, what determines the initial offer is how a rejection in period 1 affects the matching probabilities in period 2. If any firm rejects an offer, demand increases by one unit in the subsequent period. In equilibrium, all offers are accepted. The initial offers are set so that the responding party has no incentive to reject an offer. In equilibrium, each supplier receives a buyer with probability σ each period. Since each party makes the offer with probability 1/2, a supplier's expected payoffs over the two periods are

$$V_S = \sigma\left[\frac{1}{2}(1 - v_b) + \frac{1}{2}(1 - v_s)\right] + \delta\sigma(1/2). \tag{3.4}$$

Each buyer finds a supplier for one of his orders with probability β. The equilibrium discounted value of future profits for a buyer is

$$V_B = \beta x\left[\frac{1}{2}(v_b) + \frac{1}{2}(v_s)\right] + \delta\beta x(1/2). \tag{3.5}$$

Different network structures lead to different equilibrium and out-of-equilibrium matching probabilities. We first examine networks where there is always excess capacity, that is, supply always exceeds total demand, $S \geq Bx + 1$. Buyers always are able to fill all their orders, but some suppliers do not produce in either period. We then consider "capacity constrained networks," where $S \leq Bx$; here, suppliers always receive buyers, but some buyers may not be able to fill their orders for inputs.

PAYOFFS IN EXCESS CAPACITY NETWORKS   In an excess capacity network, we find that the discounted payoffs for suppliers and buyers are, respectively,

$$V_s(S,B) = \frac{1}{2}\frac{Bx}{S}\left[\frac{\delta}{2S} + 1 + \frac{\delta}{2}\right] \text{ and} \tag{3.6}$$

$$V_B(S,B) = \frac{x}{2}\left[1 - \frac{\delta}{2S} + \frac{3\delta}{2}\right]. \tag{3.7}$$

(These equations are derived in the appendix in the section titled "Payoffs in Excess Capacity Networks.") Notice that in this case a buyer's payoff is independent of B. Since there are always enough suppliers to meet demand, the buyer effectively does not compete with other buyers for suppliers. The suppliers' payoffs, however, are directly affected by the number of buyers. When B increases, the probability that a supplier receives a buyer increases: suppliers produce more often. Both the buyers' and the suppliers' payoffs depend on S. As discussed earlier, increasing the number of suppliers decreases suppliers' bargaining power. Hence, $V_S(S, B)$ is decreasing in S, and $V_B(S, B)$ is increasing in S.

PAYOFFS IN A CONSTRAINED CAPACITY NETWORK   In a constrained capacity network, in contrast, the discounted payoffs for suppliers and buyers for a network structure where $S \le Bx$ are, respectively,

$$V_s(S,B) = \frac{1}{2}[1 - (\delta/2)\gamma + \delta] \text{ and} \tag{3.8}$$

$$V_B(S,B) = \frac{S}{B}\frac{1}{2}[1 + (\delta/2)\gamma + \delta]. \tag{3.9}$$

where $\gamma \equiv \beta'(x + 1) - \beta x$ and β' is the probability a buyer finds a supplier for its units after one pair has not made an agreement in the second round; that is, γ measures the difference—from period one to period two—in the probability a buyer will find a supplier to fill all its orders. (These equations are derived in the section of the appendix titled "Payoffs in Constrained Capacity Networks.") Notice that in this case both buyers' and suppliers' payoffs depend on B and S. For the suppliers, the equilibrium payoffs depend on B because B decreases γ and, therefore, increases the amount a supplier can demand from a buyer. Buyers' payoffs respond in exactly the opposite direction to an increase in B. The number of suppliers S also affects the split of surplus. The more suppliers are available, the more likely it is that a buyer can find a supplier for its extra unit of demand when it rejects an offer. So suppliers can extract less surplus. This, obviously, increases a buyer's payoffs and decreases a seller's payoffs. Beyond these effects on bargaining power, the greater the number of suppliers, the more likely it is for a buyer to find a seller on the equilibrium path.

Buyer Optimal and Equilibrium Networks

In this section we examine firms' investments decisions given the payoffs in different networks. We first solve for the buyer optimal networks (S^*, B^*). We break the analysis down into two steps. Step

1: Bargaining payoffs in networks with constrained capacity are structurally different from those in networks with excess capacity. We, therefore, first characterize the network structure which is best for the buyers in each setting, ignoring the supplier's participation constraint. Step 2: We then consider when each type of network, excess capacity or capacity-constrained, will meet the suppliers' participation constraint. We show that there exists a critical investment cost α, which we label $\underline{\alpha}$, such that for lower investment costs excess capacity networks will satisfy the suppliers' participation constraint. For higher asset levels, excess capacity networks are not feasible and we consider constrained capacity networks. We discuss when the buyer optimal networks are equilibrium outcomes.

NETWORKS WITH EXCESS CAPACITY AND CONSTRAINED CAPACITY NETWORKS
Here we find the excess capacity network that maximizes buyers' profits, ignoring the suppliers' participation constraint. In all networks with excess capacity, buyers always find suppliers for their inputs. Buyers' payoffs are independent of the number of buyers in the network. All that matters for payoffs is the increase in a supplier's probability of receiving a buyer in the subsequent period if a supplier rejects a buyer's offer. The more suppliers there are, the smaller is the change in the probability of receiving a buyer, the less incentive any individual seller has to reject an offer. As a consequence, buyers' payoffs increase with the number of suppliers. Therefore, the excess capacity network that is best for the buyer involves infinitely many suppliers and any number of buyers:

> Proposition 1. The excess capacity network that is best for the buyers involves an infinity of suppliers and any number of buyers.[16]

We next consider constrained capacity networks. In a capacity constrained network, a buyer would always prefer to have as many suppliers as possible. Buyers want to be able to find suppliers to meet their orders. So, suppose a network has B buyers, if the network is to be capacity-constrained, the buyers would prefer to have $S = Bx$ suppliers which just meets the capacity constraint. This observation fixes the relative number of buyers and sellers. As for the absolute number of firms, we find that a buyer would also prefer to have as many buyers as possible in the network. The split of surplus depends on the ability of a buyer to find a supplier for its "extra" unit of demand if it rejects an offer. Examining γ when $S = Bx$, we see that the buyer is more likely to be able to fill its extra order in the next period the greater the number of buyers and sellers, holding fixed the relationship $S = Bx$. This increase in absolute numbers, holding fixed the relative numbers of buyers and sellers, improves a buyer's bargaining power and so increases V_B. Therefore, among capacity-constrained networks, the buyers would prefer a network that includes all the buyers, B_T, and exactly enough suppliers so that $S = B_T x$. We thus have

Proposition 2. The constrained capacity network that is best for the buyers involves $B_T x$ suppliers and B_T buyers.

SUPPLIERS' PARTICIPATION CONSTRAINTS AND FEASIBLE NETWORKS   In this section we consider the suppliers' participation constraint and determine when excess capacity networks or constrained capacity networks are feasible. We first determine the excess capacity network (S,B) that gives the highest possible payoffs to suppliers (considering, of course, B weakly less than the total number of buyers B_T). This analysis yields a critical investment cost which we label $\underline{\alpha}$ such that if and only if $\alpha > \underline{\alpha}$, no excess capacity network is feasible. We then find the constrained capacity network (S,B) that gives the highest possible payoffs to suppliers (B weakly less than the total number of buyers B_T). This analysis gives another critical investment cost, which we label $\bar{\alpha}$. If and only if $\alpha > \bar{\alpha}$, no capacity-constrained network is feasible.

In an excess capacity network, for a given number of buyers, suppliers are best off with the fewest number of suppliers. Hence, the best excess capacity network for a supplier must involve $S = Bx + 1$ suppliers. As for the absolute number of firms, the suppliers are also better off when there are more buyers. The more buyers there are the greater the chance of receiving an order for inputs in any period. The optimal excess capacity network for a supplier, then, involves B_T buyers and $B_T x + 1$ suppliers. The intuition behind this result is as follows: As the number of suppliers increases, a supplier's bargaining power decreases. But when the number of buyers increases, the supplier's probability of being matched on the equilibrium path increases. When the number of buyers and suppliers both increase, along the line $S = Bx + 1$, the second effect outweighs the first, and suppliers' payoffs increase. Hence

$$V_S(B_T x + 1, B_T) = \frac{1}{2} \frac{B_T x}{B_T x + 1} \left[\frac{\delta}{2(B_T x + 1)} + 1 + \frac{\delta}{2} \right] \qquad (3.10)$$

is the maximum a supplier can earn in an excess capacity network. These payoffs give

$$\underline{\alpha} = \frac{1}{2} \frac{B_T x}{B_T x + 1} \left[\frac{\delta}{2(B_T x + 1)} + 1 + \frac{\delta}{2} \right] \qquad (3.11)$$

(see equation 3.4). For any $\alpha > \underline{\alpha}$, the suppliers' participation constraint is not satisfied in an excess capacity network. We have:

Proposition 3. There exists an investment cost

$$\underline{\alpha} = \frac{1}{2} \frac{B_T x}{B_T x + 1} \left[\frac{\delta}{2(B_T x + 1)} + 1 + \frac{\delta}{2} \right], \qquad (3.12)$$

such that for all $\alpha > \underline{\alpha}$ excess capacity networks are not feasible and for $\alpha \le \underline{\alpha}$ there is at least one feasible excess capacity network.

Consider next when a constrained capacity network is feasible. In a capacity-constrained network (S, B) suppliers always receive orders for inputs. The suppliers care about the relative number of buyers and suppliers only to the extent that it affects γ, the ability of a buyer to find a supplier for its "extra" unit of demand if it rejects a seller's offer. For a given number of suppliers, S, as the number of buyers increases, (for $B > 2$), γ falls, and the suppliers earn greater payoffs. Hence, suppliers would earn the highest profits when there are as many buyers as possible: B_T. We then know that the capacity constrained network that gives greatest payoffs to suppliers includes all the buyers. From equation (6), we see the supplier earns

$$V_s(S, B_T) = \frac{1}{2}\left[1 - \left(\frac{\delta}{2}\right)\frac{S(B_T - 1)}{B_T(B_T x + 1)} + \delta\right].$$ (3.13)

These payoffs are clearly decreasing in S. Therefore, the constrained capacity network which yields highest payoffs for suppliers in the network is a network with a single supplier and all the buyers: $(1, B_T)$. Payoffs from this network give $\bar{\alpha}$, the critical investment cost such that no constrained capacity network is feasible.

Proposition 4. There exists an investment cost

$$\bar{\alpha} = \frac{1}{2}\left[1 - \left(\frac{\delta}{2}\right)\frac{(B_T - 1)}{B_T(B_T x + 1)} + \delta\right]$$ (3.14)

such that for $\alpha > \bar{\alpha}$, no constrained capacity network is feasible.

Simple arithmetic shows that $\bar{\alpha} > \underline{\alpha}$; hence, we can divide sellers' investment costs into three regions. For $\bar{\alpha} > \underline{\alpha} > \alpha$, feasible buyer optimal networks are excess capacity networks. For $\bar{\alpha} > \alpha > \underline{\alpha}$, feasible buyer-optimal networks are capacity-constrained networks. And for $\alpha > \bar{\alpha} > \underline{\alpha}$, no networks are feasible.

BUYER OPTIMAL NETWORKS   In this section we determine buyer optimal networks. We show first that a buyer would always prefer to be in an excess capacity network if an excess capacity network is feasible. In other words, if $\underline{\alpha} > \alpha$ the optimal feasible network for the buyers, (S^*, B), is an excess capacity network. We then consider $\alpha > \underline{\alpha}$ so that excess capacity networks are not feasible. In this case, we consider constrained capacity networks.

When the investment cost is small enough, $\underline{\alpha} \geq \alpha$, the best feasible network for buyers is an excess capacity network. To see this, consider any constrained capacity network, then add one supplier. The network is no longer capacity constrained. Comparing payoffs in the two kinds of networks, equations 3.5 and 3.7, we see that buyers earn greater payoffs in the excess capacity network. We have

Proposition 5. If $\underline{\alpha} > \alpha$, (S^*, B^*) is an excess capacity network.

We now determine the relative numbers of buyers and sellers in this case. In excess capacity networks, buyers' payoffs from ex-post bargaining are increasing in S and independent of B. When making their qualification decision, however, buyers do consider the qualification decisions of other buyers. This is because when a buyer qualifies a supplier, it must guarantee the supplier enough business to cover its fixed costs. The more buyers there are in a network, the greater is the probability that a supplier receives a buyer in each period. This increases the supplier's discounted expected payoff V_S, relaxing the participation constraint: $V_S(S, B) \geq \alpha$. Thus, the more buyers there are to generate orders for suppliers, the more suppliers can be supported in the network. Since $V_B(S, B)$ is increasing in S, buyers would prefer to have all the buyers in the same network. Thus, if $\underline{\alpha} \geq \alpha$ the feasible network that is optimal for the buyers involves the maximum number of buyers possible, B_T, and just the number of suppliers such that their participation is binding.

Proposition 6. If $\underline{\alpha} \geq \alpha$, $B^* = B_T$; that is, the best feasible network for a buyer involves all buyers in one network, and suppliers receive a payoff of $V_S = \alpha$. S^* is defined by the following equality, which derives from the suppliers' participation constraint:

$$\frac{2(S^*)^2}{(2+\delta)S^* + \delta} = \frac{B_T x}{2\alpha}.$$

No buyers are excluded and buyers prefer this network to any other-size feasible network.

In this network there is excess capacity—capacity which is not needed to meet equilibrium demand. However, we can interpret the excess capacity as a bargaining resource for buyers; it reduces the impact that any individual supplier can have on demand. Because excess capacity is never used in equilibrium, all buyers can share this resource. As the number of buyers grows, buyers are able to keep the suppliers at their participation constraint with proportionally less excess capacity. The efficiency gains from the reduction in excess capacity accrue to the buyers because suppliers just meet their participation constraint.

When investment costs are higher, $\alpha > \underline{\alpha}$, excess capacity networks are not feasible. We must then check for the feasible constrained capacity network that is best for buyers. Previously we discussed how the sellers' participation constraint implicitly defines the maximum number of suppliers for a given number of buyers such that the network is feasible, and we defined $S^*(B)$ to be the number of suppliers: $S^*(B)$ satisfies the equation $V_S(S^*(B), B) = \alpha$. Given the participation constraint binds, we ask when buyers prefer to share suppliers with other buyers or establish exclusive supply networks.

To answer this we examine how the objective function $V_B(S^*(B), B)$ changes in B. Recall from equation 3.3 that buyers prefer large networks when

$$\frac{\partial}{\partial S} V_B(S^*(B), B) \bullet S^{*\prime}(B) + \frac{\partial}{\partial B} V_B(S, B) > 0. \qquad (3.15)$$

The first term is always nonnegative. From equation 3.1, suppliers' payoffs are increasing in the number of buyers. Therefore, $S^{*\prime}(B) \geq 0$. Since buyers' payoffs are always increasing in the number of suppliers, this effect would lead to larger networks. However, the second term is nonpositive. Buyers' payoffs could be decreasing in the number of buyers because buyers may compete for the limited network supply. In the constrained capacity case, this is exactly what arises. Buyers are then better off in smaller networks. By decreasing the number of sellers and buyers, the buyers in the network can more easily meet suppliers' participation constraint. Thus we have

> Proposition 7. If $\bar{\alpha} > \alpha > \underline{\alpha}$, then the optimal feasible network for the buyers has the minimum number of buyers that will support a single supplier.

Conclusion

We provide here an economic theory of industrial-supply networks. This theory allows us to study industries in which there are small number of buyers and suppliers. We argue that networks can arise when firms on both sides of the market must make costly investments and complete long-term contracts are not feasible. By establishing links with suppliers, buyers both open up and limit their trading possibilities. On the one hand, buyers wish to establish connections with many suppliers to increase their bargaining power in later negotiations. On the other hand, if buyers allow themselves too much bargaining power, they do not guarantee suppliers sufficient returns to go into business. By committing to a limited network of suppliers, buyers guarantee suppliers a minimum return.

The chapter gives an example of how economists study network formation. We are particularly interested in how network links affect future prices and payoffs. Agents will then consider these effects when forming network links. We present a model where prices are formed through bilateral bargaining of linked firms. We find that when supplier setup costs are low, buyers choose networks with more suppliers than is necessary to meet demand. This excess capacity is a source of bargaining power for the buyers. Moreover, it is a sharable source of bargaining power. As a consequence, all buyers prefer to use the same set of suppliers. By sharing suppliers, buyers can simultaneously increase their payoffs and guarantee that suppliers invest in productive assets. When supplier setup costs are high, buyers would prefer smaller networks, where a few suppliers produce inputs for a subset of buyers. The buyers want to limit their bargaining power in order to give suppliers the incentive to invest in expensive, quality-enhancing assets.

These results can only be seen in a network model of industrial supply, and they generate simple, and possibly testable, empirical predictions. Absent coordination failures, high seller investment costs should be associated with smaller networks, with firms divided into different network components. Such industries might include biotechnology, semiconductors and computers, and automobiles. Lower seller investment costs should be associated with larger networks, with most firms in one network component. Many industries would fall into this category, including textiles and clothing, food processing, and agriculture. Empirical work guided by this theory could then shed new light on the structure of different industries.

Appendix: The Bargaining Game

Let D be the total network demand in any given period; the total network supply of inputs in any given period is equal to the number of suppliers S. Let β be the probability in any given period that a buyer finds a supplier for each of the units it demands, and let σ be the probability that a supplier is selected by a buyer in any given period. We assume that the matching process is frictionless.[17] If total demand equals the supply capacity—that is, if $D = S$—then all buyers find a supplier for each of the units of inputs they want to purchase: $\sigma = 1$ and $\beta = 1$. If network demand is above network capacity, however, the supply limits the number of matches: only S units can be sold. We assume that each buyer has an equal chance of finding a supplier for a unit of demand: $\sigma = 1$ and $\beta = S/D$. If network demand is below network capacity, the demand limits the number of matches: only D suppliers will be contacted by buyers and $\beta = 1$ and $\sigma = D/S$.

When a buyer finds a supplier for its inputs and the two firms conclude an agreement, the buyer pays the supplier the proposed amount, and the supplier produces the input for the buyer. If a buyer locates an input supplier in the first period, but they cannot conclude a deal, the buyer can either purchase inputs from a nonqualified supplier in that period (this is worth zero dollars to the buyer) or carry over the order to period two.

Bargaining

Bargaining proceeds as follows after a buyer and seller meet. Each party has an equal chance of being selected to make an offer first. Whichever party has the right to make the offer names a split of one dollar, which the other side can accept or reject. If the offer is accepted, trade takes place. If the offer is rejected, we move to period 2. Again the parties match. In a second-period match, whichever firm makes the offer will be able to extract full surplus from the other. In the first period, however, since networks consist of a small number of buyers and suppliers, firms will consider how their decision to reject an offer in the first period affects network demand in the second period. If any firm rejects an offer, it will increase demand by one unit. Of course, in equilibrium, all initial offers are accepted, since the parties anticipate the losses that would occur if they were to reject an offer. The initial offers incorporate this loss; hence, parties have no incentive to reject an offer. We next determine the equilibrium shares offered by a buyer to a supplier, and by a supplier to a buyer.

When a buyer makes the offer, let $1 - v_b$ be the share offered to the supplier, with the remainder, v_b, going to the buyer. When the supplier makes the offer, let v_s be the buyer's share and $1 - v_s$ be the supplier's share. We restrict attention to strategies that depend only on variables that directly affect firms' payoffs; that is, they do not depend on time, history, or the identity of the parties. With such strategies, the offers and the decisions whether to accept or reject offers in the first period depend only on current state of network demand and supply. Supply is always the same and equal to the number of suppliers, S. So when making an offer or deciding whether to accept or reject an offer, firms consider only how their decision will affect the relationship between network supply and network demand in the second period. Whereas rejections do not affect what offers are made in the second period, they do affect the relationship between supply and demand in the subsequent period.

In this model, then, what determines the initial offer is how a rejection affects the matching probabilities in the period two. If any firm rejects an offer, demand increases by one unit in the subsequent period. Let σ' and β' be the corresponding matching probabilities.

BUYERS' OFFERS   Consider, first, the offer a buyer makes to a supplier in a given period. If a supplier accepts the offer, it earns $(1 - v_b)$ in period 1 and has expected profits $\sigma(1/2)$ in period 2. If it rejects the offer, it earns nothing in period 1, but in the next period, $t = 2$, its probability of receiving a buyer increases to σ'. The buyer chooses $(1 - v_b)$ in period 1 so that the supplier is just indifferent between accepting the offer and rejecting it:

$$(1 - v_b) + \delta\sigma(1/2) = \delta\sigma'(1/2),$$

which yields $(1 - v_b) = \delta(\sigma' - \sigma)(1/2)$.

SUPPLIERS' OFFER   Consider next the offer a supplier makes to a buyer. If a buyer accepts the offer, it receives v_s in the current period and has expected profits $\beta x(1/2)$ in period 2. If he rejects it, he receives nothing in the current period, but carries over the order to the subsequent period. The buyer's own demand increases to $x + 1$, and the probability of being matched on any single unit becomes β'. The supplier sets v_s so that the buyer is just indifferent to accepting and rejecting the offer:

$$v_s + \delta\beta x(1/2) = \delta\beta'(x + 1)(1/2),$$

which yields $v_s = (\delta/2)\cdot\gamma$, where $\gamma \equiv \beta'(x + 1) - \beta x$.

As discussed, in equilibrium all offers are accepted. The initial offers are set so that the responding party has no incentive to reject an offer. In equilibrium, each supplier receives a buyer with probability σ each period. Since each party makes the offer with probability $1/2$, a supplier's expected payoffs over the two periods are

$$V_S = \sigma\left[\frac{1}{2}(1 - v_b) + \frac{1}{2}(1 - v_s)\right] + \delta\sigma(1/2).$$

Each buyer finds a supplier for one of its orders with probability β. The equilibrium discounted value of future profits for a buyer is

$$V_B = \beta x\left[\frac{1}{2}(v_b) + \frac{1}{2}(v_s)\right] + \delta\beta x(1/2).$$

Different network structures lead to different equilibrium and out-of-equilibrium matching probabilities. To determine the payoffs, then, we consider two types of network structures. We first examine networks where there is always excess capacity, where $S \geq Bx + 1$. Buyers always are able to fill all their orders, but some suppliers do not produce in either period. We then consider networks where there is a capacity constraint. In "capacity-constrained networks," $S \leq Bx$, suppliers always receive buyers, but some buyers may not be able to fill their orders for inputs.

Payoffs in Excess Capacity Networks

In an excess capacity network, $S \geq Bx + 1$, and there are more suppliers than needed to fulfill demand. So $\beta = 1$, and suppliers receive a buyer with probability of only $\sigma = Bx/S$. If ever a firm rejects an offer in period 1, in period 2 total network demand increases by one unit, to $Bx + 1$. There is still enough capacity in the network so that all buyers find a supplier for all of their orders: $\beta' = 1$. Suppliers, however, have an increased chance of receiving a buyer: $\sigma' = [Bx + 1]/S$.

With these probabilities, we determine the equilibrium offers of buyers and suppliers.

SUPPLIERS' OFFERS   The buyer knows that if it rejects an offer, it will be able to meet a supplier for this unit for sure in the next period. Moreover, the buyer will have a 1/2 chance of being able to make the offer himself. Since a rejection does not decrease his chances at finding a supplier, the only loss from rejecting an offer is the time delay. Since $\beta = \beta' = 1$, from equation 3.5 we have $v_s = \delta(1/2)$.

BUYERS' OFFERS   Consider next the offer a buyer will make a supplier. A supplier who rejects an offer gives up the opportunity to produce in the current period. But it increases its probability of being matched in the next period when it has 1/2 chance of being able to make an offer himself. The smaller the number of suppliers, the greater the impact one supplier can have on the future matching probabilities: $(\sigma' - \sigma) = 1/S$. From equation 3.4 we then find $(1 - v_b) = \delta(1/S)(1/2)$.

All that matters in the division of surplus between buyers and suppliers in the excess-capacity case is the increase in a supplier's probability of receiving a buyer when he rejects an offer: $(\sigma' - \sigma) = 1/S$. The fewer suppliers there are, the more impact a rejection by an individual supplier can have on network demand, the greater the surplus the supplier can extract from the buyer.

In equilibrium, suppliers receive buyers with probability $\sigma = Bx/S$, and buyers find suppliers for each of their x units with probability

$\beta = 1$. Therefore, the discounted payoffs for suppliers and buyers for a network structure such that $S \geq Bx + 1$ are, respectively,

$$V_s(S,B) = \frac{1}{2}\frac{Bx}{S}\left[\frac{\delta}{2S} + 1 + \frac{\delta}{2}\right] \text{ and }$$

$$V_B(S,B) = \frac{x}{2}\left[1 - \frac{\delta}{2S} + \frac{3\delta}{2}\right].$$

Notice that in this case a buyer's payoff is independent of B. Since there are always enough suppliers to meet demand, the buyer effectively does not compete with other buyers for suppliers. The suppliers' payoffs, however, are directly affected by the number of buyers. When B increases, the probability that a supplier receives a buyer increases: suppliers produce more often. Both the buyers' and the suppliers' payoffs depend on S. As discussed above, increasing the number of suppliers decreases a suppliers' bargaining power. Hence, $V_S(S, B)$ is decreasing in S, and $V_B(S, B)$ is increasing in S.

Payoffs in Constrained Capacity Networks

Now suppose that $S \leq Bx$. In a network with this structure, suppliers always receive buyers: $\sigma = \sigma' = 1$. Buyers, however, might not find a supplier for each of their orders. In equilibrium, total network demand is Bx, and the probability that a buyer finds a supplier for one of its units is $\beta = S/Bx$. If any firm ever rejects an offer, network demand increases to $Bx + 1$ in the subsequent period. The buyer will have more difficulty in the next period locating a supplier: $\beta' = S/[Bx + 1]$.

SUPPLIERS' OFFERS   If a buyer rejects a supplier's offer, it carries the unit of demand over to the next period, when it might be able to make the offer himself. However, it reduces the probability of being matched on any one unit to β'. Solving equation 3.5 for $v_s = (\delta/2)\cdot\gamma$.

BUYERS' OFFERS   If a supplier rejects a buyer's offer, it does not increase its chance of receiving a buyer in the next period. Therefore, a supplier has no opportunity cost of accepting an offer and producing in the current period. The buyer can offer the supplier zero surplus, and the seller will accept. Given $\sigma = \sigma' = 1$, from equation 3.4 we see that $v_{b.} = 1$.

In this case, then, the split of the surplus depends only on γ, the change in a buyer's position when it rejects an offer. As defined above, $\gamma \equiv \beta'(x+1) - \beta x$. As discussed above, it can be interpreted as the decrease in the probability that the buyer will be able to find a supplier in the next period, given it has an "extra" order. Substituting for β' and β, in this case we have $\gamma = S(B-1)/B(Bx+1)$. We can see that for $B > 2$, γ is decreasing in B, holding fixed the number of sellers. That is, holding fixed S, the greater the number of buyers, the less one buyer's actions affect the matching probabilities. As B increases, the matching probability in period 2 depends essentially on the relative number of buyers and sellers. Increasing the number of buyers, holding the number of sellers fixed, this probability is lower, and the seller can extract more surplus from the buyer. We therefore have $v_s = (\delta/2)\cdot\gamma$ (the buyer's payoff when the seller makes an offer) is decreasing in B for $B > 2$.

On the equilibrium path suppliers receive buyers with probability $\sigma = 1$, and buyers find suppliers for each of their x units with probability β. The discounted payoffs for suppliers and buyers for a network structure where $S \leq Bx$ are, respectively,

$$V_s(S,B) = \frac{1}{2}[1 - (\delta/2)\gamma + \delta] \text{ and}$$

$$V_B(S,B) = \frac{S}{B}\frac{1}{2}[1 + (\delta/2)\gamma + \delta].$$

Notice that in this case both buyers' and suppliers' payoffs depend on B and S. For the suppliers, the equilibrium payoffs depend on B because B decreases γ and, therefore, increases the amount a supplier can demand from a buyer. Buyers' payoffs respond in exactly the opposite direction to an increase in B. The number of suppliers S also affects the split of surplus. The more suppliers are available, the more likely it is that a buyer can find a supplier for its extra unit of demand when it rejects an offer. So suppliers can extract less surplus. This, obviously, increases a buyer's payoffs and decreases a seller's payoffs. Beyond these effects on bargaining power, the greater the number of suppliers, the more likely it is for a buyer to find a seller on the equilibrium path.

Proofs of Propositions

PROOF OF PROPOSITION 1   Maximize the buyer's payoffs in an excess capacity network:

$$Max\ V_B(S,B) = \frac{x}{2}\left[1 - \frac{\delta}{2S} + \frac{3\delta}{2}\right]\ s.t.\ S \geq Bx + 1$$

$V_B(S, B)$ is independent of B and increasing in S. Therefore, for any B the buyer's payoff approaches its maximum as $S \to \infty$.

PROOF OF PROPOSITION 2   Maximize the buyer's payoffs in a constrained capacity network:

$$Max\ V_B(S,B) = \frac{S}{B}\frac{1}{2}[1 + \delta\gamma(1/2) + \delta]\ s.t.\ S \leq Bx$$

Since γ is increasing in S, for any B, $V_B(S, B)$ is increasing in S. Therefore, the constraint will bind. The optimal network must involve $S = Bx$ suppliers. Given this, consider how buyers' payoffs change as we increase the number of buyers and suppliers along the line $S = Bx$. Consider $V_B(Bx, B)$:

$$V_B(Bx,B) = \frac{x}{2}[1 + \delta] + \frac{\delta}{4}\left[\frac{x^2(B-1)}{Bx + 1}\right]$$

Differentiating with respect to B shows that $V_B(Bx, B)$ is increasing in B. Therefore, a buyer is best off when $B = B_T$ and $S = B_T x$.

PROOF OF PROPOSITION 3   Consider the maximum payoffs a supplier can earn from an excess capacity network:

$$Max\ V_S(S,B) = \frac{1}{2}\frac{Bx}{S}\left[\frac{\delta}{2S} + 1 + \frac{\delta}{2}\right]\ s.t.\ S \geq Bx + 1.$$

For any B, $V_S(S, B)$ is decreasing in S. Hence, the solution to this problem must involve a network where S is as small as possible: $S = Bx + 1$. Given this, consider how suppliers' payoffs change as we increase the number of buyers and suppliers along the line $S = Bx + 1$. Consider $V_S(Bx + 1, B)$:

$$V_S(Bx+1,B) = \frac{1}{2}\frac{Bx}{Bx+1}\left[\frac{\delta}{2(Bx+1)}+1+\frac{\delta}{2}\right].$$

Differentiating with respect to B shows that $V_S(Bx + 1, B)$ is increasing in B. Hence, the most a supplier can earn from an excess-capacity network is when $B = B_T$ and $S = B_T x + 1$. Let $\underline{\alpha} = V_S(B_T x + 1, B_T)$. Since $\underline{\alpha}$ is the maximum suppliers can earn in an excess capacity network, for any $\alpha > \underline{\alpha}$, excess capacity networks are not feasible. For $\alpha \leq \underline{\alpha}$, the network $(B_T x + 1, B_T)$, an excess capacity network is feasible.

PROOF OF PROPOSITION 4   If $\underline{\alpha} > \alpha$, both capacity-constrained and excess-capacity networks are feasible. Consider the highest payoffs a buyer can earn in a constrained capacity network. From proposition 2, these payoffs are in a network with B_T buyers and $B_T x$ suppliers. Now consider the excess capacity network $(B_T, B_T x + 1)$. In this network, suppliers receive $V_S (B_T x + 1, B_T x) = \underline{\alpha}$. So, by hypothesis, this network is feasible. This network has the same number of buyers and one more supplier. It can be shown that buyers receive a higher payoff in this network: $V_B(B_T x + 1, B_T x) - V_B(B_T x, B_T x) > 0$. Therefore, buyers prefer this network to any capacity-constrained network.

PROOF OF PROPOSITION 5   We find the feasible excess capacity network that is best for buyers when $\alpha = \underline{\alpha}$. Seller feasibility requires $V_S(S,B) = \alpha$. Buyers prefer more sellers (other things being equal), so for any B, the buyer optimal feasible $S(B)$ is the S that solves

$$V_S(S,B) = \frac{1}{2}\frac{Bx}{S}\left[\frac{\delta}{2S}+1+\frac{\delta}{2}\right] = \alpha$$

Solving this equality for S gives a quadratic equation for $S(B)$. There are two roots. One is positive and one is negative. The positive root is the correct root. It is

$$S(B) = \frac{1}{8\alpha}\left[2Bx + \delta Bx + \sqrt{4B^2x^2 + 4B^2x^2\delta + B^2x^2\delta^2 + 16\alpha\delta Bx}\right]$$

If $S(B) \geq Bx + 1$, the network $(S(B),B)$ is an excess capacity network.
    From equation 3.8 we have

$$V_B(S(B),B) = \frac{x}{2}\left[1 - \frac{\delta}{2S(B)} + \frac{3\delta}{2}\right]$$

$$= \frac{x}{2}\left[1 - \frac{4\alpha\delta}{\left(2Bx + \delta Bx + \sqrt{4B^2x^2 + 4B^2x^2\delta + B^2x^2\delta^2 + 16\alpha\delta Bx}\right)} + \frac{3\delta}{2}\right].$$

We find that

$$\frac{\partial V_B(S(B),B)}{\partial B} = 2x^{3/2}\alpha\delta$$

$$\left[\frac{(2+\delta)\left(\sqrt{B}\sqrt{x}\sqrt{4Bx + 4Bx\delta + Bx\delta^2 + 16\alpha\delta}\right)}{\sqrt{B}\sqrt{4Bx + 4Bx\delta + Bx\delta^2 + 16\alpha\delta}} \middle/ \left(2Bx + Bx\delta + \sqrt{4B^2x^2 + 4B^2x^2\delta + B^2x^2\delta^2 + 16\alpha\delta Bx}\right)^2\right] > 0$$

So of all networks $(S(B),B)$, the buyers prefer the network $(S(B_T),B_T)$.
    Therefore, if $(S(B_T),B_T)$ has excess capacity, then it is the buyer optimal feasible network. It is straightforward to check that $S(B_T) = B_Tx + 1$ when $\alpha = \underline{\alpha}$ and $S(B_T) > B_Tx + 1$ when $\alpha < \underline{\alpha}$.

PROOF OF PROPOSITION 6   Sellers must earn α, so considering the equation for the participation constraint from equation 3.10 we have

$$V_S(S,B) = \frac{1}{2}\left[1 - \frac{\delta}{2}\gamma + \delta\right] = \alpha,$$

rewriting

$$\frac{\delta}{2}\gamma = 1 - 2\alpha + \delta, \tag{3.1a}$$

where $\gamma = \dfrac{(B-1)}{(Bx-1)}\dfrac{S}{B}$. Substitute the expression for γ into equation 3.1a to find $S(B)$, the number of sellers that can be in a network of size B, given the seller's participation constraint.

$$S(B) = \frac{B(Bx+1)}{(B-1)}\frac{2}{\delta}(1 - 2\alpha + \delta).$$

Since we can only have a positive number of sellers, we need $S(B) > 0$, which requires

$$\frac{(1+\delta)}{2} > \alpha.$$

Substitute equation 3.1a into the buyer's payoff function, as given in equation 3.11:

$$V_B(S,B) = \frac{S}{B}\frac{1}{2}[1 + (\delta/2)\gamma + \delta] = \frac{S(B)}{B}[1 - \alpha + \delta]$$

$$= \frac{(Bx+1)}{(B-1)}\frac{2}{\delta}(1 - 2\alpha + \delta)(1 - \alpha + \delta).$$

Define the ratio of sellers to buyers in a constrained capacity network with B buyers and $S(B)$ sellers:

$$R(B) = \frac{S(B)}{B} = \frac{(Bx+1)}{(B-1)}\frac{2}{\delta}(1 - 2\alpha + \delta).$$

Then $V_B(S(B),B) = R(B)[1 - \alpha + \delta]$.

If $R'(B) < 0$, then the buyer optimal network involves the fewest buyers possible subject to the constraint that $S(B) \geq 1$. Note that $S'(B) > 0$ so long as $B \geq 3$. Although $S'(B) < 0$ at $B \leq 2$, we still always have that $S(2) \leq S(3)$. The inequality is strict if $x > 1$.

When $R'(B) < 0$, we find that

$$R'(B) = \frac{-(x+1)}{(B-1)^2} \frac{2}{\delta} (1 - 2\alpha + \delta).$$

This is negative so long as $\frac{(1+\delta)}{2} > \alpha$, which is the condition we had before.

Notes

1. There is a growing game-theoretic literature on network formation.
2. Long-term contracts are not possible; rather, a noncooperative price-setting mechanism determines the terms of trade. The limitation on firms' ability to write contracts creates an incentive for firms to organize production through networks. In a more complex contractual environment, firms could write long-term contracts on the link, the investment, and the price. The inability to write long-term contracts captures contracting difficulties in a stylized setting as in Sandford J. Grossman and Oliver Hart (1986), Hart and Moore (1990), and Patrick Bolton and Michael Whinston (1993).
3. One of the first papers we know of on this topic is Susan Helper and David Levine's (1992) study of long-term supplier relations in the automobile industry. Their study differs from ours in that they compare two extreme market structures, whereas we allow for intermediate numbers of competing suppliers.
4. Quality is often cited as an important concern to buyers. Suppliers often must make up-front investments to improve quality, and quality can be difficult to specify in a contract.
5. These choices cannot be changed in the production stage. Although in reality the structure of buyer-supplier networks changes over time, these changes occur less frequently than production decisions. We therefore view network formation as a long-term decision, and production as a short-term decision.
6. Asymmetries would not add to the basic insights we obtain here concerning supplier investment incentives.

    Rachel Kranton and Deborah Minehart (2001) consider buyers' decisions to make investments in particular suppliers, where buyers ultimately compete for inputs in a stylized representation of price competition (an ascending-bid auction).

7. The extent to which buyers know the identity of their suppliers' other customers, and vice versa, can vary. For instance, computer companies often clearly specify suppliers of specific parts (for example, chips, hardware, and software) in the product information accompanying a personal computer. In other industries, input suppliers and buyers are not openly advertised. But firms can sometimes obtain this information through espionage.

8. Because we wish to focus exclusively on the input market, we assume that buyers do not compete strategically in the output market. This assumption would correspond to textile manufacturers, for example, that sell their output on the world market but procure inputs from local suppliers (see Dore 1987).

9. To be precise, this will be true in our bargaining game for $B = 2$.

10. Notice that there are integer constraints for both the number of buyers and the number of suppliers. To avoid excess notation, throughout this chapter we will conduct the analysis as if there were no integer constraint. Of course the actual solutions to the various maximization problems in the chapter would involve the closest integers that still satisfy the participation constraint.

11. For example, according to many observers, the "just-in-time" management structure employed in the Japanese auto industry facilitates high standards. This system rests on closer relationships between the firms in the industry supply chains and complex coordination of daily shipments between input suppliers and buyers.

12. We have not formally defined payoffs for buyers and sellers in overlapping networks. We could make basic assumptions about these payoffs so that we can write precise equilibrium conditions for buyers forming nonoverlapping networks. This precision would not change the basic insights we derive here concerning sellers' investment incentives.

13. Networks that are not optimal for buyers could also be equilibria. For example, given that each buyer chooses to qualify a different set of suppliers, the best response for an individual buyer could be to do the same. It could be an equilibrium for each buyer to have his own group of suppliers, even though it would be optimal for all buyers to qualify the same set of suppliers.

14. This bargaining model is a simplified version of an infinite-horizon bargaining game we developed for this setting.

15. While a supplier's quality investment is not contractible over time periods, the actual delivery of an input within one period is contractible.

16. All formal proofs are provided in the appendix.

17. Because the numbers of buyers and suppliers are small, we believe

that it should be easy for buyers and suppliers to contact one another quickly to determine who has made contact with whom.

References

Bolton, Patrick, and Michael Whinston. 1993. "Incomplete Contracts, Vertical Integration, and Supply Assurance." *Review of Economic Studies* 60(1): 121–48.

Demski, Joel, David E. M. Sappington, and Pablo T. Spiller. 1987. "Managing Supplier Switching." *RAND Journal of Economics* 18(1): 77–97.

Dore, Ronald. 1987. *Taking Japan Seriously*, London: Athlone Press.

Farrell, Joseph, and Nancy T. Gallini. 1988. "Second-Sourcing as a Commitment: Monopoly Incentives to Attract Competition." *Quarterly Journal of Economics* 103(4): 673–94.

Grossman, Sanford J., and Oliver D. Hart. 1986. "The Costs and Benefits of Ownership: A Theory of Vertical and Lateral Integration," *Journal of Political Economy* 94(4): 691–719.

Hart, Oliver, and John Moore. 1988. "Property Rights and the Theory of the Firm." *Journal of Political Economy* 98(6): 1119–58.

———. 1990. "Property Rights and the Nature of the Firm." *Journal of Political Economy* 98(6): 1119–58.

Helper, Susan, and David Levine. 1992. "Long-Term Supplier Relations and Product-Market Structure." *Journal of Law, Economics, and Organization* 8(3): 561–81.

Horn, Henrick, and Asher Wolinsky. 1988. "Bilateral Monopolies and Incentives for Merger." *RAND Journal of Economics* 19(3): 408–19.

Jackson, Matthew, and Asher Wolinsky. 1994. "A Strategic Model of Social and Economic Networks." Discussion paper no. 1098. Evanston, Ill.: Northwestern University.

Kranton, Rachel, and Deborah Minehart. 2001. "A Theory of Buyer-Seller Networks." *American Economic Review*. 91(3): 485–508.

Lazerson, Mark. 1993. "Factory or Putting-Out? Knitting Networks in Modena." In *The Embedded Firm: On the Socioeconomics of Industrial Networks*, edited by Gernot Grabher. New York: Routledge.

McAfee, R. Preston, and John McMillan. 1987. "Auctions and Bidding." *Journal of Economic Literature* 25(2): 699–738.

Riordan, Michael. 1994. "Contracting with Qualified Suppliers." Unpublished paper. Boston, Mass.: Boston University.

Saxenian, Annalee. 1994. *Regional Advantage: Culture and Competition in Silicon Valley and Route 128*. Cambridge, Mass.: Harvard University Press.

Williamson, Oliver. 1975. *Market and Hierarchies: Analysis and Antitrust Implications*. New York: Free Press.

Part II

The Sociology Approach

Chapter 4

The Formation of Inter-Organizational Networks

Toby Stuart

In this chapter I will offer a literature review and some thoughts on processes that may systematically account for the formation networks among economic actors. After reviewing why sociologists (and, increasingly, economists) see networks as essential to the functioning of markets, and then review much of the work that has been done in economic sociology on the formation of networks and a smaller portion of the research on the subject in economics and applied mathematics. Although I describe research on networks at both the organizational and the individual level, I focus on the organization level. In the interest of brevity, I emphasize horizontal relationships among organizations, rather than vertical (that is, buyer-supplier) transactions.

What, exactly, is meant by "horizontal inter-organizational networks"? To fix ideas, imagine a venture capital firm that has identified a promising young company that it wishes to finance. Further, suppose that the venture capitalist chooses to form a syndicate—a small group composed of other high-risk investors—to finance the startup company. Although not all venture investments are made in syndicates, the majority of them are. In the context of the venture capital industry, the question of where inter-organizational networks come from translates into a question about the mechanisms that guide venture capital firms in the search for and selection of syndicate partners. To give another example that has been the site of much empirical research, consider the case of a pharmaceutical firm that has a promising drug candidate but lacks sufficient internal capacity to launch a worldwide marketing campaign. What regularities guide its selection of a marketing partner? Both of these examples are about the formation of horizontal inter-organizational networks.

Why examine the question of what determines the formation of particular transactions, or of patterns of connections, in inter-organizational networks? The most straightforward answer is that we believe we know that the shapes of networks—the particular structures of relations in place—is consequential for important outcomes experienced by the actors in networks. Research on social and economic networks has thrived during the last few decades, but the overwhelming thrust of the empirical literature has been to document the consequences of occupancy of different locations in established networks on outcomes of all types. In the economic sociology and organization theory literature—the area in which the author works—there are literally hundreds of studies that examine "network effects." For instance, in the tradition of Mark S. Granovetter (1973), a number of studies consider the role of networks in the job search process (see Fernandez, Castilla, and Moore 2000) and in the process of securing promotions inside firms (Podolny and Baron 1997). Extending classic work on the diffusion of innovations (Coleman, Katz, and Menzel 1966; Burt 1987), a large number of studies have assessed the influence of interfirm networks on explaining patterns of adoption of practices and processes (Mizruchi 1992). Building from network-based conceptions of market structure, a third thrust of the literature has been to show that firm positions influence performance outcomes, ranging from sales growth (Podolny, Stuart, and Hannan 1996; Ingram and Roberts 2000) to market valuation (Stuart, Hoang, and Hybels 1999) to innovation rates (Ahuja 2000).

Can we be certain that the findings from this body of work are valid? It is possible to take issue with any one of these studies on empirical grounds. In particular, the vast majority of published work treats measures of network position as exogenous to the outcome variable under examination and in many cases does little adequately to account for plausible unobserved correlates of particular network positions. As is discussed at some length in chapter 6 in this volume, by Ray E. Reagans, Ezra Zuckerman, and Bill McEvily (and is implied in chapter 3, by Rachel Kranton and Deborah Minehart, and chapter 8, by James E. Rauch and Joel Watson), the endogeneity of network position may be particularly problematic in studies seeking to document the effects of networks on actors' performance (see Durlauf and Fafchamps 2004 for an introduction to the issues). The reason why unadjusted empirical estimates of network effects may be confounded is simple. If actors are aware that benefits accrue to those who possess certain network configurations, they have an incentive to elbow in to certain regions of a social structure. Conversely, if actors differ in their ability to create or benefit from certain types of links, apparent network effects may in fact be caused by some underlying, unobserved characteristic of the actors.

One reason why questions loom about the empirical accuracy of studies of network effects is that the vast and growing body of research that documents them belies our quite limited knowledge of how networks emerge and evolve. To put it succinctly, without a reasonably rich understanding of how networks emerge and change—without a theory of where networks come from and how they evolve—the ground underneath the findings of network effects will always be at least a little shaky. Therefore, I see the literature on inter-organizational networks as facing something of a crossroads. It might continue as it has developed, with the vast majority of work looking at how heterogeneous network positions affect outcomes. Hopefully, the focus will shift to considering in greater depth the more difficult question of understanding the social and organizational principles that govern the formation of networks. These understandings may in turn inform the empirical work on the causal influence of network positions on outcomes of interest.

I also describe the theoretical foundations for the basic claim that networks should matter for how markets behave and how outcomes in markets are shaped. There is far more to say on this point than there is space available, so I focus on the well-known argument that there is often considerable uncertainty in market exchanges, and that a consequence of this uncertainty is that networks among market participants play a prominent role in shaping patterns of exchange, or more precisely, which pairs of actors engage in exchange. I then describe the research on endogenous network formation in economic sociology. This research has adapted network-theoretic models to examine how the structure of an inter-organizational network in one period adumbrates the creation of next-period ties. In this section I also briefly describe work in economics, statistics, and mathematics that address the question of how networks change. Section IV offers a brief conclusion.

Why Networks Matter

Governing inter-organizational relationships poses challenges. The literatures in economics on transaction costs and on the theory of incomplete contracts have taught us that because the explicit contracts that govern many market transactions are insufficiently detailed (i.e., inadequately forward-looking) to eliminate all possible opportunities for firms to violate the spirit of an exchange agreement (Williamson 1975), participants in economic exchanges are often exposed to the risk that their trading partners will behave opportunistically. As the early-twentieth-century Viennese economist Friedrich von Hayek (1945/1984) famously explained, economic markets are rife with information problems.

This basic insight—that contractual mechanisms often cannot eradicate all transactional risk—is often invoked in sociological work on why established networks affect the creation of new market-based relationships. While the transaction-costs literature has counterposed hierarchical control and market-based exchange as alternative forms of governance, structural sociologists have responded that market participants have an option other than hierarchical control for mitigating transactional risks. Specifically, actors routinely respond to market uncertainty by exploiting their social networks to select transaction partners who, on the basis of semiprivate information available to them from the network, they believe will behave honorably, even if they are not required to under the terms of the formal contract governing the relationship (Macauley 1963; Granovetter 1985). In short, in many market contexts, social networks are a means to redress inefficiencies caused by imperfect information of various kinds.

How, exactly, does a network function to reassure would-be exchange partners that a particular partner will behave with integrity? Five possible mechanisms have been proposed to explain why networks matter for trade:

Information diffusion
Attributions of competence
Brokerage
Obligations
Sanctions

Most network-based studies posit that one or more of these mechanisms produce "trust," as formally articulated by James S. Coleman (1990, chapter 5): to a focal actor, the network serves to establish the anticipation that a certain set of actors will execute tasks competently and behave cooperatively in exchange relations, even without the assurance of contractually specified enforcement mechanisms (see also many of the chapters in Gambetta 1988). Clearly, other things being equal, actors would prefer to have transactions with trusted exchange partners—and this would be evidence of the network's impact on exchange structures.

Information Diffusion
A basic function of the network is to disseminate information; the many ramifications of the restricted propagation of information through networks have been established in a number of domains. With respect to relationship formation, social ties that are already in place affect patterns of affiliation because the paths that actors in the network traverse to other actors determine who has access to information about the characteristics of other actors (see Granovetter 1985 for a programmatic discussion; Podolny 1994; Gulati 1995a; see Walker, Kogut, and Shan 1997 for evidence on inter-organizational relationships). For example, Ranjay Gulati (1995a, 1995b) describes how managers of firms communicate with one another to

exchange information about prospective alliance partners. In another instance, Paul Ingram and Peter W. Roberts (2000) describe forms of information exchange that extend across the friendship network among managers of nearby hotels in one city. These channels of information flow affect exchange patterns because knowing about a potential partner may reduce the perceived risk of transacting with that person, and dealing only with known associates lowers the cost of searching for and screening potential partners. Because social systems tend to be stratified, however, relying on information gathered from one's network to select exchange partners often effectively leads to a clustering of relations within and around particular locations in a social structure. Where access to information is restricted by disconnects in the network, new relationships are less likely to form.

Attributions of Competence

A closely related process concerns the network's effect on attributions of competence. In the search for worthwhile exchange partners, the relative structural positions of two actors may affect their assessments of one another's quality when competence is difficult to discern—as it frequently is. As the task of assessing a potential partner's competence becomes more difficult, evaluators' appraisals of quality begin to open to the influence of indirect signals, such as the proximity and social status of the actors under scrutiny, as well as the prestige of their affiliates (Podolny 1994; Stuart, Hoang, and Hybels 1999). To the extent that the social structural proximity of other actors becomes a basis for making quality inferences, the estimates of the potential value of an exchange with an alter (another member of a network), in addition to expectations of his or her trustworthiness, may be positively influenced when a potential exchange partner is near to a focal actor in social space.[1]

Brokerage

A third stream of the literature on information dissemination emphasizes bridging ties and the brokerage role. The theoretical and empirical discussion in this area is most developed in Ronald S. Burt

(1992; see also chapter 5, this volume), who expounds on the opportunities created by actors who span disconnected social clusters. Although one function served by these "third parties" is simply to transfer information between two otherwise disconnected groups (Granovetter 1973), Burt (1992) articulates a more active role often performed by the third party, envisioning an entrepreneur who identifies opportunities for synergistic trades and induces the trust of several parties to produce new resource combinations. In this case, the intermediary often also performs the role of guarantor (Coleman 1990, chapter 8); he or she may participate in dispute resolution and offer assurances about another's reliability, and thus add value to the relationship he or she brokers. Hence, the profit-seeking motive of the third party becomes an additional factor in the network's effect on relationship formation.

Obligations

Work on the embeddedness of economic transactions is the source of the fourth perspective on why established networks impact the formation of next-period exchanges. Studies in this area observe that personal relationships inevitably come to overlap with repeated economic exchanges, and these friendships promote trust between and feelings of obligation toward trading partners. As a consequence, transgressing the terms of an explicit or implicit contract in an embedded economic exchange is tantamount to cheating a friend (Granovetter 1985). Brian Uzzi (1996) discusses the advantages of embedded ties: they often facilitate information exchange and joint problem solving, and the fact that they are characterized by a level of trust obviates the need for rigid contracts and active monitoring (see also Dore 1983; Larson 1992). As a result, embeddedness scholars are apt to highlight the efficiencies engendered in exchanges immersed in webs of prior transactions—namely, relationships are more flexible and possibly encompass a greater range of activities than would be possible if transaction governance was limited to written contracts. This of course has implications for patterns of exchange: if embedded exchanges are advantageous, actors will favor transactions with those with whom they have established relationships.[2]

Sanctions

Until now we have discussed network mechanisms that are for the most part historically oriented, insofar as consideration of how one's current behavior may affect future trading opportunities is not strictly necessary to the functioning of any of the mechanisms. By contrast, rational-choice models (in economics and sociology) rely on the incentives created by the possibility of future exchanges to explain how the information-transmitting capacity of the network might affect patterns of trade (see especially Raub and Weesie 1990; also, Granovetter 1985; Coleman 1990; Kandori 1992; Robinson and Stuart forthcoming). Because the network effectively widens the observability of actors' conduct, the potential gains one might obtain by violating the spirit of a current transaction must be weighed against the damage to one's reputation that would result if the offended trading partner informs his or her affiliates of the infringement. Building from this insight, Werner Raub and Jeroen Weesie (1990) develop a model of how the level of connectedness in a network affects the potency of the incentive structures created by reputational considerations. In the model, the structural properties of a network determine the extent to which deliberations about future exchange opportunities influence present-day conduct.

Where Do Networks Come From?

Clearly, there are compelling theoretical reasons for the existence of network effects, and subject to the aforementioned caveat of the prevalent, all-too-often implicit and questionable assumption that network positions are exogenous, there is reason to believe that network positions have real consequences. As important influences on the attainment of desired outcomes, the question of how networks are configured and how actors sort into different positions within them is central both for understanding individual-level stratification processes and performance of actors—whether individuals or collectivities—in economic markets.

Sociological Approaches

In most of the sociologically inspired research on inter-organizational networks the process of "intra-network" evolution has been considered. "Intra-network evolution" refers to the fact that most studies have examined the development of a network as if it could be characterized as a Markov process, one in which the analyst can begin to study the evolutionary process at any arbitrary point in the network's development.[3] In effect, the prototypical study analyzes panel network data in which multiple (typically, annual) observations of a network are made, and the researcher analyzes the probability that two nodes in the network establish a link in time $t \pm 1$ as a function of the shape of the network at t.[4] Thus, an already existing network is an antecedent in the empirical analyses. For example, Gulati (1995a) studies the formation of strategic-alliance networks in three industries during a nine-year window. In his study the shape of the alliance network in one year forms the antecedent that influences the creation of new alliance ties in the following year.

Sociologically inspired studies of network-tie formation have put forth three primary arguments to explain the pattern of emergence of connections among social and economic actors: trust, reciprocity, and homophily. The importance of trust-related considerations for the formation of economic exchange relations are outlined in the preceding section. In practice, researchers have explored trust-based considerations by assuming that certain social structural configurations can be treated as proxies for the level of trust among the actors in a network. Uzzi's (1996) and Gulati's (1995a, 1995b) studies are representative, arguing that pairs of actors that have previous exchange relationships or are connected through a common third party (each one has a relationship with the same third organization) are more likely to enjoy mutual trust (see also Powell, Koput, and Smith-Doerr 1996). There are now numerous relationship-level studies showing that, relative to randomly chosen pairs of actors in a network, pairs of organizations with past ties are highly likely to form "repeat" deals, and pairs with common third parties similarly are more likely to initiate relations. These results exist both in the United States and in studies of developing economies (for example, Stark 1996; Keister 2001). The fact that pairs of actors that have transacted in the past are particularly likely to form subsequent ties is taken as evidence that trust is a central consideration in the formation of new ties.

A number of criticisms can be levied at the empirical research claiming to demonstrate that trust is a mechanism explaining the formation of economic exchange relations. First, most of the existing research does little to cleanly identify trust as the operative mechanism; as I will describe, there are (obviously) other possible mechanisms that could cause the empirical relationships that network researchers have attributed to trust. Second, there is a pervasive assumption in the sociological literature on intra-network evolution that connections in networks represent positive relationships among the participating actors. In other words, actors, we typically assume, have uniformly positive assessments of their past contacts. Hence, the information that passes from node to node along the links in a network is assumed to affirm the worth of past exchange partners. Yet as individuals, we know that much information conveyed to or heard from trusted partners is intended to encourage avoiding transactions with certain third parties. Moreover, sociologists have given scant attention to the fact that actors may have systematic incentives to distort or simply not convey information to other members of a social system. As sociologists have moved from studying noneconomic to economic relationships, there has been minimal effort to modify theories to account for contextual differences between arenas.

A second line of argument on network formation is that actors have a strong tendency to interact with homophilous others, that is, people and organizations select exchange partners who are like themselves. Of course, since long before Peter M. Blau's (1977) systematic treatment, sociologists have observed that individuals are far more likely to associate with sociodemographically and geographically proximate others. In human ecology, the law of distance-interaction states that the probability of interaction between social elements declines as a multiplicative function of the distance between them (Hawley 1971). Sociologists believe this "law" arises for a number of reasons. First, geographic and social distance decreases the likelihood of a chance meeting. Second, the costs of interacting—including finding and screening exchange partners and maintaining relationships—increase with distance (Zipf 1949). The seminal studies of Leon Festinger, Stanley Schacter, and Kurt W. Back (1950) and the work of the human ecologists have refined these insights by showing an increased interaction frequency when actors meet in "functional" space (for example, when the tenants in an apartment complex meet in the laundry room).

It is not surprising that individuals gravitate toward sociodemographically similar others, but this line of argument has been extended to the study of patterns of interaction among organizations. If we take a number of firms that are at risk of forming transactions with one another and characterize each one by a vector of attributes (such as its geographic location, specific areas of expertise, birth or industry entry cohort, status level, and so forth), it is possible to construct multiple or summary measures of pairwise proximities and distances for all of the organizations in the group. The resulting similarity or distance matrices can then be used to gauge the influence of proximity on the formation of economic ties. A number of studies have taken this approach. In an examination of the formation of bond-underwriting syndicates in the investment banking industry, Joel M. Podolny (1994) argues that organizations' trading patterns will exhibit status-based homophily, especially in the junk bond market. In other words, Podolny argues (and finds) that pairs of high-status banks affiliate to jointly manage securities-underwriting syndicates, and pairs of low-status banks collaborate, but pairings of high- with low-status banks are infrequent. Using a completely different dimension of distance, Toby Stuart (1998) finds that in technology-based industries, horizontal strategic alliances cluster among firms with relatively similar technological expertise. In a study of investment syndicates in venture capital, Olav Sorenson and Toby Stuart (2006) find that investment syndicates form in the presence of common geographic locations, common industry expertise, and common status levels. Examining the formation of strategic alliances in the biopharmaceuticals sector, W. W. Powell et al. (2005)

test for the effects of inter-firm similarities along the dimensions of age, size, location, and ownership status as determinants of the likelihood of collaboration.

The fact that organizations appear to exhibit the tendency to establish exchange relationships with proximate partners underscores the challenge of econometrically singling out particular social mechanisms as driving the formation of relationships in intra-network studies. In particular, if similarities along certain dimensions are antecedent to the formation of economic ties, then the fact that organizations that have exchanged in the past or that share common third parties are more likely to initiate new deals could be the simple result of unobserved similarities among the transacting organizations. Thus, to convince skeptical readers, intra-network evolutionary studies in which the shape of the network at t is used to predict the emergence of ties at $t + 1$ must address the possibility that findings on lagged network attributes are driven by omitted variables related to unobserved similarities among transacting organizations. There are few studies in sociology that meet this challenge.

Another social mechanism that has been examined for its capacity to shape inter-organzational transactions is reciprocity. The so called "norm of reciprocity" has long been recognized as a principle for organizing patterns of exchange in a network. Of course, to study reciprocity it is necessary that transactions be directional; in other words, opportunities for exchange are sent from i to j, or vice versa. James R. Lincoln, Michael L. Gerlach, and Peggy Takahashi (1992) study partial equity stakes and interlocking ties among Japanese company directors. Their argument, which is rooted in the institutional context of Japanese industrial organization, is that equity ownership is likely to be reciprocal—shareholding patterns will be cross-firm—but director interlocks will be unidirectional. In a recent paper, Matthew Bothner, Salih Z. Ozdemir, and Scott Meadow (2005) examine the norm of reciprocity in the venture capital industry. This paper looks at the social structural conditions that contour the probability that a partner who joins a lead investor's syndicate will reciprocate with a follow-on offer to the former lead to join a syndicate that it assembles.

A Brief Comparison with Economic Approaches

Not surprisingly, economic approaches to network formation fundamentally differ from sociological studies. First, the literature in economics is predominantly theoretical, whereas recent work in sociology is overwhelmingly empirical. Probably in large part because of the theoretical focus, the recent literature on network formation is larger in economics than in sociology, where, in my view, fresh empirical modeling approaches and theoretical insights have not been forthcoming. Second, economic approaches assume that agents are self-interested and strategic, and that there are both costs and incentives associated with agents' attempts to form links in a network. Thus, in economic arenas at least, relationships are strategic rather than social, and self-interest drives the extension and reciprocation of offers to interact. In sociological accounts of the emergence of network, by contrast, incentives and strategies to form ties for subsequent purposes play secondary roles.

Chapter 3 in this volume, by Rachel Kranton and Deborah Minehart, is representative of the economic approach and illustrative of the differences between the disciplines. Kranton and Minehart develop a theoretical model of network formation in which the outcomes that the network will influence are central explanatory factors in the formation of the network itself. In other words, they jointly model the formation and consequences of an economic network. Agents who negotiate with their counterparties at the second stage (in Kranton and Minehart's case, buyers and sellers) anticipate that the pattern of links in the network will influence their bargaining power; thus agents seek to establish links that they anticipate will position them advantageously in future negotiations.

It is worth highlighting a few studies that bridge the disciplinary divide. It is encouraging to see that the emerging literature in economics on network formation often includes a few references to and borrows insights from sociological research, which is not the case in many areas of economics that broadly relate to work that has been done in sociology. (Zuckerman [2003] reports disheartening base rates for citations of sociological research in prominently placed economics papers.) Notable in my view are papers by James Montgomery. Montgomery (1996) develops a game-theoretic model of the stability of exchange patterns; his (1998) paper presents a game-theoretic formalization of embeddedness that is rooted in classic work on role theory. In both cases, the inspiration for Montgomery's formalizations are important works in sociology; respectively, Blau's (1964) theory of social exchange and Granovetter's (1985) essay on embeddedness.

Large Networks

In recent years, the area of research on network formation that has experienced the largest growth is work in statistical physics and applied mathematics on the topological properties of very large networks (see, for example, Watts and Strogatz 1998; Barabasi and Albert 1999). In particular, the distribution of the number of links of the nodes in a network (called the degree distribution) and the extent to which the nodes in a network are embedded in dense, local clusters of relations have been commonly studied attributes of networks. From studies of these and other network-level topographic features, the literature on large networks has evolved to incorporate models of microlevel dynamics that could potentially generate structures that approximate those actually observed in large-network studies, as well as studies of the consequences of macrostructural configurations for individual-, community-, and network-level outcomes.

The research on large networks draws more heavily on theories and empirical regularities in sociology than in economics. For instance, a recent paper (Boguna et al. 2004) formulates a mathematical model of network formation based on the sociological notion that relationships appear disproportionately among socially proximate actors. Marian Boguna and collaborators find that the microlevel process of matches formed on the basis of minimizing social distance can yield a macro network with commonly observed statistical properties, in particular, a high clustering coefficient and homophily among the degree scores of interacting nodes. In another example, Roger Guimera et al. (2005) present a model of team self-assembly in which three parameters govern the demographic composition of newly created teams: the number of agents in the population; the strength of the preference of agents to repeat past ties; and the probability that network incumbents (versus new entrants) are selected to join a new team. In simulations, topographic features of the macrostructures that emerge from this three-parameter model are similar to those empirically observed in five different networks. Likewise, Duncan J. Watts, P. S. Dodds, and M. E. J. Newmann (2002) develop a model of search across networks that is rooted in sociological insights about the connections of individuals with common identities.

Endogeneity

Well-specified empirical models of how actors come to occupy specific network positions represent a promising avenue for making headway on the endogeneity problems that beleaguer most of the empirical studies of network effects in sociology. In the typical setting that has engaged the interest of organizational sociologists, the researcher neither can randomly assign actors to network positions nor have at his or her disposal a strong instrumental variable that can be used to identify the causal effect of (an often time complex) network position.

Given the lack of both the ability to implement an experimental design and a strong instrumental variable, the most appealing general option to identify causal effects may be to use sample selection corrections or other selection-on-observables type estimators (for examples, see Robinson and Stuart forthcoming; Azoulay, Ding, and Stuart forthcoming; for development of a compelling, general approach, see Robins 1999). Although there are limitations to this empirical approach (which are beyond the scope of this chapter), if the researcher can generate a strong baseline model of the likelihood that actors maneuver into particular types of network positions, it may be possible to use a sample weighting procedure to estimate a causal effect of network positions.

Future Directions

I believe that we are on the verge of rapid progress in our understanding of the social mechanisms that underlie the formation of economic networks. In all likelihood, theoretical work on network formation processes in economics will gain momentum. Similarly, there is a fast-growing community of scholars with interests in large social networks in the disciplines of applied mathematics, physics, bioinformatics, and computer science. Not surprisingly, researchers from these fields have become interested in applying mathematical models to the analysis of social and economic networks (in addition to nonsocial networks, such as neural networks). Thus, there is cause for optimism regarding the future development of research on the formation of networks.

Within organizational sociology, it also seems that attention to processes of network formation is gaining momentum. In one recent endeavor, Baum and his colleagues (2005) examine the formation of investment syndicates in Canadian investment banking. In their effort to explain the emergence of relationships among dissimilar organizations, Baum et al. (2005) argue that organizations are driven by aspiration-level search: when a firm fails to perform up to its assumed aspiration level, it is driven to search for syndicate partners beyond its roster of familiar partners. Taking a very different approach, Sorenson and Stuart (2006) argue that Scott Feld's (1981) ideas about the role of social foci in organizing social structures have promise for explaining the formation of inter-organizational networks. In particular, because many organizational associations arise from two firms' joint participation in an event—for example, when members of two different organizations serve on the same board of directors or participate in the same investment syndicate—properties of the occasion that precede interaction may play a causal role in explaining which pairings of firms actually occur. Translating this into the context they analyze, Sorenson and Stuart argue that the probability that two venture capitalist firms will join a syndicate together significantly depends on each one's relationship with the "event," or early-stage company, in which they both invest.

Finally, there is remarkably little research on the role of interpersonal relationships as the foundation upon which interfirm transactions are built. (Perhaps the sole recent exception to this in the organizational sociology literature is Paul Ingram and Peter Roberts's 2000 study of the Sydney hotel industry.) Although there are no general statistics on the mobility of management-ranked employees between firms, we do know from surveys of graduates from MBA programs that most MBAs do spells with multiple employers in their careers. Thus, the career paths of managers and other members of the professional workforce (such as engineers) generate dense interpersonal linkages between members of different organizations. This is especially true in spatially concentrated industries; for example, mobility rates among Wall Street investment bankers and Silicon Valley electronics firms are known to be particularly high. Although some of this personnel mobility may be endogenous to the patterns of formal interfirm relations, I would anticipate that the causal arrow typically points in the opposite direction. With better information on flows of people between firms, it may well be possible to gain significant insight into the formation of economic relationships between organizations.

Notes

1. The idea here is that, ceteris paribus, actors may be more likely to be generous in their attributions of competence when they have been well informed about a potential partner from their acquaintances. Ronald S. Burt and Marc Knez (1995) argue that opinions become amplified in relatively closed social systems (social locations with relatively high network density), so that actors are likely to reach consensus regarding their assessments of others. If this is the case, then there is likely to be little (at least, perceived) uncertainty about the competence of particular trading partners in comparatively closed social systems. Thus, when competence is otherwise ambiguous, the network helps resolve uncertainty about partner quality.

2. Olav Sorenson and David Waguespack's (2005) recent paper on the feature film industry offers a dissenting view. They argue that the outcomes of embedded exchanges are conditionally worse than the outcomes of new partnerships in the context they study, feature films in Hollywood. In particular, they argue that the unconditional, average performance of films created from repeated pairings of distributors and key personnel are superior to the average results achieved by first-time pairings, but the sign reverses when the amount of resources invested in the film is taken into account.

3. James M. Podolny and Karen Paige (1997), Ranjay Gulati and Martin Garguilo (1999), and others have used the phrase "endogenous" to de-

scribe studies of network formation in which the pattern of links in one period is considered to be the central predictors of the ties that are formed in the next period. Because properties of the network itself form the (lagged) right-side variables, the process is one of endogenous network change. However, to avoid confusion with the earlier (and subsequent) discussion of endogeneity as a methodological challenge in the estimation of network effects, I will use the term "intranetwork" instead of "endogenous" to refer to the studies that consider how the network at time t influences the formation of relations at $t + 1$.

4.   In recent work, Gueorgi Kossinets and Duncan J. Watts (2006) describe more sophisticated methods for recovering the instantaneous shape of a network that evolves in continuous time.

References

Ahuja, Gautam. 2000. "Collaboration Networks, Structural Holes, and Innovation: A Longitudinal Study." *Administrative Science Quarterly* 45(3): 425–57.

Azoulay, Pierre, Waverly Ding, and Toby Stuart. Forthcoming. "The Impact of Academic Patenting on the Rate, Direction, and Quality of (Public) Research Output." *Journal of Economic Behavior & Organization*.

Barabasi, Albert-Laszlo, and Reka Albert. 1999. "Emergence of Scaling in Random Networks." *Science* 286(5439): 509-12.

Baum, Joel, Timothy Rowley, and Andrew Shipilov. 2005. "Dancing with Strangers: Aspiration Performance and Search for Underwriting Syndicate Partners." *Administrative Science Quarterly* 50(4): 536-575.

Blau, Peter. 1964. *Exchange and Power in Social Life*. New York: Wiley.

——— 1977. *Inequality and Heterogeneity: A Primitive Theory of Social Structure*. New York: Free Press.

Boguna, Marian, Romualdo Pastor-Satorras, Albert Diaz-Guilera, and Alex Arenas. 2004. "Models of Social Networks Based on Social Distance Attachment." *Physical Review E* 70(5): 056122-30.

Bothner, Matthew, Salih Z. Ozdemir, and Scott Meadow. 2005. "Social Constraint and the Rate of Reciprocal Exchange Among Venture Capital Firms." Working paper, University of Chicago Graduate School of Business.

Burt, Ronald S. 1987. "Social Contagion and Innovation: Cohesion Versus Structural Equivalence." *American Journal of Sociology* 92(6): 1287–1335.

———. 1992. *Structural Holes*. Cambridge, Mass.: Harvard University Press.

Burt, Ronald S., and Marc Knez. 1995. "Kinds of Third-Party Effects on Trust." *Rationality and Society* 7(3): 255–92.

Coleman, James S. 1990. *Foundations of Social Theory.* Cambridge, Mass., and London: Harvard University Press/Belknap Press.

Coleman, James S., Elihu Katz, and Herbert Menzel. 1966. *Medical Innovation: A Diffusion Study.* Indianapolis, Ind.: Bobbs-Merrill.

Dore, Ronald. 1983. "Goodwill and the Spirit of Market Capitalism." *British Journal of Sociology* 34(4): 459-82.

Durlauf, Steven N., and Marcel Falchamps. 2004. "Social Capital." NBER working paper no. W10485. Washington: National Bureau of Economic Research.

Feld, Scott L. 1981. "The Focused Organization of Social Ties." *American Journal of Sociology* 86(5): 1015–35.

Fernandez, Roberto, Emilio Castilla, and Paul Moore. 2000. "Social Capital at Work: Networks and Employment at a Phone Center." *American Journal of Sociology* 105(5): 1288–1356.

Festinger, Leon, Stanley Schacter, and Kurt W. Back. 1950. *Social Pressure in Informal Groups.* New York: Harper & Bros.

Gambetta, Diego, ed. 1988. *Trust: Making and Breaking Cooperative Relations.* New York: Blackwell.

Granovetter, Mark S. 1973. "The Strength of Weak Ties." *American Journal of Sociology* 78(6): 1360–80.

———. 1985. "Economic Action and Social Structure: The Problem of Embeddedness." *American Journal of Sociology* 91(3): 481–510.

Guimera, Roger, Brian Uzzi, Jarrett Spiro, and Luis Amaral. 2005. "Team Assembly Mechanisms Determine Collaboration Network Structure and Team Performance." *Science* 308(5722): 697–702.

Gulati, Ranjay. 1995a. "Social Structure and Alliance Formation Pattern: A Longitudinal Analysis." *Administrative Science Quarterly* 40(4): 619–42.

———. 1995b. "Does Familiarity Breed Trust? The Implications of Repeated Ties for Contractual Choice in Alliances." *American Management Journal* 38(1): 85–112.

Gulati, Ranjay, and Martin Garguilo. 1999. "Where Do Interorganizational Networks Come From?" *American Journal of Sociology* 104(5): 1439-93.

Hawley, Amos H. 1971. *Human Ecology.* New York: Ronald Press Company.

Hayek, Friedrich A. 1945/1984. "The Use of Knowledge in Society." In *The Essence of Hayek,* edited by Chiaki Nishiyam and Kurt R. Leube. Palo Alto, Calif.: Stanford University, Hoover Institution Press.

Ingram, Paul, and Peter W. Roberts. 2000. "Friendships Among Competitors in the Sydney Hotel Industry." *American Journal of Sociology* 106 (2): 387–423.

Kandori, Michihiro. 1992. "Social Norms and Community Enforcement." *Review of Economic Studies* 59(1): 63–80.

Keister, Lisa A. 2001. "Exchange Structures in Transition: Lending and

Trade Relations in Chinese Business Groups." *American Sociological Review* 66(6): 336–60.

Kossinets, Gueorgi and Duncan J. Watts. 2006. "Empirical Analysis of an Evolving Social Network." *Science* 311(5757): 88–90.

Larson, Andrea. 1992. "Network Dyads in Entrepreneurial Settings: A Study of the Governance of Exchange Relationships." *Administrative Science Quarterly* 37(1): 76-104.

Lincoln, James R., Michael L. Gerlach, and Peggy Takahashi. 1992. "Keiretsu Networks in the Japanese Economy: A Dyad Analysis of Intercorporate Ties." *American Sociological Review* 57(5): 561–85.

Macauley, Stewart. 1963. "Non-Contractual Relations and Business: A Preliminary Study." *American Sociological Review* 28(1): 55–69.

Mizruchi, Mark S. 1992. *The Structure of Corporate Political Action: Interfirm Relationships and Their Consequences.* Cambridge, Mass.: Harvard University Press.

Montgomery, James D. 1996. "The Structure of Social Exchange Networks: A Game-Theoretic Reformulation of Blau's Model." *Sociological Methodology* 26(1): 193–225.

———. 1998. "Toward a Role-Theoretic of Embeddedness." *American Journal of Sociology* 104(1): 92–125.

Podolny, Joel M. 1994. "Market Uncertainty and the Social Character of Economic Exchange." *Administrative Science Quarterly* 39(3): 458–83.

Podolny, Joel M., and James N. Baron. 1997. "Resources and Relationships: Social Networks and Mobility in the Workplace." *American Sociological Review* 62(5): 673–93.

Podolny, Joel M., and Karen L. Page. 1997. "Network Forms of Organization." *Annual Review of Sociology* 24(1): 57-76.

Podolny, Joel M., Toby Stuart, and Michael Hannan. 1996. "Networks, Knowledge, and Niches: Competition in the Worldwide Semiconductor Industry, 1984–1991." *American Journal of Sociology* 102(3): 659–89.

Powell, Walter W., Kenneth Koput, and Laurel Smith-Doerr. 1996. "Interorganizational Collaboration and the Locus of Innovation: Networks of Learning in Biotechnology." *Administrative Science Quarterly* 41(1): 116–45.

Powell, Walter W., Douglas R. White, Kenneth W. Koput, and Jason Owen-Smith. 2005. "Network Dynamics and Field Evolution: The Growth of Interorganizational Collaboration in the Life Sciences." *American Journal of Sociology* 110(4):1132–1205.

Raub, Werner, and Jeroen Weesie. 1990. "Reputation and Efficiency in Social Interactions: An Example of Network Effects." *American Journal of Sociology* 96(3): 626–54.

Robins, James M. 1999. "Association, Causation, and Marginal Structural Models." *Synthese* 121(1-2): 151–79.

Robinson, David, and Toby Stuart. Forthcoming. "Network Effects in the Governance of Strategic Alliances." *Journal of Law, Economics, and Organization.*

Sorenson, Olav, and Toby Stuart. 2006. "The Evolution of Venture Capital Investment Networks." Working paper.

Sorenson, Olav, and David Waguespack. 2005. "Social Networks and Exchange: Self-Confirming Dynamics in Hollywood." Paper presented at the annual meeting of the American Sociological Association.

Stark, David. 1996."Recombinant Property in Eastern European Capitalism." *American Journal of Sociology* 101(4): 993–1027.

Stuart, Toby E. 1998. "Network Positions and Propensities to Collaborate: An Investigation of Strategic Alliance Formation in a High-Technology Industry." Administrative Science Quarterly 43(3): 668–98.

Stuart, Toby E., Ha Hoang, and Ralph C. Hybels. 1999. "Interorganizational Endorsements and the Performance of New Ventures." *Administrative Science Quarterly* 44(2): 315–49.

Uzzi, Brian. 1996. "The Sources and Consequences of Embeddedness for Economic Performance of Organizations." *American Sociological Review* 61(4): 674–98.

Walker, Gordon, Bruce Kogut, and Weijian J. Shan. 1997. "Social Capital, Structural Holes and the Formation of an Industry Network." *Organization Science* 8(2): 109–25.

Watts, Duncan J., and Steven Strogatz. 1998. "Collective Dynamics of 'Small-World' Networks." *Nature* 393(6684): 440–42.

Watts, Duncan J., Peter S. Dodds, and M. E. J. Newmann. 2002. "Identity and Search in Social Networks." *Science* 296(5571): 1302–5.

Williamson, Oliver. 1975. *Markets and Hierarchies.* New York: Free Press.

Zipf, George K. 1949. *Human Behavior and the Principle of Least Effort.* Reading, Mass.: Addison-Wesley.

Zuckerman, Ezra W. 2003. "Some Notes on the Relationship Between Sociology and Economics (and Political Science): Cross-Disciplinary Citation Patterns over the 20th Century." MIT website, http://web.mit.edu/ewzucker/www.

Chapter 5

Closure and Stability—Persistent Reputation and Enduring Relations Among Bankers and Analysts

Ronald S. Burt

As the network around a set of people closes, it creates a competitive advantage known as social capital. The gist of the argument—found in economics (Tullock 1985; Greif 1989), political science (Putnam 1993, 2000), and sociology (Coleman 1988, 1990; Granovetter 1985, 1992)—is that closed networks create a reputation cost for inappropriate behavior, which facilitates trust between people in the network. A network is closed to the extent that the people in it have strong relations with one another or can reach one another indirectly through strong relations to mutual contacts. Information travels quickly in such networks. People wary of news reaching colleagues that might erode their reputation in the network are careful to display appropriate opinion and behavior. With a reputation cost for inappropriate opinions and behavior, trust is less risky within the network, people are self-aligning to shared goals, transactions occur that would be difficult outside the closed network, and production efficiencies result from donated labor and the speed with which tasks can be completed (see Burt 2005, 93–166, for review and diverse examples).

Questions about network formation and decay are central to the social capital of network closure because stability is essential to the mechanism. For reputation to have its salutary effects, there has to be a credible threat that a person's reputation will persist to affect future relationships. From a woman's work in one project group, word gets around defining her reputation, which precedes her into her next project group. If negative reputation quickly dissolves, reputation loses its coercive power because yesterday's poor behavior is too soon forgotten. "Too soon" is relative. It could be a day, a month, a year. Relative stability is the key. Reputation has to persist longer than the productive relations it facilitates and the hurtful relations it protects against.

Stability cannot be taken for granted. Network closure varies from low to high, so closure-induced stability must vary. But how does stability co-vary with closure? Current answers to this question are typically little more than assumptions convenient for formal models or speculation from cross-sectional evidence. Yet the question is central to any theoretical model that invokes a reputation mechanism and the question has broad substantive relevance. Consider Kaivan Munshi and Mark Rosenzweig's work on community support networks in India (2005). They explain that people connected in the same village or by subcaste (*jati*) across villages have traditionally had a social obligation to support one another (428): "The fundamental marriage rule in Hindu society is that no individual can marry outside the *jati*. Marriage ties thus link all the members of the *jati*, either directly or indirectly, improving information flows and ensuring that members of the network do not renege on their obligations." For example, "An individual making a job referral for another member of his *jati* will have a good idea of his ability, solving the basic information problem facing firms in labour markets with high rates of labour turnover. At the same time, the individual making the job referral can expect to receive similar support from his *jati* when he is unemployed in the future, giving rise to a decentralized reciprocal arrangement that only a long established and closed-knit community can provide" (428). Munshi and Rosenzweig describe a decline in social obligation due to trends eroding attachment to community networks, a point to which I will return later in the chapter. The point here is that readers familiar with James S. Coleman's (1988) social-capital argument will immediately recognize closure's reputation mechanism in Munshi and

Rosenzweig's setting. Where Coleman discusses social obligation within rotating credit associations, Munshi and Rosenzweig discuss social obligation within *jati* and caste. All are concerned with reputation within a closed network, within the association, within the village, within the *jati*. Social obligation is enforced through a threat of losing face, eroded reputation, if one does not meet one's obligation of helping people who have a legitimate right to one's help. Which raises questions about variably-strong reputation costs in variably-closed networks: How closed must a network be to make reputation cost credible? How weak can closure in the *jati* beyond the local community become before *jati*-based reputation dissolves, whereupon felt obligation to the *jati* disappears?

To answer such questions, I studied four years of colleague networks around the upper-level bankers and analysts in a large financial organization. I measure reputation as the organization does, by the average evaluation a person receives from colleagues in the annual evaluation process. Reputation consistent in adjacent years I call reputation stability. "Decay" refers to the tendency for colleague relations to disappear from one year to the next. The empirical question is why certain reputations are less stable and certain relationships are prone to decay.

Consistent with received wisdom, closure is associated with stability: where relations are more deeply embedded in a closed network, reputation is more stable and relationships are less subject to decay.

Beyond the fact of association, three conclusions from the analysis describe the way in which stability co-varies with closure:

1. Reputation stability increases quickly with closure. I find that reputation has no stability from one year to the next in networks of colleagues who have little contact with one another. However—and this is an intriguing parallel to the social conformity induced by four peers in S.E. Asch's (1951) classic laboratory experiment—do the same work when you have four mutual contacts with colleagues, and reputation this year is a good predictor of reputation next year. With respect to the people studied here, Coleman (1988, 107) had it exactly right when he said, "Reputation cannot arise in an open structure."

2. Closure's stability effect is concentrated in new relationships.

Closure is associated with more positive relations and relations are more impervious to decay when they are embedded in closed networks. By the third year of a relationship, however, closure is less important than the strength of the relationship that has built up between the two people. In other words, closure keeps people in new relations longer than they would stay otherwise, thus protecting new relations from decay.

3. Closure's stabilizing effect operates at a distance from the stabilized network element. Closure among direct contacts, and closure among indirect contacts (friends of friends), make independent and statistically significant contributions to stability.

My summary conclusion is that closure creates an endogenous force for the status quo that secures and expands the boundary around a network, protecting new relations until they are self-sustaining, and doing so even for people only indirectly connected at the periphery of the network.

Study Population

My study population is upper-level people in two divisions of a large American financial organization during the late 1990s, just before the dot.com bubble burst. The people in one division craft investments and offer advice on investments. I will call them bankers. People in the second division work in the back office doing research to make predictions about the market value of investments. I will call the second group of people analysts.[1] The bankers and analysts play distinct but related roles. Beginning in the 1970s, market pressure on commissions for buying and selling stocks led to analysts' work becoming increasingly tied to investment banking. Especially through the 1990s, analysts became a prominent and powerful factor in the investment business. The trend intensified a conflict of interest between analyst accuracy and analyst support of employer-sponsored investments. The conflict of interest drew public attention when the dot.com bubble burst in 2000, and it became apparent over the next couple years that analysts' opinions, expressed in emails with colleagues, were sometimes sharply more negative than the opinions they expressed in published reports. These points are relevant here in that analysts rose during the period of my data above their traditional back-room staff role to become contenders in the bonus pool and subject to peer evaluation, just like bankers and other people with leadership responsibilities in financial organizations. The peer evaluations are one reason why the bankers and analysts are an attractive site for studying closure and stability: the evaluations provide annual panels of network data.

Annual Network Data

As in other organizations moving to more adaptive, less bureaucratic structures during the 1990s, work in financial organizations required flexible cooperation between employees. And as in other organizations during the period, it was difficult, if not impossible, to monitor cooperation through bureaucratic chains of command because people were cooperating across chains of command. Many organizations began to use multisource evaluation processes, processes in which employees were evaluated by their immediate supervisor as well as colleagues above, below, and around them. Rare in the 1970s, multisource evaluation swept through corporate America during the 1980s and 1990s to help managers adapt to the ambiguity of flatter organizations in which bureaucratic chains of command were replaced with networks of negotiated influence. Estimates at the end of the century had as many as 90 percent of the Fortune 1,000 using some form of multisource evaluation (Atwater and Waldman 1998). Such evaluations create data on the social network in an organization, each evaluation indicating a relationship between the employees evaluating and being evaluated. In the organization from which this chapter's study population is drawn, bonus-eligible people were instructed in an annual evaluation process to identify colleagues with whom they had worked closely during the preceding year, then were asked to describe their experience with the colleague as poor, adequate, good, or outstanding (my synonyms for the words actually used). All of the evaluations were averaged and the average evaluation of an employee became a factor in promotion and bonus decisions.

I have four years of evaluations with which to measure an annual network around each analyst and banker. As network data, each evaluation is a claim that the person making the evaluation had substantial contact with the person evaluated—they probably communicated, coordinated, and were otherwise "in touch" during the year. I do not know what they did, or what roles they played to one another (other than the broad divisional roles of banker, analyst, sales, administration, and so forth), or how much they gained from the interaction. The evaluation data measure an employee's opinion about which people were colleagues during the year, and what it was like to work with each. The data reveal a global network of bankers and analysts centered on headquarter offices in the United States and Europe (see Burt 2007 for sociograms).

Not knowing what people were doing with one another raises a question about how much discretion people had in the relations. At one extreme, people could have been assigned to work with certain colleagues, whereupon network decay is determined exogenously; you work with whomever you are assigned to. At the other extreme, people could have been free to select the colleagues with whom they worked.

The truth is some mixture of exogenous assignment and endogenous choice, with different mixes for different individuals. Nevertheless, an attractive feature of this study population is that the network data on average are probably closer to the endogenous alternative. I cannot prove this, but I have two reasons for thinking it. First, there is the nature of the work. These are upper-level bankers and analysts. The analysts received average annual incomes of several hundred thousand dollars and the bankers averaged well over a million dollars a year. They were not paid that level of compensation to take orders. They were expected to find ways to create value. In fact, the company invests substantial resources in annual peer evaluations precisely because it is otherwise difficult to keep track of collaborations. The relations of bankers and analysts so often cut across vertical chains of command that a supervisor cannot know how her direct reports are working with other employees. The only way to monitor collaborations is to survey the upper-level employees, asking each to name the people with whom they had substantial work contact during the year. Second, evaluations determined by exogenous assignment should be symmetric and correlated within dyads. People assigned to the same project would evaluate each other and project factors they have in common would create correlation between their evaluations (more positive evaluations, perhaps, in more successful projects). Instead, the evaluations are asymmetric and contradictory. Less than half of evaluations are reciprocated (38 percent), and when reciprocated, they are inconsistent—one person saying the relationship was good while the other says it was okay (.27 correlation between reciprocated evaluations scored 1 to 4). In short, I believe that the bankers and analysts had wide latitude in naming colleagues with whom they had substantial work contact.

Relationship Turnover

Relations among the bankers and analysts change rapidly, which also makes the study population an attractive site for research on closure and stability. With respect to the network endogeneity issue (discussed by Ray E. Reagans, Ezra Zuckerman, and Bill McEvily in chapter 6 of this volume), rapid change makes my time ordering consequential. With respect to Joel Podolny and James E. Rauch's two categories of network formation (see chapter 1, this volume), this chapter falls into the category of structure observed at one time period affecting structure observed at the next time period. Let "causal interval" refer to the time interval over which routine change occurs in a structure. If two observation periods are closer together than the "causal interval," structure will not appear to change. The two observation periods would be ordered in time, but their similarity would be less about stability than about measurement reliability. High turnover in relations between annual observations means that I am in a stronger position to draw causal inference from evidence of closure in one year preserving structure into the next year.[2]

Turnover is illustrated in table 5.1. The values are the percentage of row evaluations this year that become the column evaluation next year. Evaluations are not independent between years. The diagonal cells for continuing relations are the largest in each row (for example, 21.3 percent of relations judged "outstanding" this year are again rated "outstanding" next year), and percentages are

Table 5.1 Turnover in Colleague Relations[a] (Based on 46,231 Relations)

Colleague Relation this Year	Colleague Relation Next Year					
	Poor	Adequate	Good	Outstanding	Not Cited (Decayed)	Total (Percentage)
Poor	9.2	6.4	3.2	1.3	79.9	100
Adequate	3.1	10.5	8.9	1.7	75.8	100
Good	0.7	4.9	14.4	6.6	73.4	100
Outstanding	0.3	1.3	8.1	21.3	69.0	100
Total	1.5	4.9	10.6	10.1	72.9	100

Source: Author's compilation.
[a] Row relations this year that receive column evaluation next year.

smaller in cells more removed from the diagonal (for example, 1.3 percent of "poor" relations this year become "outstanding" relations next year). However, decay is the typical transition. Seven of ten colleagues cited are new each year (72.9 percent at the bottom of table 5.1). Banker relations are slightly more prone to decay than analyst relations, but decay is the typical outcome for relations in both groups: 73 percent for bankers, 71 percent for analysts. Strong relations are less subject to decay, but decay is the most likely outcome for strong and weak: of relations judged "outstanding" this year, 69 percent are not cited next year. Of "poor" relationships this year, 80 percent are not cited next year. Life in the financial organization involves some long-term colleague relationships, but most relations fade as employees move to new projects: Of 16,505 relations to the bankers and analysts in the first of the four years, 4,418 are cited again in the second year, 1,233 continue to the third year, and 567 make it to the fourth year (see table 5.2). And these are the relations substantial enough to be cited in the peer evaluations. Less substantial relations must pass by like faces in a train going the other direction.

With such high turnover, it is not surprising to see that evaluations are more about the pair of people involved than about either person individually. Only 12 percent of variance in the evaluations can be attributed to agreement on the person evaluated. In fact, the

Table 5.2 Network Closure and Reputation Stability

Network This Year	Analysts		Bankers	
	Zero-Order	Partial	Zero-Order	Partial
Intercept	—	−.501	—	−.183
Risk year (2, 3, 4)	.112 (.009)**	.105 (.013)**	−.049 (.007)**	.015 (.009)
Number of colleagues in risk year (/10)	.080 (.011)**	.010 (.006)	.087 (.007)**	.015 (.006)*
Relational embedding				
Number of colleagues this year (/10)	.098 (.007)**	−.023 (.007)**	.070 (.004)**	−.032 (.007)**
Number of continuing colleagues (/10)	.152 (.010)**	−.009 (.009)	.113 (.006)**	.009 (.008)
Reputation this year (absolute score)	−.043 (.025)	−.007 (.018)	.020 (.017)	−.009 (.016)
Extreme reputation this year (dev. score)	−.023 (.017)	.023 (.009)*	−.019 (.012)	.025 (.008)*
Years reputation observed (1, 2, 3)	.120 (.011)**	.017 (.008)*	−.005 (.008)	−.010 (.008)
Direct structural embedding				
Number of positive two-step connections	.124 (.004)**	.070 (.012)**	.105 (.005)**	.075 (.012)**
Number of negative two-step connections	.127 (.004)**	.035 (.010)**	.096 (.005)**	.034 (.009)**
Indirect structural embedding				
Number of three-step connections	.170 (.009)**	.074 (.012)**	.164 (.011)**	.074 (.015)**
Holds senior rank	.146 (.021)**	.026 (.020)	.110 (.011)**	−.006 (.018)
Percentage of colleagues at senior rank	−.002 (.0003)**	−.0004 (.0004)	.002 (.0002)**	−.0001 (.0003)
Percentage of colleagues in division	−.003 (.0006)**	−.0007 (.0003)*	.0004 (.0004)	−.0000 (.0002)
Percentage of colleagues in geographic region	−.002 (.0006)**	−.0002 (.0003)	.0002 (.0003)	−.0004 (.0002)*

Source: Author's compilation.

Note: These are regression models predicting reputation stability from this year to next from network variables measured this year. Stability is measured for a person by the subcorrelation between reputation in adjacent years (see note 4). Connections 2-step and 3-step are log scores. There are 623 annual observations of analysts and 1,179 annual observations of bankers. "Zero-Order" columns refer to models containing only a single row variable. Standard errors in parentheses are adjusted for autocorrelation between stability scores on the same person, but they are only a heuristic since routine statistical inference is not applicable for subsample correlations as a criterion variable.

*p < .05

**p < .001

Figure 5.1 Banker's Direct and Indirect Colleagues

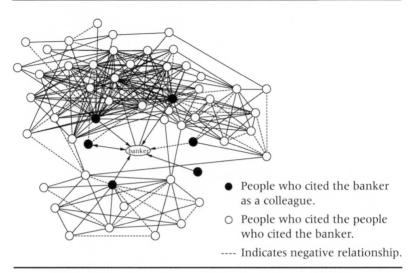

● People who cited the banker as a colleague.

○ People who cited the people who cited the banker.

---- Indicates negative relationship.

Source: Author's configuration.

best predictor of the number of positive evaluations a person receives is the number of negative evaluations received. Another 23 percent of evaluation variance can be traced to rater differences. Some colleagues give positive evaluations on average. Others have a more negative frame of reference. The remaining variance in evaluations, 65 percent, is unique to the two people connected by an evaluation. The employee whom one colleague considers outstanding can be incompatible with another colleague.[3]

Measuring Closure: Direct and Indirect Embedding

I compute annual closure measures from the evaluation data. To illustrate, figure 5.1 displays the colleague network around one of the bankers. Dots are employees, lines connect employees where one cited the other in the annual evaluation process, and a solid line indicates a positive evaluation.

Shaded dots indicate the six colleagues who provided evaluations of the banker. The six colleagues are disconnected from each other.

Thus, if limited to the immediate network around the banker, one could argue that there is no reputation cost to the banker for poor behavior. The banker could drop a disgruntled colleague from the network without worrying about his reputation being tarnished by the erstwhile colleague talking to the other five.

The six colleagues are embedded in a broader network through which they are all connected indirectly. Beyond the six colleagues who evaluated the banker are forty-seven other employees who evaluated one or more of the six people who evaluated the banker. These are the banker's contacts of contacts, friends of friends, or more simply, indirect contacts. The forty-seven are the hollow dots in figure 5.1. The broader network clearly shows two clusters. The primary cluster, at the top of figure 5.1, is composed of other investment bankers. These contacts are frequently connected indirectly through mutual ties to other bankers in the cluster. Further, the banker's one contact disconnected from everyone in figure 5.1 is in another banker cluster, but newly hired to a junior rank so no one in the banker's primary cluster cited her as a colleague. That leaves one contact to a senior person outside the banker's own cluster, in the cluster at the bottom of figure 5.1, which is a group of people who specialize in a kind of financial instrument. Three people in the instrument-specialist cluster are connected to bankers. The specialist who cited the banker in figure 5.1 is a central person, directly connected with every one of the other people in the instrument-specialist cluster.

Following Mark Granovetter's (1985, 1992) discussion of relations in context, there are three ways to think about a network closed around a relationship: relational embedding, structural embedding, and what I will call indirect structural embedding.

Relational Embedding

Relational embedding refers to the relation accumulated between two people. It would be indicated in figure 5.1 by the strength of the banker's relationship with each of his colleagues. Peter M. Blau (1968, 454) summarizes the process as follows: "Social exchange relations evolve in a slow process, starting with minor transactions in which little trust is required because little risk is involved and in which both partners can prove their trustworthiness, enabling them to expand their relation and engage in major transactions. Thus, the process of social exchange leads to the trust required for it in a self-governing fashion." In proposing the term "relational" embeddedness, Granovetter (1992, 42) offers the following (see Granovetter 1985, 490): "That trustworthy behavior may be a regularized part of a personal relationship reflects one of the typically direct effects of relational embeddedness and explains the widespread preference of all economic actors to deal with those they have dealt with before. Our information about such partners is cheap, richly detailed, and probably accurate." The information advantage is illustrated in Brian Uzzi's fieldwork on relational embedding in apparel (Uzzi 1996), banking (Uzzi 1999; Uzzi and Gillespie 2002), and law (Uzzi and Lancaster 2004). Peter Leung-Kwong Wong and Paul Ellis (2002) describe how Hong Kong companies entering China decide more quickly between alternative venture partners when their information comes from family or close friends rather than casual friends or acquaintances.

Structural Embedding

Imagine a network of interconnected people telling stories; not stories in the sense of deception, just stories in the sense of personal accounts about people—in other words, gossip. Gossip is the sharing of news, the catching up, through which we build and maintain relations (Dunbar 1996; Gambetta 1994). Reputations are defined by people monitoring and discussing individual behavior, and by defining reputations, mutual friends and colleagues constitute an adaptive control on behavior. The stronger and more numerous the connections between two people through mutual contacts, the more closed the network around the two people, and the greater their vicarious experience of one another. Alternative, redundant communication channels let numerous tellings of a story get around quickly, ensuring reliable, early warning. The omnipresent hydra-like eyes of a closed network make it difficult for misbehavior to escape detection. The more closed the network, the more penetrating the detection and so the lower the risk of misplaced trust. Where trust is an advantage, therefore, closure is social capital. This is the argument with which I began the chapter.

Coleman's (1988, 1990) closure argument is the most prominent with respect to social capital (some derived from Putnam's [1993] widely cited application of Coleman's argument to regional government in Italy), but it is not alone in predicting that closure facilitates trust (see Stuart's review, chapter 4, this volume; see also Burt 2005, chapter 3). Anthropologists have long reported on gossip and trust in small communities. Sally Engle Merry (1984) offers a review and ethnographic illustrations that foreshadow Coleman's argument (Coleman 1990, 283–85). There is a closure argument familiar in economics, in which mutual acquaintances make behavior more public, creating an incentive for good behavior to maintain reputation, which decreases the risk associated with trust and so increases the probability of trust (for example, Tullock 1985; Greif 1989). The other prominent closure argument in sociology is Granovetter's (1985, 1992) discussion of embeddedness. "Structural" embeddedness refers to the relationship between people who share mutual friends (Granovetter 1992, 44): "My mortification at cheating a friend of long standing may be substantial even when undiscovered. It may increase when the friend becomes aware of it. But it may become even more unbearable when our mutual friends uncover the deceit and tell one another."

Indirect Structural Embedding

The closure that Coleman calls social capital and Granovetter calls structural embedding is more precisely "direct" embedding in the sense that contacts are directly connected so as to monitor each other. Completely consistent with Coleman's and Granovetter's discussions, perhaps implicit in both, is a broader domain of closure in which contacts are connected through people further removed in the network. The banker in figure 5.1 illustrates the point. Closure can exist between people not because of their many connections with mutual colleagues but because of dense connections farther removed. In keeping with Granovetter's (1992) discussion, I will call closure through indirect contacts indirect structural embedding. There are degrees. Continuing to more remote indirect connections eventually leads from network analysis to institutional analysis, but

I limit myself in this analysis to the initial distinction between direct and indirect structural embedding.

Measures of indirect structural embedding can capture an important aspect of network closure missed by measures of direct structural embedding: the lack of choice. Closure means closed to alternatives. The network of a person connected to two or more groups is less closed than the network of a person similarly connected to only one of the groups. To the extent that reputation-protection is a motivation, people in a closed network have a single source of reputation and can be expected to protect it. As Coleman (1988, S107–8) summarizes, "The consequence of this closure is, as in the case of the wholesale diamond market or in other similar communities, a set of effective sanctions that can monitor and guide behavior. Reputation cannot arise in an open structure, and collective sanctions that would ensure trustworthiness cannot be applied." It is easy to imagine how closure and reputation work in the small face-to-face groups measured by direct structural embedding. Not doing your share is quickly apparent and immediately embarrassing.

But how effective is closure in creating reputation in the larger groups in which it is assumed—such as the Indian *jati* with which I began the chapter, or Greif's Maghribi traders, or Putnam's Italian regions, or contemporary professional groups, or business groups more generally? In these larger groups, most people are only connected indirectly, through colleague intermediaries.

With respect to the Indian example, Munshi and Rosenzweig (2005) describe a decline in social insurance (what Coleman and Putnam would term community social capital), which they attribute to two events that have eroded attachment to community networks. One was a farming innovation that created an economic advantage for one group over others, which made the advantaged group disproportionately wealthy and likely to be asked for favors, which in turn encouraged the advantaged group to marry outside the *jati*. Marriage ties outside the *jati* eroded felt obligation to the *jati*, thus explaining the decreased interpersonal economic assistance previously provided within the *jati*. The second event was the liberalization of the Indian economy in the 1990s, which led to higher incomes in commercial and corporate jobs, thus encouraging parents to move their children to English-language schools (in preference to indigenous-language schools) so the children could better compete for the desired jobs. More able children were more likely to matriculate in the English-language schools, thus removing the more able participants in job referrals previously provided within the local network. Munshi and Rosenzweig's two disruptive events both eroded obligation to a group by creating attachments outside the group.

Back in the United States, Frank Ellis of Shasta County, California, is an excellent example of this dynamic. Ellis was one of the largest landowners who was a prominent character in Robert C. Ellickson's (1991) study of disputes resolved informally in closed networks. Ellis was a rancher and real estate broker in his late fifties when he bought his large tract of land in Shasta County. He had risen to prosperity outside Shasta County, and his primary affiliations were elsewhere. Ellis stands out in Ellickson's analysis for his immunity to the reputation mechanism by which Shasta County landowners resolved disputes. The area, wrote Ellickson (1991, 57–58) remained

> distinctly rural in atmosphere. People tend to know one another, and they value their reputations in the community. Some ranching families have lived in the area for several generations and include members who plan to stay indefinitely. Members of these families seem particularly intent on maintaining their reputations as good neighbors. . . . [Residents] seem quite conscious of the role of gossip in their system of social control. One longtime resident, who had also lived for many years in a suburb of a major California urban area, observed that people in the Oak Run area "gossip all the time," much more than in the urban area. Another reported intentionally using gossip to sanction a traditionalist who had been "impolite" when coming to pick up some stray mountain cattle; he reported that application of this self-help device produced an apology, an outcome itself presumably circulated through the gossip system.
>
> The ranchette residents who were particularly bothered by Ellis'[s] cattle could see that he was utterly indifferent to his reputation among them. They thought, however, that as a major rancher, Ellis would worry about his reputation among the large cattle operations in the county. They therefore reported Ellis'[s] activities to the Board of Directors of the Shasta County Cattlemen's Association. This move proved unrewarding, for Ellis was also surprisingly indifferent to his reputation among the cattlemen.

Figure 5.2 Network Closure from Direct and Indirect Embedding

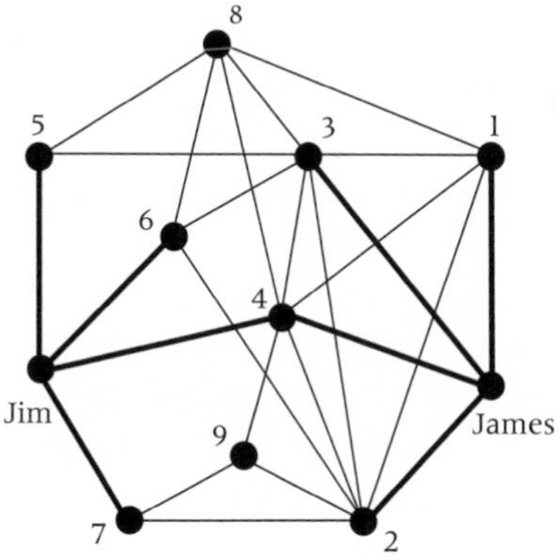

	Number of Two-Step (Direct) and Three-Step (Indirect) Connections			
	Jim		James	
	Direct	Indirect	Direct	Indirect
Person 1	1	3	3	0
Person 2	3	1	3	0
Person 3	3	1	3	0
Person 4	0	3	3	0
Person 5	0	2	1	3
Person 6	0	3	2	2
Person 7	0	2	1	3
Person 8	3	0	2	2
Person 9	1	2	1	3
Jim	—	—	1	3
James	1	3	—	—
Mean number per Contact (in box)	0.0	2.5	3.0	0.0

Source: Author's configuration.

Network Measures

To estimate the relative contributions of direct and indirect connections to closure, I measure both among the bankers and analysts. The measures are illustrated in figure 5.2. Let a two-step connection refer to a connection between two people through a mutual contact. For example, the 1 under D for Jim in the first row of the table in figure 5.2 refers to person 4 in the sociogram. Person 4 is the only contact linked directly to Jim and person 1. The 3 underneath the 1 in the table refers to three mutual contacts between Jim and person 2. The mutual contacts are persons 4, 6, and 7. Two-step connections are this chapter's measure of direct structural embedding.

Indirect structural embedding is measured in this chapter with three-step connections. For example, the 1 under I for Jim in the second row of the table in figure 5.2 refers to persons 5 and 3 in the sociogram. Jim's connections to person 2 through persons 4, 6, and 7 are 2-step connections. Jim's fourth contact, person 5, is not connected to person 2, but is connected to person 3, who is connected to person 2, so Jim has a three-step connection to person 2 via person 5. In graph-theoretic terms, I am looking for geodesics linking two people through one intermediary (direct structural embedding) or two intermediaries (indirect structural embedding). Since I want to know how indirect embedding adds to direct embedding, I only count distant connections in the absence of closer connections. For example, Jim is connected to person 6 who is connected to person 3 who is connected to person 2, which is a three-step connection between Jim and person 2. However, Jim reaches person 2 through person 6 directly, so the table reports one three-step connection (the 5-3-2 connection).

To the extent that direct structural embedding provides stability, I expect stability to increase with counts of two-step connections. James illustrates direct structural embedding. I put a box around James's four contacts. He has three two-step connections with each of his contacts. For example, the relationship between James and person 1 is embedded in their mutual connections to persons 2, 3, and 4. With all four contacts directly embedded in one another, there is no additional embedding recorded through indirect connections.

To the extent that indirect structural embedding adds to the stabilizing effect of direct embedding, I expect stability to increase with counts of three-step connections that link contacts in the absence of more direct connection. Jim illustrates indirect closure. None of Jim's four contacts are connected to one another. Like the banker in figure 5.1, Jim's contacts are only connected indirectly. For example, Jim's relationship with person 4 is embedded in three three-step connections. Jim is indirectly connected to person 4 through his connection with person 5 (via 8 or 3). Jim is indirectly connected through person 6 (via 2, 3, or 8). Jim is indirectly connected through his connection with person 7 (via 2).

Results on Reputation Stability

Given the substantial turnover in banker and analyst relations, and the large proportion of evaluation variance unique to individual relationships, I expected to see reputations bounce up and down from one year to the next.

Instead, reputation last year is a good predictor of reputation this year. The four levels of evaluation in table 5.1 are scored in the organization as 1 to 4, then averaged for each employee to measure the employee's reputation with colleagues. An average evaluation of 1.0 indicates an employee who is consistently judged "poor" by colleagues. An average of 4.0 indicates an employee who is consistently judged "outstanding." Across the bankers and analysts, reputation next year is clearly contingent on reputation this year (.54 correlation, 20.7 t-test adjusted for repeated observations, $p < .001$).

Intrigued by stable reputations in chaotic networks, I raised the issue over drinks with one of the senior people in the financial organization. He took on a puzzled look, then patiently explained to me that "of course" employee reputations are stable. They are the company's market index of employee quality. A good employee this year is a good employee next year, regardless of the colleagues with whom the employee works. Reputations are expected to go up and down a little depending on personalities and business opportunities, but good employees continue to be good employees, and weak employees are weeded out.

In other words, the division head had a human-capital explanation for reputation stability. Able people receive good evaluations. Weak people receive poor evaluations. Reputation is correlated over time because human capital continues over time, certainly between adjacent years.

I, on the other hand, had a social-capital explanation. Evaluations are based on limited personal experience mixed with the experiences of colleagues with whom work is discussed. The more connected the colleagues evaluating an employee, the more likely they share stories about the employee. In fact, their story-sharing activity is essential to the argument in the first paragraph of this chapter that closed networks constitute social capital.

The human-capital and social-capital explanations can be tested against each other. If individual ability is the reason for reputation stability over time, then stability should be independent of connections between colleagues. An able employee should receive good evaluations whether the colleagues who made the evaluations work together or work in separate parts of the organization. On the other hand, if reputation stability is defined by colleagues sharing stories about the employee, then stability should be higher when colleagues are more interconnected so they are more likely to have shared stories about the employee.

Closure in the Aggregate

Results in figure 5.3 support the social-capital explanation: reputation stability increases in proportion to network closure. Closure is measured on the horizontal axis by the extent to which an employee is evaluated by interconnected colleagues. The measurement was illustrated in figure 5.2. For each colleague citing an employee in a particular year, the number of mutual contacts is the number of people citing the employee that year and connected to the colleague by an evaluation. An employee's score on the horizontal axis in figure 5.3 is the employee's average number of mutual contacts with evaluating colleagues (for example, 0.0 for Jim and 3.0 for James, in figure 5.2). In figure 5.3, I rounded scores to the nearest of the eleven integer categories on the horizontal axis.

Reputation stability is measured on the vertical axis by a correlation between banker reputations in adjacent years.[4] The dashed line describes stability when stability is measured independent of closure.[5] In random samples of employees, stability is about the same at each level of closure.

The solid line in figure 5.3 shows how stability increases with closure. The correlation between reputations in adjacent years increases from a .09 correlation for employees whose colleagues do not cite one another to a .73 correlation for employees who share ten or more mutual contacts with the colleagues evaluating them. Where colleagues evaluating an employee are strongly connected, the employee's reputation continues over time. When the evaluating colleagues are not connected, reputation is quickly forgotten.

Consider two hypothetical employees who work well with ten colleagues this year. One works with colleagues segregated in the organization so they do not cite one another in the annual peer evaluations (illustrated by the sociogram at the bottom-left in figure 5.3).

Figure 5.3   Closure and Reputation Stability from This Year to the Next

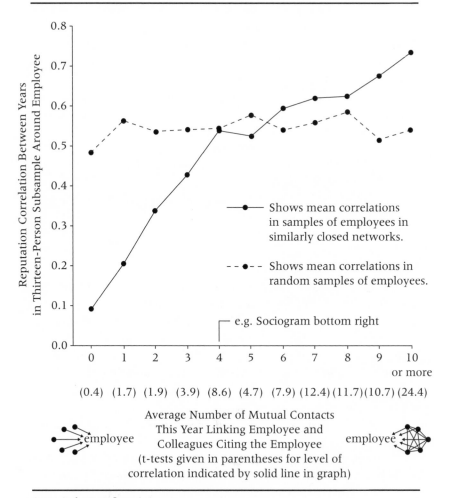

That employee would be over the zero on the horizontal axis in figure 5.3. The second employee works with five colleagues who work together in one division and another five colleagues who work together in a second division (sociogram at the bottom right in figure 5.3). The second employee would be over the 4 on the horizontal axis.

Both employees do good work, but it is the second employee's work that will be remembered. The solid line in figure 5.3 shows that an employee doing good work for colleagues not connected with each other can expect to be forgotten. The exact correlation expected between the employee's reputation this year and next year is given by the level of the solid line over the zero on the horizontal axis. The correlation is indistinguishable from random noise.[6] The employees work with so many new contacts each year that their work is quickly forgotten—unless the people with whom they work talk to each other. For the second employee, the one who worked with two groups of connected colleagues, reputation has an expected correlation of .57 over time. What carries an employee's reputation into the future is people talking about the employee.

Distinguishing Kinds of Closure

Figure 5.4 presents the figure 5.3 aggregate closure-stability association for categories of bankers and analysts. Table 5.2 contains regression models predicting the level of stability between years from closure and other variables. Zero-order associations are presented with partial effects to show by their similar direction that there are no complex interactions to explain.[7] Routine standard errors are no more than a heuristic here because the subsample measure of reputation stability (see note 4) is based on combinations of thirteen observations assumed to be independent under routine statistical inference.

The most obvious point in figure 5.4 is that closure and stability are linked for both the bankers and the analysts. The closure-stability association was lowest for analysts in the first year, when they began to participate in the peer evaluations, then highest for analysts in the last years, after they were a routine part of the peer evaluations. The difference is substantial (−10.64 routine t-test for the lower association in first year), but the difference is negligible when the factors in table 5.3 are held constant (−10.64 t-test drops to .47), so I do not include the adjustment in table 5.2.

Table 5.3   Decay in Colleague Relations

Years Observed (T)	Panel in Which First Cited (P)	Relations at Risk[a]	Relations That Decay[b]	Decay Rate[c]
Year 1	Year 1[d]	16,505	12,087	.732
Year 2	Year 1[d]	4,418	3,185	.721
Year 3	Year 1[d]	1,233	666	.540
Year 1	Year 2[e]	11,528	9,355	.811
Year 2	Year 2[e]	2,173	1,247	.574
Year 1	Year 3[f]	10,374	7,147	.689
	Total	46,231	33,687	.729

Source: Author's compilation.
Note: [a] Relations cited this year that are at risk of not being cited next year.
[b] Relations at risk that were not re-cited.
[c] Column e divided by d, in other words, the proportion of relations at risk that decayed.
[d] This row describes colleague relations cited in the first panel.
[e] This row describes relations cited in the second panel, but not in the first panel.
[f] This row describes relations cited in the third panel, but not in the second.

The stability association with direct structural embedding is about the same as the association with indirect structural embedding. Both have strong associations in table 5.2, holding the other constant along with the control variables.[8] In other words, the banker in figure 5.1 can expect the closure among his indirect contacts to improve the stability of his reputation from one year to the next. There is also a result in table 5.2 corroborating the earlier characterization of bankers integrating across geography and analysts integrating across functions. Analyst reputation is less stable when it comes primarily from other analysts ("Percentage of colleagues in division"). Banker reputation is less stable when it comes primarily from colleagues in the same region ("Percentage of colleagues in geographic region").

The stability association with closure is consistent across positive and negative evaluations. The hollow dots in figure 5.4 refer to stability in the reputations of people with above-average reputations this year. The solid dots refer to stability in the reputations

Figure 5.4   Detail on Closure-Stabilizing Reputation

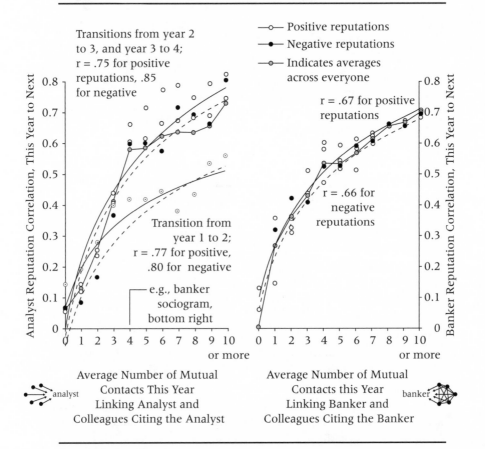

Source: Author's configuration.

of analysts in the bottom 25 percent of analysts and bankers in the bottom 25 percent of bankers. The hollow and solid dots have very similar distributions in figure 5.4. For example, the right-hand graph in figure 5.4 shows that stability in banker reputation has a .67 correlation with closure for bankers with a positive reputation and a .66 correlation with closure for bankers with a negative reputation.

Relational embedding is not as strong a consideration here as it will be for the stability of individual relationships in the next section. Positive reputations are not more likely to be stable, but extreme reputations—extremely negative or extremely positive—are more likely to continue from year to year.

Results on Network Decay

Closure's stabilizing effect can be traced down to the level of individual relationships. Table 5.3 reports hazard rates for decay. Of 16,505 relations cited in the first of the four years (first row of table 5.3), 12,087 were not cited in the second year, which defines a .73 decay rate for the first year. The surviving 4,418 relations were at risk of decay in the third year. Of those, 3,185 were not cited in the third year, which defines a .72 decay rate. The surviving 1,233 were at risk of decay in the fourth year. Of those, 666 were not cited, defining a .54 decay rate. A large number of new relations were reported in the second period (11,528), of which a large proportion decayed before the third period (9,355). Aggregating across time periods and survival durations, the 46,231 relations at risk of decay had a .73 decay rate, which is reported at the bottom of table 5.3 just as it was reported at the bottom of table 5.1.

The rates in table 5.3 illustrate a decay baseline analogous to the "liability of newness" in population ecology (Hannan and Freeman 1989, 80). Relations decay over time, but more slowly in surviving relations. The decay process begins with people becoming acquainted as a function of random chance and exogenous factors. People who would not otherwise seek one another out can find themselves neighbors, colleagues in the same company, assigned to the same project team, or seated next to one another. It is rude not to strike up a relationship (see Feld 1981, on the social foci from which relations emerge). The relations can be bridges to other groups when they result from events that bring people together from separate groups, events such as cross-functional teams, inter-department committees, or inter-organizational conventions and professional meetings. People in these relationships often discover that they do not enjoy one another, or cannot work well together, so they disengage in favor of more compatible contacts. The selection process in which new, hoped-to-be compatible contacts replace existing known-to-be incompatible ones means that relations on average weaken and decay over time. There is a liability of newness because the longer a relationship has survived, the more likely that it connects people who have learned to appreciate one another, which increases the probability of the relationship continuing into the future. This is illustrated in table 5.3 by the .73 decay rate in relations during the first year, and the .54 decay rate in relations that survived to a third year. Learning is more than an accompanist to selection processes. There is also learning from your current relationships to identify kinds of people with whom you are likely to be compatible. Whatever the average probability of a new relationship disappearing next year, that probability should be lower for more experienced people in the study population because experienced people have learned to identify partners with whom they can be compatible.

Thus, aging is a factor twice in decay functions. First is the age of a relationship, call it tie age, for which the liability of newness is evident from slower decay in older relationships. Second is the time that the person citing a relationship has spent in the study population (or in a specific role within the study population), call it node age, for which the liability of newness is evident from slower decay in relations cited by people with more experience.

Closure in the Aggregate

Figure 5.5 shows the association between closure and stability in the banker and analyst relationships. Bankers and analysts are combined because they have similar decay functions. Logit models in table 5.4 predict the vertical axis in figure 5.5 from the horizontal axes with various controls. Relations to analysts are more negative (−.385 coefficient divided by .079 standard error yields a test statistic of −4.87, $p < .001$) and decay faster (4.76 logit test statistic, $p < .001$), but factors that predict next year's relation to an analyst similarly predict next year's relation to a banker, so I combined the two groups for this analysis. The point illustrated in figure 5.5 is that closure is associated with more positive relations and relations are more robust to decay when embedded in closed networks, but closure stabilizes by protecting new and old relations differently.

Figure 5.5 Closure Strengthens and Prevents Decay in New Relations

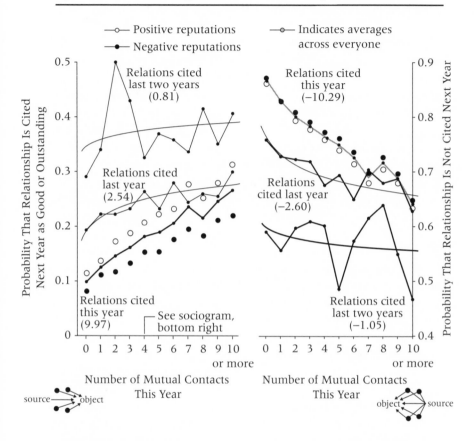

Source: Author's configuration.

The horizontal axes in figure 5.5 distinguish relationships this year by the number of mutual contacts between the two people connected by the evaluation. The measurement was illustrated in figure 5.2 and sociograms at the bottom of figure 5.5 illustrated here. The vertical axes show the state of the relationship next year. The upward-sloping lines in the graph to the left in figure 5.5 show the increasing probability of a positive evaluation next year between two people with mutual contacts this year. Downward-sloping lines in the graph to the right show the decreasing probability of decay in a relationship between people with mutual contacts this year.

Distinguishing Kinds of Closure

Relational embedding increases stability. The more positive the relationship this year, or the longer it has been reported in the peer evaluations, the more likely it will be positive next year and the more robust it is to decay. There is also a crowding effect related to the concentration effects that Uzzi (1996, 1999) has made familiar. The more relationships a person has this year, the less likely they will be positive next year, and the more prone they are to decay.[9]

Direct structural embedding increases stability. Holding relational embedding constant, relations are more likely to be positive next year and less subject to decay in the presence of mutual colleagues. Table 5.4 shows the statistical significance of the associations and figure 5.5 shows the associations working equally for people with positive and negative reputations (hollow and solid dots, respectively). The stabilizing effect of closure is limited to positive third-party ties (friends of friends or enemies of enemies), but even negative third-party ties slow decay (friends of enemies), though they are not a statistically significant decay factor. My causal language notwithstanding, causal order is not demonstrated. It is equally accurate to say that people who continue to work together accumulate mutual contacts.

The slower decay in embedded relations is consistent with other studies. Scott Feld (1997) analyzes network data on 152 students enrolled in a small college, at the beginning and end of their freshman year. Of 5,345 initial sociometric citations for recognition, 54 percent were observed again in the second survey, but the percentage increases significantly with mutual acquaintances. David Krackhardt (1998) analyzes network data gathered over a semester on seventeen sophomore college students living together. He too finds that a relationship is more likely to continue when the two students have mutual friends. Complementing the analysis here of evaluations received by an employee, I analyze change in evaluations made and find that bankers are more likely to continue relations to colleagues with whom they have mutual colleagues (Burt 2002).

Table 5.4   Network Closure, Positive Relations, and Decay

Network This Year	Positive Relation Next Year		Relation Decayed Next Year	
	Zero-Order	Partial	Zero-Order	Partial
Intercept	—	−5.045	—	2.920
Risk year (2, 3, 4)	.152 (.036)**	.086 (.046)	−.175 (.038)**	−.105 (.048)*
Marginals in risk year (/10)	.073 (.005)**	.085 (.009)**	−.089 (.006)**	−.097 (.011)**
Evaluated person is analyst (vs. banker)	.122 (.064)	−.385 (.079)**	−.071 (.064)	.428 (.090)**
Relational embedding				
Marginals this year (/10)	−.017 (.004)**	−.077 (.008)**	.014 (.005)*	.076 (.010)**
Positive relationship this year (1, 2, 3, 4)	.604 (.030)**	.582 (.029)**	−.178 (.023)**	−.130 (.024)**
Years relationship observed (1, 2, 3)	.457 (.043)**	.470 (.070)**	−.403 (.044)**	−.450 (.071)**
Direct structural embedding				
Number of positive two-step connections	.093 (.007)**	.058 (.011)**	−.084 (.008)**	−.056 (.012)**
Number positive two-step for new relations	.059 (.007)**	.060 (.014)**	−.056 (.007)**	−.054 (.014)**
Number of negative two-step connections	.015 (.009)	−.002 (.022)	−.065 (.008)**	−.025 (.020)
Number negative two-step for new relations	−.007 (.009)	.062 (.023)*	−.045 (.010)**	−.082 (.022)**
Indirect structural embedding				
Number of positive three-step connections	.045 (.003)**	.036 (.005)**	−.042 (.003)**	−.032 (.005)**
Number of negative three-step connections	−.003 (.004)	−.027 (.005)**	−.003 (.003)	.025 (.005)**
Both people hold senior rank	.218 (.053)**	.023 (.054)	−.209 (.049)**	−.043 (.056)
Same division	.275 (.054)**	.100 (.076)	−.260 (.054)**	−.065 (.086)
Same geographic region	.395 (.042)**	.158 (.050)**	−.485 (.042)**	−.237 (.050)**

Source: Author's compilation.

Note: These are logit models predicting a relation next year from network variables this year for people cited in both years. "Positive" predicts which of this year's relations are cited next year as good or outstanding. "New" relations are relations in their first year. "Decay" predicts which of this year's relations are not cited again next year. "Zero-Order" columns refer to logit models containing only a single-row variable. Standard errors are adjusted for autocorrelation between citations from the same person and given in parentheses (chi-square statistics of 1166.0 and 827.5 for the "positive" and "decay" predictions with 15 d.f. and 27,364 observations).

* $p < .05$
** $p < .001$

The results in figure 5.5 and table 5.4 extend previous studies in showing a shift from structural to relational embedding as the aspect of closure associated with stability. As relations age, they become self-sustaining. I have data on four years of the banker relations so I can distinguish relations that are one, two, or three years old. Some relations are older still, but I do not know when each relationship started. Fortunately, relations change so quickly in this population that "this year" is the first year for most colleague relationships. The lines in figure 5.5 labeled "relations cited this year" describe stability in relations first cited this year. They are new relationships. The lines labeled "relations cited last year" describe stability in relations that are two years old when at risk of decay next year. The lines labeled "relations cited last two years" describe stability in relations that are three years old when at risk of decay next year.

The lines of association in figure 5.5 show two patterns. First, older relations are more stable. The line for three-year-old relations at the top of the left-hand graph shows a high probability of positive relationship next year. The line for three-year-old relations at the bottom of the right-hand graph shows a low probability of decay next year. These are the relational embedding effects captured in table 5.4.

Second, the stabilizing effect of structural embedding decreases with the age of a relationship. The lines in figure 5.5 for "relations cited this year" are steeper than the lines for "relations cited last two years." The interaction effects under "Direct Structural Embedding" in table 5.4 capture this effect. Above and beyond the association between mutual contacts and stability in general, mutual contacts around a new relationship are associated with significantly more stability in the form of a more positive evaluation next year and higher resistance to decay next year. In short, structural embedding creates stability by carrying relations through the initial period of a relationship, when the risk of decay is highest.

Finally, indirect structural embedding is also associated with stability. Having contacts who are indirectly connected (as illustrated in Figure 5.2) adds significantly to the stability associated with direct structural embedding. Relations next year are more likely to be positive and less likely to decay. Embedding in positive and negative third-party ties are both decay factors. Having a broader network of positive connections among one's separate contacts increases the probability of our positive relationship next year and decreases the probability of decay. Having a broader network of my contacts disliking the people connected to your contacts decreases the probability of your and my having a positive relationship next year, and increases the probability of our connection this year disappearing next year.

Conclusions and Discussion

My summary conclusion is that closure creates an endogenous force for the status quo that secures and expands the boundary around a network, protecting new relations until they are self-sustaining, and doing so even for people only indirectly connected at the periphery of the network. More specifically, I draw three conclusions from the material presented here.

Reputation Contingent on Closure

Reputation stability increases with network closure, increasing from completely unstable to stable in the span of a few mutual contacts (figures 5.3 and 5.4). In networks of colleagues who have little contact with one another, reputation this year has no correlation with reputation next year. Do the same work with interconnected colleagues, and reputation this year is a good predictor of reputation next year. It is striking to see how quickly closure has its effect. The speed is reminiscent of S.E. Asch's (1951) laboratory results on conformity to a group standard: reputation stability among the bankers and analysts increases from nothing to the full closure effect within four mutual colleagues.[10] And the closure effect is separate from quality of work, measured by average colleague evaluation: as illustrated in figure 5.4, the stability of positive and negative reputations increases similarly with closure.

An implication is that you do not own your reputation. The possessive pronoun in "your reputation" refers to the subject of the reputation, not the owner. The people who own your reputation are the people in whose conversations it is built, and the goal of those conversations is not accuracy so much as bonding between the speakers (Burt 2005, chapter 4). You are merely grist for the gossip mill through which they strengthen their relationships with each other.

Ownership has implications for managing reputation. First impressions are critical for the gossip chain they set in motion. Reputations do not emerge from good work directly so much as from colleague stories about the work. Good work completed for people who don't talk about it is work quickly forgotten. This is striking in figures 5.3 and 5.4, where banker and analyst reputations are no more stable than random noise if they work with colleagues who have no connection with one another. The key to building reputation is to close the network around colleagues talking to one another (known in word-of-mouth marketing as "building the buzz"; see Gladwell 2000; Rosen 2000).

Closure Reinforces Status Quo by Selective Protection for New Relations
Closure's stabilizing effect is concentrated in new relationships (figure 5.5). Closure is associated with more positive relations and relations are more robust to decay when embedded in closed networks. However, by the third year of a relationship, mutual friends are less important than the strength of the relationship built up between the two people. Relational embedding is the stronger component in closure's stabilizing effect (table 5.4), but structural embedding plays a unique role in protecting new relations from decay, which gives new relations in closed networks a survival advantage in becoming self-sustaining strong relations.

Summarizing the age-specific decay rates in figure 5.5, figure 5.6 describes decay across age. As a relationship ages across the horizontal axis in figure 5.6, lines in the graph show the probability that the relationship will be gone next year. The risk of decay increases quickly after colleagues first meet, peaks, then declines.[11] For bridge relations—relations that reach across groups—the risk peaks a little after a year. There is less risk of decay for relations embedded in a closed network. Embedded relations have a longer honeymoon period, with decay risk peaking at one and a half years. Decay is slower still for the 25 percent of banker relations most embedded in a net-

Figure 5.6   Effect of Closure in Slowing Network Decay, Especially in New
Relationships

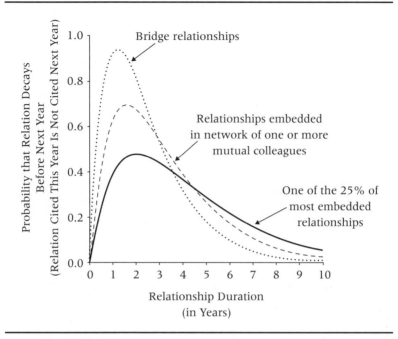

Source: Author's configuration.

work of mutual colleagues. In other words, closure has its strongest
effect protecting new relations from decay. After the first three
years, a bridge relation is less subject to decay than an embedded relation—but few bridges survive to age three. Relations in this population changed dramatically from year to year, so the decay functions in figure 5.6 are probably higher than such functions in other
populations. I expect three points about the functions to generalize:
decay decreases with closure, decay has a kinked functional form,
and closure slows decay primarily by carrying relations through the
initial period of a relationship, when the risk of decay is highest.
With strong relations less subject to decay, and new relations between friends of friends more likely to survive to maturity, the existing structure is reinforced, increasing density within groups and

deepening the structural holes between groups. The summary result is that closure reinforces the status quo.

Closure Reaches Beyond the Immediate Network

My third conclusion is that indirect contacts matter (tables 5.2 and 5.4). Closure among direct contacts, as well as closure among indirect contacts, friends of one's friends, make independent and statistically significant contributions to stability. The coordination-inducing stability benefits of closure depend on monopoly control over reputation. Closure means no alternatives. Structural holes in the network are backdoors through which deviants can escape, weakening the coercive pressure that reputation can exert (recall the rancher Frank Ellis). It is not too surprising to find among the bankers and analysts that dense connections among friends of friends increase the stability of reputation and relations.

This result is in sharp contrast to brokerage, however, for which friends of friends seem to be irrelevant. Table 5.5 contains summary evidence on the contrast. Each row corresponds to an equation in which the row criterion variable is predicted by a person's network of direct contacts, various control variables, and the person's network of indirect contacts. The first four rows of table 5.5 are from this chapter. For example, when I estimate the stability model in table 5.2 for analysts, measuring closure among direct contacts by the combined number of positive and negative two-step connections to direct contacts and holding constant the other variables in table 5.2, I get the results in the first row of table 5.5: a 12.0 t-test for the reputation-stability association with direct structural embedding and a 8.3 t-test for the association with indirect structural embedding. The bottom four rows in table 5.5 are taken from an analysis of returns to brokerage reported elsewhere (Burt 2007), using data on the bankers and analysts in this chapter along with data on a more segmented network of supply-chain managers.

The contrast is between the two columns. The first column contains test statistics for associations with the network of direct contacts. All are statistically significant. The second column contains test statistics for associations with the network of indirect contacts. Only the associations with closure are statistically significant. The

Table 5.5   Brokerage and Closure for Direct and Indirect Network Effects

	Statistical Test for Network of Direct Contacts	Statistical Test for Network of Indirect Contacts
Closure association with stable analyst reputation (table 5.3)	12.0	8.3
Closure association with stable banker reputation (table 5.3)	11.5	8.0
Closure association with decay in analyst relationships (table 5.4, logit)	–9.7	–4.0
Closure association with decay in banker relationships (table 5.4, logit)	–5.4	–3.1
Brokerage association with manager salary	4.3	1.6
Brokerage association with manager annual evaluation	2.9	0.7
Brokerage association with banker compensation	3.4	1.5
Brokerage association with analyst election to All-America Research Team	3.2	0.2

Source: Author's compilation.
Note: Except where logit z-score tests are noted, these are t-tests for the association in the row with various control variables held constant. The closure results are from the indicated tables in this chapter. The brokerage results are taken from analyses reported elsewhere (see Burt 2007, tables 1, 3, and 5).

results for brokerage in the lower right of table 5.5 show no evidence of returns to brokerage among friends of friends. Returns to brokerage are concentrated in direct contacts while closure has its stabilizing effect at further remove, through friends of friends as well as direct contacts.[12]

Two implications follow. With respect to research design, brokerage can be studied with standard survey network designs in which survey respondents are asked to name contacts and relations among their contacts (for example, Marsden 2005, on name generators and interpreters). There is no need to measure structure among friends of friends since returns to brokerage are concentrated in the network of direct contacts. This means that network measures of brokerage can be incorporated easily in survey research with stratified probability samples of disconnected respondents. The same is not true for closure, according to the results in this chapter. Closure among friends of friends contributes significantly to closure's stability effect, so research designs to estimate closure effects should include friends of friends as in cluster and saturation samples of interconnected survey respondents (Coleman 1958). Given the costs of clustering respondents in survey research, it is worth noting that standard survey network methods can capture the effects of closure among direct contacts, but the effects will be conservative. The additional closure effect from indirect connections among friends of friends is unobserved.

Second, the significance of indirect connections among friends of friends raises coordination issues for closure studies. For example, Robert K. Merton (1957) describes factors that limit the visibility of beliefs and behavior such that ordinary people are more able to play complex roles (Merton 1968, 390–411, for detail). If you typically see Bill in Chicago during the autumn and Beverly in Singapore during the winter, your exchanges with Bill and Beverly are segregated in time and space. Bill and Beverly will have difficulty coordinating their demands on you, relative to their ability to coordinate if they met with you at the same time in the same place. Indirect connections are that much more complicated to coordinate. For example, James Moody (2002) describes complications due to time as a segregation factor. If a connection between persons A and B happens today and a connection between persons B and C happens tomorrow, A's news can travel to C through the A–B–C indirect connection, but C's news will not travel to A through the C–B–A connection because the A–B discussion is finished by the time C's news reaches B. Sequence is an obvious issue in the networks of sexual relations that Moody (2002) describes. In a discussion network, B can remember C's news and relay it in B's next conversation with A. Coordination is still an issue: How much time will elapse before B has another conversation with A? Will B remember to transmit C's news in subsequent conversations? These kinds of questions are relevant to closure studies, in a way they are not to brokerage studies, because connections through friends of friends contribute to closure's stability effect. In general, any factor that disrupts information flow through indirect connections creates structural holes between friends of friends, eroding the coordination-inducing stability that closure can provide.

Interdisciplinary Research on Reputation

It is difficult to draw a clear line between economic and sociological reasoning, but the two communities of work often have distinct focuses, and in that spirit it is fair to say that economists have focused on reputation effects, in contrast to sociologists, who have focused on reputation origins.

For a specific example, consider the issue of how to price the risk of an institution's debt. The economist Gary Gorton (1996) uses Douglas W. Diamond's (1989) reputation argument to describe the value of reputation to banks created during the 1838 to 1860 Free Banking Era in the United States. To put the argument in its original vernacular (Diamond 1989, 690): "Reputation effects eliminate the need for monitoring when the value of future profits lost because of the information revealed by defaulting on debt is large. Borrowers with higher credit ratings have a lower cost of capital, and such a rating needs to be maintained to retain this source of higher present value of future profits." Gorton shows that the debt of new banks is discounted more heavily than that of otherwise similar banks, and the discount declines over time as the new banks become reputable. In Gorton's analysis, reputation is indexed by time in a market, the assumption being that reputation will somehow emerge and have its effect as a bank spends time in the market.

In contrast, Joel Podolny (1993), a sociologist, studies a similar reputation effect but with respect to the network structure responsible for reputation. Adopting a status metaphor to distinguish investment banks with respect to their reputation for quality, and reasoning that "tombstone" advertisements for investments display more prominently the higher-status banks involved in an offering, Podolny measures relative status by the frequency with which bank

A is displayed higher, in larger print, than bank B. More reputable (higher-status) investment banks can raise capital at lower cost, and Podolny argues that "higher-status banks should take advantage of their lower cost to underbid their competitors for the bonds that they wish to underwrite" (848). He shows for several thousand investment-grade offerings in the 1980s that higher-status banks enjoy lower costs (a point generalized to other products and situations in Podolny 2005). Going a step further to study returns to affiliation with status, Toby E. Stuart, Ha Hoang, and Ralph C. Hybels (1999) show that biotechnology start-up companies with higher-status alliance partners and equity investors speed to IPO at a younger age and with higher market valuations.

These analyses are productive to compare because they illustrate the distinct focuses of economic and sociological analyses at the same time that they illustrate inherent overlap. Studies of reputation origins adjudicate between alternative models using reputation effects as a criterion. Podolny (1993) and Stuart, Hoang, and Hybels (1999) estimate reputation effects to test hypotheses about the origins of reputation in network structure. There is a three-variable chain: network-reputation-performance, in which sociologists have focused on the network-reputation link and economists have focused on the reputation-performance link. Sociological work is strengthened when it incorporates the reputation-performance link (for example, Podolny 1993, 2005; Stuart, Ha Hoang, and Hybels 1999) and economic work is strengthened when it incorporates the network-reputation link (for example, Greif 1989, 2006). There is reason to expect—from the evidence presented here and from pioneering studies such as Munshi and Rosenzweig's (2005)—that estimates of reputation effects will vary with network closure. Stated in a more cautionary tone, reputation effects will be dramatically inconsistent across populations without controls for the network closure sustaining reputation.

I do not wish to make too much of the economist-sociologist contrast. There are sociologists who analyze reputation effects without analyzing reputation's etiology in network structure, and there are economists who articulate the way that reputation is dependent on network closure. I suspect that economists and sociologists can agree that reputation production involves information diffusion, and therefore must be affected by social factors that inhibit diffusion to this group while speeding diffusion elsewhere (see, for example, Raub and Weesie 1990). Reputations do not spring to life without people talking to one another, and anything that depends on people talking to one another will be affected by networks of people who have variable contacts.

Notes

1. Nothing is revealed in this chapter that could be awkward for the organization, but to honor management's wish for anonymity, I am deliberately vague on job ranks in the study population, and on the number of people in lower ranks with whom study-population people had relations. The people I discuss as bankers and analysts could be described with other job labels. I use "banker" and "analyst" because the labels are short and not inappropriate.

2. High relationship turnover makes the study population analytically attractive for another reason, but it is not productive to mention until I have introduced, in the next section, Granovetter's distinction between relational and structural embedding. See note 9.

3. The percentages in this paragraph were computed from a regression equation predicting the evaluations from colleague i to employee j, e_{ij}, from the average evaluation made by the colleague (row mean, e_i) and the average evaluation of the employee (column mean, $e_{.j}$). The 23 percent of evaluation variation due to rater differences is the variance predicted by the row mean. The 12 percent due to agreement on the employee is the variance predicted by the column mean. The remaining 65 percent is the residual variance unique to colleague i paired with employee j. The same percentages result if evaluations are standardized within years, and they only differ slightly if evaluations of analysts are predicted separately from the evaluations of bankers (63.0 percent residual variance for analysts versus 66.1 percent for the bankers). The tendency for relations to be more about the pair of people than either person individually is consistent with the substantial turnover in relationships in this study population, but it could be a more general phenomenon. David A. Kenny and Linda Albright (1987, 399) report a similar pattern in networks of college students.

4. The vertical axis is the correlation within a subsample around each employee. Bernard Finifter (1972) is a good introduction to the subsampling strategy. Rank-order the employees present in two adjacent years by their average number of two-step and three-step connections

with colleagues (the mean scores for Jim and James in figure 5.2). The six employees above and below person *i* on the list are drawn as a subsample around person *i*. Person *i*'s score on the vertical axis in figure 5.3 is the correlation, for the thirteen people in the subsample, between reputation this year and next year. I settled on subsamples of a dozen colleagues after testing alternatives. The association with closure in figure 5.3 increases sharply through subsamples of four, six, and eight colleagues (decreasing sampling error), more slowly through subsamples of ten and twelve colleagues, then little for larger subsamples. I took twelve as the inflection point. With subsamples of thirteen, I lose the first six and last six employees in the rank order.

5. For each employee, I drew a random sample of twelve other employees and correlated reputation scores for adjacent years across the thirteen employees. The subsample size of thirteen is arbitrary. I set the subsample size at thirteen to match the subsamples of similarly embedded employees (see previous note). In essence, the squares in figure 5.3 are random subsamples from the sampling distribution around the population correlation between reputation in adjacent years.

6. Test statistics are reported at the bottom of figure 5.3. For example, there are 121 observations of employees who have an average of 3 mutual contacts with the colleagues evaluating them (20 employees in the first and second years, 42 employees in the second and third years, and 59 in the third and fourth years). Regressing reputation next year over reputation this year yields a coefficient of .432 across the 121 observations, with a standard error of .111 (adjusted for repeated observations of some employees over time), which yields the 3.9 t-test reported in figure 5.3. I repeated the computation to get a test statistic for reputation stability in each of the other ten categories of network closure in the figure.

7. The one exception is "number of colleagues this year." Stability is higher for bankers and analysts cited by many colleagues this year, but the partial effect shows a crowding effect of stability eroded by numerous colleague evaluations. Number of colleagues is highly correlated with direct structural embedding. The more colleagues who cite an employee, the more two-step connections possible among the colleagues. There is a .84 correlation between "number of colleagues this year" and "number of positive two-step connections" this year. Just holding constant the number of positive two-step connections changes the strong positive association between stability and "number of colleagues" to a strong negative association (routine t-test statistics of 23.6 versus –3.8). The multicolinearity is much less at the level of individual relations so I do not make much of the crowding effect in table 5.2 in preference to raising it in the discussion of table 5.4.

8. I combined positive and negative three-step connections in table 5.2 because they are so highly correlated when aggregated across an individual's relationships. There is a .92 correlation between positive three-step connections and negative three-step connections, and their respective correlations with the reputation stability measure in table 5.2 are .63 and .63. There is nothing to distinguish the two kinds of three-step connections aggregated across an individual's relations so I combine them in table 5.2. I report them separately in table 5.4 because they are less redundant at the level of individual relationships.

9. High turnover in relationships also makes the bankers and analysts an attractive research site because relational embedding is not as influential as it would be in a population of people who work with the same colleagues over time (see note 2). In other words, the bankers and analysts are nicely suited for studying the relative stabilizing effects of direct versus indirect structural embedding.

10. I do not wish to make too much of the analogy because it is only an analogy, but it is worth noting because analogy between the Asch results and the results reported here implies that the closure results for bankers and analysts could generalize to the many diverse situations in which Asch's results have been replicated and that Asch's laboratory methods could be a productive way to study closure's effect on stability. Asch (1951, 188) reports the frequency with which subjects make errors in the direction of an obviously wrong peer opinion as the number of peers increases. He reports an average of 3.75 errors with 16 peers, 3.84 errors with 8 peers, 4.20 errors with 4 peers, 4.00 errors with 3 peers, 1.53 with 2 peers, .33 with 1 peer, and .08 errors for people alone in the lab. Conformity increases quickly with 3 or 4 peers (after which the small lab became crowded). In figure 5.3, there is a .09 correlation between reputations in adjacent years for people evaluated by colleagues with whom they share no mutual colleagues. Add one mutual contact and the correlation rises from .09 to .20, a 122 percent increase in stability. With two mutual contacts, the correlation rises from .20 to .34, which is a 70 percent increase. The marginal increases then begin to decline, to 26 percent for three mutual contacts, and 26 percent for four mutual contacts. Marginal increases are small after four mutual contacts. This is apparent in figure 5.4 from the steep bold line for zero to four mutual contacts and the less-steep line thereafter. Similarly, the marginal effect of the fifth, sixth, or seventh mutual contact on a relation being positive next year (left graph in figure 5.5) or decaying next year (right graph in figure 5.5) is smaller than the marginal effects of one, two, or four mutual contacts.

11. Banker and analyst relations are combined in figure 5.6. I use a two-parameter model to describe kinked decay: $r(T) = (aT)exp(-T/b)$,

where $r(T)$ is the risk of decay at time T, and a and b are parameters, b the time of the peak in decay risk (see Diekmann and Mitter 1984; Diekmann and Engelhardt 1999, 787). If detailed data were available through the first year, I would want to separate level, shape, and time of peak decay (for example, Brüderl and Diekmann 1995, 162), but the two-parameter model is sufficient for illustration here. Details on creating the decay functions in figure 5.6 from the decay data are given in Burt (2002, 361n). For bridge relations, a is 2.055, and b is 1.236 years (which, times twelve, puts the peak risk of decay at 14.8 months). For embedded relations, a is 1.160 and b is 1.612 (which puts the peak decay risk at 19.3 months). For the most embedded relations, a is 0.616 and b is 2.095 (which puts the peak risk of decay at 25.1 months).

12. A quick note is in order to avoid misinterpretation if these results are juxtapositioned with James E. Rauch and Joel Watson's argument in chapter 8. Rauch and Watson explore a model in which the probability of someone's becoming an entrepreneur is increased by having a colleague who became an entrepreneur. The results in table 5.5 might be interpreted as implying no benefit to having network brokers as friends. In fact, the benefit is indirect, as implied by Rauch and Watson's model. People who have brokers as colleagues are likely to be brokers themselves: there is a .74 correlation between direct and indirect brokerage for the bankers in this chapter, and .71 for the analysts. However, there are people who are friends of brokers but not themselves brokers. The results in table 5.5 reflect the fact that being the friend of a broker does not have a performance benefit (the "indirect contacts" column in table 5.5) until a person becomes a broker him- or herself ("direct contacts" column in table 5.5). This point is discussed in Burt (2007).

References

Asch, S.E. 1951. "Effects of Group Pressure upon the Modification and Distortion of Judgments." In *Groups, Leadership and Men*, edited by Harold Guetzleow. Pittsburg, Pa.: Carnegie Press.

Atwater, Leanne, and David Waldman. 1998. "Accountability in 360 Degree Feedback." *HR Magazine* 43(2): 96.

Blau, Peter M. 1968. "Interaction: Social Exchange." In *The International Encyclopedia of the Social Sciences*, edited by David L. Sills. New York: Free Press and Macmillan.

Brüderl, Josef, and Andreas Diekmann. 1995. "The Log-Logistic Rate Model: Two Generalizations with an Application to Demographic Data." *Sociological Methods and Research* 24(2): 158–86.

Burt, Ronald S. 2002. "Bridge Decay." *Social Networks* 24(4): 333–63.

———. 2005. *Brokerage and Closure.* New York: Oxford University Press.

———. 2007. "Second-Hand Brokerage: Evidence on the Importance of Local Structure for Managers, Bankers, and Analysts." *Academy of Management Journal* 50(1): 119-48.

Coleman, James S. 1958. "Relational Analysis: The Study of Social Organization with Survey Methods." *Human Organization* 17(4): 28–36.

———. 1988. "Social Capital in the Creation of Human Capital." *American Journal of Sociology* 94(supplement): S95–S120.

———. 1990. *Foundations of Social Theory.* Cambridge, Mass.: Harvard University Press.

Diamond, Douglas W. 1989. "Reputation Acquisition in Debt Markets." *Journal of Political Economy* 97(4): 828–62.

Diekmann, Andreas, and Henriette Engelhardt. 1999. "The Social Inheritance of Divorce: Effects of Parents' Family Type in Postwar Germany." *American Sociological Review* 64(6): 783–93.

Diekmann, Andreas, and Peter Mitter. 1984."A Comparison of the 'Sickle Function' with Alternative Stochastic Models of Divorce Rates." In *Stochastic Modeling of Social Processes,* edited by Andreas Diekmann and Peter Mitter. Orlando, Fla.: Academic Press.

Dunbar, Robin. 1996. *Grooming, Gossip, and the Evolution of Language.* Cambridge, Mass.: Harvard University Press.

Ellickson, Robert C. 1991. *Order Without Law.* Cambridge, Mass.: Harvard University Press.

Feld, Scott L. 1981. "The Focused Organization of Social Ties." *American Journal of Sociology* 86(5): 1015–35.

———. 1997. "Structural Embeddedness and Stability of Interpersonal Relations." *Social Networks* 19(1): 91–95.

Finifter, Bernard M. 1972. "The Generation of Confidence: Evaluating Research Findings by Random Subsample Replication." *Sociological Methodology* 4: 112-75.

Gambetta, Diego. 1994. "Godfather's Gossip." *Archives Européennes de Sociologie* 35(2): 199–223.

Gladwell, Malcolm. 2000. *The Tipping Point.* New York: Little, Brown.

Gorton, Gary. 1996. "Reputation Formation in Early Bank Note Markets." *Journal of Political Economy* 104(2): 346–97.

Granovetter, Mark S. 1985. "Economic Action, Social Structure, and Embeddedness." *American Journal of Sociology* 91(3): 481–510.

———. 1992. "Problems of Explanation in Economic Sociology." In *Networks and Organization,* edited by Nitin Nohria and Robert G. Eccles. Boston, Mass.: Harvard Business School Press.

Greif, Avner. 1989. "Reputation and Coalitions in Medieval Trade: Evidence on the Maghribi Traders." *Journal of Economic History* 49(4): 857–82.

————. 2006. *Institutions and the Path to the Modern Economy*. New York: Cambridge University Press.

Hannan, Michael T., and John H. Freeman. 1989. *Organizational Ecology*. Cambridge, Mass.: Harvard University Press.

Kenny, David A., and Linda Albright. 1987. "Accuracy in Interpersonal Perception: A Social Relations Analysis." *Psychological Bulletin* 102(3): 390–402.

Krackhardt, David. 1998. "Simmelian Ties: Super Strong and Sticky." In *Power and Influence in Organizations*, edited by Roderick M. Kramer and Margaret A. Neale. Thousand Oaks, Calif.: Sage.

Marsden, Peter V. 2005. "Recent Developments in Network Measurement." In *Models and Methods in Social Network Analysis*, edited by Peter J. Carrington, John Scott, and Stanley Wasserman. New York: Cambridge University Press.

Merry, Sally Engle. 1984. "Rethinking Gossip and Scandal." In *Toward a General Theory of Social Control*, edited by Donald Black. Volume 1. New York: Academic Press.

Merton, Robert K. 1957. "The Role-Set: Problems in Sociological Theory." *British Journal of Sociology* 8(2): 106–20.

————. 1968. *Social Theory and Social Structure*. New York: Free Press.

Moody, James. 2002. "The Importance of Relationship Timing for Diffusion." *Social Forces* 81(1): 25–56.

Munshi, Kaivan, and Mark Rosenzweig. 2005. "Economic Development and the Decline of Rural and Urban Community-Based Networks." *Economics of Transition* 13(3): 427–43.

Podolny, Joel M. 1993. "A Status-Based Model of Market Competition." *American Journal of Sociology* 98(4): 829–72.

————. 2005. *Status Signals*. Princeton, N.J.: Princeton University Press.

Putnam, Robert D. 1993. *Making Democracy Work*. Princeton, N.J.: Princeton University Press.

————. 2000. *Bowling Alone*. New York: Simon & Schuster.

Raub, Werner, and Jeroen Weesie. 1990. "Reputation and Efficiency in Social Interactions: An Example of Network Effects." *American Journal of Sociology* 96(3): 626–54.

Rosen, Emanuel. 2000. *The Anatomy of Buzz*. New York: Doubleday.

Rosnow, Ralph L., and Gary Alan Fine. 1976. *Rumor and Gossip*. New York: Elsevier.

Stuart, Toby E., Ha Hoang, and Ralph C. Hybels. 1999. "Interorganizational Endorsements and the Performance of Entrepreneurial Ventures." *Administrative Science Quarterly* 44(2): 315–49.

Tullock, Gordon. 1985. "Adam Smith and the Prisoner's Dilemma." *Quarterly Journal of Economics* 100(supplement): 1073–81.

Uzzi, Brian. 1996. "The Sources and Consequences of Embeddedness for the

Economic Performance of Organizations: The Network Effect." *American Sociological Review* 61(4): 674–98.

———. 1999. "Embeddedness in the Making of Financial Capital: How Social Relations and Networks Benefit Firms Seeking Finance." *American Sociological Review* 64(4): 481–505.

Uzzi, Brian, and J. J. Gillespie. 2002. "Knowledge Spillover in Corporate Financing Networks: Embeddedness and the Firm's Debt Performance." *Strategic Management Journal* 23(7): 595–618.

Uzzi, Brian, and Ryon Lancaster. 2004. "Embeddedness and the Price of Legal Services in the Large Law Firm Market." *American Sociological Review* 69(3): 319–44.

Wong, Peter Leung-Kwong, and Paul Ellis. 2002. "Social Ties and Partner Identification in Sino-Hong Kong International Joint Ventures." *Journal of International Business Studies* 33(2): 267–89.

Part III

Melding the Economics and Sociology Approaches

Chapter 6

On Firmer Ground: The Collaborative Team as Strategic Research Site for Verifying Network-Based Social-Capital Hypotheses

Ray E. Reagans, Ezra Zuckerman, and Bill McEvily

Social networks command the interest of scholars and others because these relational patterns are assumed to have causal force. In particular, network theories typically adopt the premise that such patterns often lead to individual or collective outcomes that cannot be fully ascribed to the exogenous forces that determined such configurations. When this premise of network exogeneity is undermined, network analysis may be a useful tool for viewing the operation of other forces, but it cannot fulfill the network analyst's ambition of demonstrating how social networks shape important outcomes. Moreover, network analysts must concede that network structures are always subject to manipulation by actors and can thus never be considered exogenous to the same degree as are, say, a person's natural endowments and fixed characteristics, such as age, gender, or innate ability. Thus, to place network theories on firmer ground, there must be strong theoretical and empirical reasons for adopting the premise of network exogeneity with confidence.

In this chapter we focus on a key class of network hypotheses that is particularly vulnerable to the criticism that networks do not have causal force: claims that differential success or performance may be attributed to an actor's position in a social network.[1] Such hypotheses have gained considerable popularity in recent years and may be summarized as hypotheses regarding social capital.[2] Examples of such hypotheses include the claim that individuals whose networks are better (or more poorly) constructed are more (or less) likely to achieve their goals—say, obtaining a job (Granovetter 1974/1995) or advancing through a corporate hierarchy (Burt 1992). The general difficulty that such analyses face is that, to the extent that certain network positions are more advantageous than others, all actors should be expected to strive for them. And to the extent that such efforts are made by all actors but that only some succeed, this suggests that occupancy of differentially valuable network positions reflects prior differences among actors that are responsible both for observed differences in performance and for network position. In short, the premise of network exogeneity can be undermined by "unobserved heterogeneity," or the possibility that the variation in social capital reflects differences in intrinsic attributes; and by "reverse causality," or the possibility that prior performance differences (or even the prior anticipation of future performance differences) are responsible for the social capital attained.

It is crucial to note that the fact that hypothesized network effects might be endogenous in a particular case does not mean that they always are. Indeed, we shall argue that there are ample theoretical reasons to expect network exogeneity in many cases. The challenge is to find nonexperimental research contexts that may serve as "strategic research sites" (Merton 1987) for testing social-capital hypotheses. The primary objective of this chapter is to make progress in meeting this challenge.

In particular, we argue that contexts that include sets of overlapping collaborative teams represent such a strategic research site under certain conditions. Such teams, which may be defined as collective actors that comprise multiple individuals who are responsible for a joint product, include film projects, academic or scientific collaborations, and work groups in organizations—even organizations themselves. The hypothesis that a given team—like an individual—outperforms others because of how it is positioned in a wider social network is weakened by the possibility that the team's network is not causally responsible for the outcome. For instance, the observed performance differences could be due to differences in composition—for example, a team with more highly skilled members both succeeds at its task and attracts many useful ties, but the latter does not actually cause the former. Alternatively, it could be that teams that either have a history of past success or who experience success at the beginning of a project develop effective networks as a result.

How can these quite reasonable objections be countered? We show below that teams can have two features that make them useful for countering such objections and thereby serving as strategic research sites for testing hypotheses about social capital. Such teams have relatively short lives and contain members with multiple and overlapping team memberships. The team's having a short life means that it will not have a prior performance record and its members will not be able to anticipate its future success and thus shape their social networks in light of the outcome. This means that one can collect social network data regarding the team members well before the team comes into existence. Multiple and overlapping team membership is important because it means that we can identify each person's average contribution to team performance. That is, we can recover baseline fixed effects for each of the team members (and even subsets of these members) and thereby deal with the problem of unobserved heterogeneity. Put simply, this strategy helps determine whether a team is really more than the sum of its parts.

Validating Network Exogeneity: Ideal and Reality

Before considering the difficulties of validating the premise of network exogeneity, it bears reminding why it may make sense to invoke this premise. Network analysts are rarely explicit in stating their rationale, but there appear to be two main justifications for the premise. The first is based on the recognition that actors typically are involved in multiple arenas and roles and that the network observed for one arena is, at least in part, a by-product of relations in other arenas. This notion of network-as-by-product is at the heart of Mark Granovetter's (1985) discussion of embeddedness in market interactions. Granovetter argues that the social-network overlay on economic exchange may often have functional (and also dysfunctional) consequences. However, the origins of such networks often reside in more "primordial" affiliations (as in the archetypical example of the Hasidic diamond traders; see also Coleman 1988), which are essentially exogenous (but see Zuckerman 2003, 558). In this example, the social network observed in the economic sphere is a by-product of activity in an exogenous sphere. And the reverse may occur as well. For example, a common theme in the "embeddedness" literature is that once actors become members of an economic network, they acquire a commitment to the relationships that can no longer be reduced to self-interest (see Sgourev and Zuckerman 2006 for a test of this argument; see also Granovetter 1974/1995, 463–5; Lawler 2001; Uzzi 1997, 55). In such cases then, a social network develops as a by-product of economic interests.

Another possibility is a situation where networks in each of multiple arenas may arise endogenously, but, since each privileges a different type of network and networks cannot be adjusted quickly, it is effectively impossible for the actor to design a network that works for both arenas. For example, Ezra W. Zuckerman (1999, 2000) argues that firms suffer a price penalty when their egocentric network of coverage by securities analysts implies a mismatch between the firm's industrial participation and the way it has been classified by analysts. Why would a firm not endeavor to eliminate such a penalty by realigning its corporate strategy in a way that induces a more favorable position in the coverage network? The answer may be that such a change would require the firm to realign its corporate strategy in a way that hurts profits in the long term, even if it removes the financial-market penalty in the short-term. Thus, if firms optimize for profits, their position in the analyst coverage network will be at least somewhat exogenous.

A second rationale for treating networks as exogenous relies on principles of path dependence similar to those familiar from studies of technological networks. Although prior forces may be responsible for "seeding" a network, the initial configuration unleashes a dynamic that reinforces such initial conditions, thereby imputing causal force to the resulting network. Such models are prominent in the literature on status hierarchies, which can be considered social networks where the links are relations of deference from one party to another. For example, Joel M. Podolny (2005) argues that, whereas the initial status hierarchy results from initial differences in quality, the "loose linkage" between the two implies that over time, initial quality differences are solidified as substantial differences in status that are then relatively insensitive to changes in quality. Roger V. Gould's (2002) model of status hierarchy implies a similar decoupling of status from quality. Key to both models is a rationale for why low-status actors remain in their positions even though they suffer from lower performance. In both cases, the rationale relies on the paradox that a high-status actor risks losing status if he competes with low-status actors because he will thereby become affiliated with them. So a network structure with greater returns accruing to particular positions may exist in a steady state. And this means that the resulting network can be treated as exogenous.

How Exogenous?

Thus, the primary challenge to the premise of network exogeneity is not theoretical but empirical. Since in virtually all cases, it is possible to derive both a social network-based and a network-free explanation for the observed association between network position and performance, the challenge is to find research contexts in which network position may indeed be treated as at least partly exogenous.

In attempting to meet this challenge, it is useful to consider the experimental design necessary to demonstrate the causal impact of social-network position on performance. Such an experiment must satisfy two straightforward conditions. First, the experimenter should assign network positions to individual subjects (collectivities) rather than allowing networks to emerge from interaction. Second, such assignments should be conducted in a manner that is random with respect to underlying differences in quality or ability or any other factor that might be correlated with performance. If an experiment that is designed in such a manner (see, for example, Cook et al. 1983; Willer 1999) finds that network position affects performance, such results provide unambiguous evidence that network position is causal.

Researchers who analyze processes outside the laboratory are rarely able to engineer social networks (but see Karlan 2004; Rubineau 2007; Sacerdote 2001 for exceptions). The challenge that confronts most analysts, then, is to analyze observational data using methods that help them to isolate the causal impact of network position. In particular, the experimental conditions given may be translated into two directives for analysis of observational data. First, one must measure social networks prior to the measurement of performance. Second, one must demonstrate that the observed association between network position at time t and performance (at time $t + 1$) could not have been spuriously produced by one or more prior variables that affect both network position and performance (see Davis 1985).[3] Such prior variables may be classified into three types: measures of underlying differences in ability or quality; past performance; and expectations of future performance. Elimination of the first type of variable solves the problem of unobserved heterogeneity; elimination of the second and third solves the problem of reverse causality. In general, to the extent that the analysis establishes the temporal priority of network position and succeeds either in controlling for the three types of spurious effects or in eliminating them via experimental design, we may be confident that the observed association between network position and performance indeed reflects causation. Yet these directives are extremely hard to fulfill in practice, as we show next in a review of how past research has struggled to justify the premise of network exogeneity.

Eliminating Reverse Causality

The difficulty of eliminating the problem of reverse causality is perhaps best illustrated by the fact that researchers have been hard-pressed even to meet the basic directive that network data be collected before the observation of performance. Indeed, the challenge of collecting data over time has forced many studies (for example, Burt 1992; McEvily and Zaheer 1999; Reagans and Zuckerman 2001; Uzzi 1996) to analyze cross-sectional data and to make the unverified assumption that the causal arrow runs from network position to success rather than vice versa. Yet gathering network data prior to the observation of performance is not enough to rule out the possibility that the network position resulted from past performance or the anticipation of future performance. For example, to support his assumption that the positive association between "structural autonomy" and organizational success reflects a causal effect of the former on the latter, Burt (1997, 349; see also Burt 1992, 173–80) replicates the result with data from a study for which the network data were collected six months prior to the observation of performance. However, it is quite possible that either (unobserved) performance at or prior to the collection of the network data affect both network position and future performance or that performance six months hence may be anticipated by actors with some accuracy and therefore may affect how they manage their relationships. Thus, it is insufficient to verify network exogeneity simply by measuring networks prior to that of performance.

A related study that makes progress in solving the reverse causality problem is Podolny and James N. Baron (1997). Podolny and Baron observe performance (mobility in a corporate hierarchy) over a period that begins prior to and includes their survey window, but they are also careful to include in their analysis only relationships that were reported to have begun one year prior to the survey. In addition, Podolny and Baron report that they conducted robustness tests that showed that the observed associations between egocentric network patterns and performance did not become stronger when more recent ties are included. Since the performance effects are more salient with network data from the more distant past, this suggests to Podolny and Baron that the networks must be causal. This creative strategy weakens but does not eliminate the possibility that the observed relationship is produced by past performance differences or the anticipation of future ones. In particular, Podolny and Baron did not obtain the respondent's full network one year prior to the survey, but only a selection based on the criteria presented to the respondent at the time of the survey. As a result, their network data are a subset of the respondent's network from the prior year that could have been selected in a way that is related to past or in anticipation of future performance. Indeed, it is not unreasonable to expect older ties to be more strongly associated with performance because they have proved themselves to be more valuable (and were therefore selected by the respondent), whereas newer ties may be generated by more temporary, short-lived needs.

The possibility that the anticipation of future performance drives observed relationships between network position and future performance is particularly problematic where the network data can be construed as patterns of endorsement or certification. For example, several studies have shown that endorsement by the state or a prominent firm may increase the survival or valuation of a firm (Singh, Tucker, and House 1986; Baum and Oliver 1991, 1992). Other studies posit effects of network position on performance where the network is interpreted alternatively as involving the transfer of resources (for example, Powell, Koput, and Smith-Doerr 1996; Ahuja 2000) or as conferring implicit endorsements (for example, Stuart, Hoang, and Hybels 1999). All such studies face the possibility that the certification of an actor has no independent effect on her performance but merely reflects the anticipation on the part of the certifier that the actor will perform at a high level. And, unless one is willing to entertain the possibility that endorsements are handed out randomly, it is a reasonable working hypothesis that they are at least correlated with forecasts of future performance. A similar difficulty confronts studies that examine the positive impact of organizational status on profits or returns (Podolny 1993; Benjamin and Podolny 1999) in that one may receive greater deference when one performs (or is expected to perform) at a higher level. The challenge faced by all such research involves demonstrating that the positive relationship between certification, or deference, and performance is not spuriously produced by that between interpretations of performance on the part of the observer, and performance itself.

Paul Ingram and Peter Roberts's (2000) analysis of the effect on hotel performance (yield) by friendship ties among hotel managers deserves attention for its creative attempt to eliminate the possibility that prior performance is responsible for the observed effects. In particular, they endogenize the network by regressing the existence of a friendship from manager i to j on a series of covariates that are presumed to be unrelated to performance. This then allows them to use an instrumental-variables (IV) regression technique (see for example, Hanushek and Jackson 1977; Greene 1997) to identify the portion of the relationship between the network variables and performance that is not due to performance differences. This analytic strategy should be widely emulated in future research. However, one must recognize that IV regression techniques are only as good as the identifying assumptions. In particular, one must be willing to believe that the covariates used to explain network position are truly unrelated to performance. For example, one might wonder whether hotel managers who have shown themselves to be (or display indications that they will be) high performers are also more likely to have more friends, a variable Ingram and Roberts (2000, 414) use to identify network exogeneity. In general, it is extremely difficult to find covariates that are clearly responsible for the development of the network but are unrelated to performance (but see Munshi 2001), which limits the cases for which IV techniques will be applicable.

Eliminating Unobserved Heterogeneity
Clearly, eliminating reverse causality is difficult. However, the challenge of eliminating unobserved heterogeneity may be even more daunting. Short of random assignment (for example, Karlan 2004; Rubineau 2007; Sacerdote 2001), which is obviously not feasible in most research contexts and can rarely generate substantial variation in network structure, how can we be sure that network structure is independent of the actors' underlying characteristics? Most researchers have tried to solve this problem by controlling for human-capital variables that might be responsible for the observed relationship between network position and performance (for example, Burt 1992, 1997; Podolny and Baron 1997). But the observable indicators of human capital are typically general variables such as years of education and age rather than the specific forms of human capital (for example, knowledge of organizational routines or managerial ability), which are more likely to affect performance in a local context. An alternative strategy to using observable indicators of human capital, often applied to panel data, involves using fixed effects or the inclusion of a dummy variable for each of the actors (see, for example, Burt 1992, 283–84; Zuckerman 1999). This strategy helps eliminate underlying differences between actors in both perfor-

mance and network position. Yet, while fixed effects can be useful for addressing unobserved heterogeneity, it cannot solve the problem of reverse causality: changes in an actor's (present or expected) performance over time could produce observed change in its network position.

Two papers are noteworthy for having made exemplary progress in solving the challenge of unobserved heterogeneity. In particular, Ingram and Roberts's paper (2000) deserves attention not only because of its advances in addressing reverse causality but because it is quite comprehensive in controlling for a wide set of variables that could affect a hotel's yield. One is hard put to imagine unobserved variables that might be missing from their analysis. Beth A. Benjamin and Podolny's (1999) analysis of firm status on the price of a bottle of wine also merits attention. This study is particularly unusual because it includes quality measures based on blind taste tests. In addition, Benjamin and Podolny control for indicators of a wine's cost structure, the second of the two underlying characteristics that should govern price and that might relate to status. With such controls in place, it becomes quite difficult to argue that a firm's position in the status hierarchy can be reduced to underlying characteristics. Thus, both studies serve as models because they make it difficult (though not impossible) for the skeptic to assert that unmeasured underlying differences among actors (in these cases firms) undermine the premise of network exogeneity. At the same time, the uniqueness of these two studies is testament to the difficulty of obtaining a comprehensive set of controls that can definitively rule out unobserved heterogeneity.[4]

Proposed Research Strategy

Although the research just summarized has made some progress in addressing the challenges of reverse causality and unobserved heterogeneity, the approaches thus far are largely idiosyncratic to the particular cases studied. Thus, more general-purpose strategies are needed to help test social-capital hypotheses in nonexperimental settings. In the next section we discuss the particular social-capital hypotheses that we wish to consider. In this section, we discuss a strategy for validating such hypotheses.

Our strategy applies to social units that are collections of individuals. Two distinctive features of collectivities are useful for the purpose at hand. First, many collectivities are short-lived relative to the time frame of performance. In particular, the collectivity itself may be formed to carry out a defined task within a particular time frame. Such groups' performance may be affected by their members' internal and external networks of relations, but prior performance of the group per se cannot be responsible for observed effects for the simple reason that the group did not exist previously. In addition, it is feasible to eliminate the possibility that expectations of future performance (by the actors themselves as well as others, such as their managers) are responsible for such a group's success by measuring networks that were formed prior to any expectation that the group will be constituted.

Of course, all collectivities have at least an initial endowment of resources that predates their existence and could be responsible for their relative success. For example, an observed association between an organization's network structure and its subsequent success could reflect the fact that the organization has employees who are particularly skilled, and such skills facilitate the formation of the observed networks. Furthermore, expectations that certain employees, who may have more effective preexisting networks, will be more successful could lead to their inclusion in the group, thereby generating a spurious association between the members' networks and its performance. In sum, unobserved heterogeneity remains an issue even if analysis of collectivities helps resolve the problem of reverse causality.

Yet this brings us to a second distinguishing feature of certain collectivities. In various contexts, substantial overlap in human-resource elements may be found in numerous collectivities. Examples include academic collaborations, short-term project organizations such as films (Soda, Usai, and Zaheer 2004) or conventions, professional service firms (for example, consulting, legal, accounting) and even organizations themselves, when viewed over a longer period of time. Imagine an organization where each individual is a member of a unique set of teams and whose memberships partially overlap with many other individuals. Such a population aids in the identification of person-level and even higher-order (dyadic, triadic) effects that are distinct from those at the level of the collectivity.

Hedonic models in econometrics (for example Griliches 1961; Rosen 1974), which specify a product's quality as a weighted average of the product's underlying attributes, provide a useful analogy for such identification. Since the same attributes are observed in different combinations across multiple products, it is possible to recover baseline effects for each characteristic and specify the extent to which outcomes for the products exceed or fall short of a level that is expected, given the characteristics included in the product. Although we do not know of a precedent for applying this logic to human collectivities, such an extension seems compelling. If individuals in a population (for example, an organization) are each members of multiple collectivities (such as work groups), it is possible to produce an expected level of performance on the basis of such human-capital endowments and then to observe deviations from such a level. In particular, such a strategy allows one to make good on the conceptual distinction between individual and position that is basic to structural sociology (Gould 2002; Sørensen 1977; Podolny 1993). Analytically separating associations with individual attributes from positional effects is notoriously difficult at the individual level (see Zuckerman et al. 2003). Yet assuming that the social-capital hypothesis applies at the collective level, it affords such a separation at the collective level—and thereby helps address the problem of unobserved heterogeneity for analyses of such collectivities.

We illustrate this approach with the hypothetical population of teams presented in tables 6.1 to 6.3. In table 6.1, we present ten five-person teams and their performance on tasks of equal difficulty. In table 6.2 we present the mean performance score for a given actor, taken over the teams in which she participates. To what extent can the differences in team performance be explained by differences in the skills that their members bring to the table? This can be estimated by trying to compute estimated team performance from the individual-level means. In this case, the correlation between ex-

Table 6.1   Hypothetical Projects: Membership and Performance

	A	B	C	D	E	F	G	H	I	J
Members	Abe	Abe	Bea	Chris	Chris	Fred	Abe	Bea	Chris	Don
	Chris	Bea	Don	Don	Eve	Greg	Bea	Chris	Don	Eve
	Eve	Chris	Fred	Eve	Greg	Helen	Don	Eve	Fred	Greg
	Greg	Don	Helen	Fred	Helen	Ike	Eve	Fred	Greg	Helen
	Ike	Eve	Joe	Greg	Ike	Joe	Greg	Helen	Ike	Joe
Observed Performance	1	4	2	3	5	5	2	3	4	1

Source: Authors' compilation.

pected and actual performance is considerable, though there is much variance that remains to be explained. And this residual performance could be due to the way that the social-capital available to each individual team member aggregates to become a team-level characteristic that is greater or less than the sum of its parts. That is, if we find that team social capital (measured according to our hypothesis) explains performance beyond the person-level fixed effects, this would imply strong, if not conclusive, validation of the social-capital hypothesis. In the language of the counterfactual model of causality (see, for example, Winship and Morgan 1999; Stuart,

Table 6.2   Hedonic Scores for each Actor

Actor	Number of Projects	Mean Performance
Abe	3	2.33
Bea	4	2.75
Chris	6	3.33
Don	6	2.67
Eve	6	3.00
Fred	5	3.40
Greg	7	3.00
Helen	5	3.20
Ike	4	3.75
Joe	3	2.67

Source: Authors' compilation.

Table 6.3   Hedonic Prediction for Teams

	A	B	C	D	E	F	G	H	I	J
Hedonic prediction[a]	3.08	2.82	2.94	3.08	3.06	3.20	2.75	3.14	3.23	2.91
Actual minus prediction	−2.08	1.18	−0.94	−0.08	1.94	1.80	−0.75	−0.14	0.77	−1.91

Source: Authors' compilation.
[a] Correlation between predicted and actual = 0.42.

chapter 4, this volume), our strategy identifies sets of teams that are observationally equivalent in the sense of having the same hedonic prediction—for example, teams A and D—but display different outcomes, which are potentially explicable by reference to supra-individual differences—that is, the social-capital variables.

Note that, assuming sufficient degrees of freedom are available (owing to the size and number of teams), our strategy can easily be extended to include dyadic and other higher-order fixed effects to serve as baselines. That is, let us imagine that Abe and Bea have skills that are compatible or complementary such that each is more productive when working with the other. This would not be fully reflected in the hedonic predictions in table 6.3. Thus, these predictions could be augmented by computing hedonic scores for each dyad and incorporating them into the hedonic predictions. A downside of this extension of the strategy that is especially worrisome as one includes ever higher-order effects is that it likely means that we will assign network effects to the hedonic baselines. Indeed, the reason that Abe and Bea are so productive together may be precisely because their network positions are compatible.

In sum, we propose a general-purpose research strategy for testing social-capital hypotheses. The cornerstone of the strategy is the unit of analysis: temporary collectivities composed of individuals who participate in partially overlapping sets of such collectivities. Since there is no prior performance for these types of collectivities and the network data are collected well prior to the formation of the team, observed associations between the team's network position and performance are relatively uncontaminated by reverse causality. In addition, since each collectivity is composed of a unique set of individuals, individual-level effects can be distinguished from collectivity-level effects, thereby helping to address the concern of unobserved heterogeneity.

Team Social Capital: Internal Density and External Range

Our hedonic approach promises to test whether team social capital is causally responsible for performance; this raises the question of the specific mechanisms by which a team's social network affects its performance. Following our earlier work (Reagans and Zuckerman 2001; Reagans, Zuckerman, and McEvily 2004), we focus on two key variables: the extent to which the team has a high degree of internal network density, and the extent to which the team has a high degree of external network range.

The first of these variables is often cited in the social-capital literature as well as in research on organizational work teams. In this work, density is often measured in terms of the demographic homogeneity of a team owing to the common assumption that homophily (or the tendency of people with similar attributes to form ties more easily than those who are dissimilar) operates. A common metaphor in both literatures is the mutual support and coordination often found in cohesive ethnic communities (for example, Aldrich and Zimmer 1986; Portes and Sensenbrenner 1993). Network density, or "closure," in such communities is thought to facilitate mutual identification among members of a collectivity (for example, Portes and Sensenbrenner 1993) and to promote a degree of trust sufficient to support social exchange and collective action (Coleman 1988). To the extent that closure promotes the development and enforcement of norms and insofar as these norms emphasize high performance, increasing network closure can be expected to have a positive effect on performance (Homans 1950).

The absence of network closure—or the presence of "structural holes" (Cross and Cummings 2004; Oh, Chung, and Labianca 2004)—is problematic within a team. Meanwhile, a second strand of the social-capital literature focuses on the advantages of structural holes between external contacts or external range. Cohesion and range are thought by many scholars to be in tension (for example,

Figure 6.1   Local Versus Global Structural Holes

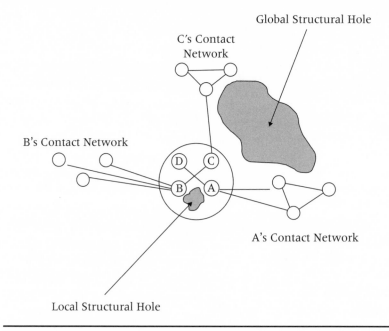

Source: Reagans, Zuckerman, and McEvily (2004).

Podolny and Baron 1997, pp. 674; Adler and Kwon 2000; Ahuja 2000; Bae and Gargulio 2003). Yet Ray Reagans and Ezra W. Zuckerman (2001) clarify that each applies at different locations in the social network (see also Burt 2001; Gabbay and Zuckerman 1998, 195–96; Ingram and Roberts 2000, 395–96; Reagans and McEvily 2003, 263; see also Burt 1980; Burt 1982, chapter 7; Burt 1992, chapter 3). Figure 6.1 reproduces these researchers' distinction between internal (or local) and external (or global) structural holes. Although local structural holes may hinder internal coordination and the team's capacity for collective action, ties that bridge holes outside the team generate "information benefits" because they represent points of contact into different network clusters, each of which tends to represent a relatively nonredundant concentration of information and resources (Burt 1992, 13–16). Therefore, the most productive teams are characterized by both high internal density and high external range.

Two notes are in order here. First, Rauch and Watson's chapter in this volume could be interpreted as assuming that a team that is high on internal density must necessarily be low on structural holes. In particular, if all founders of an entrepreneurial venture originate from the same organization, they can be expected to have preexisting relationships that facilitate coordination but to lack wide-reaching links to the environment that are crucial for securing resources and information. This tension can be reconciled when we recognize that the internal density hypothesis focuses on direct relationships between team members. Insofar as the members of a team have such direct relationships, they should be able to coordinate more easily. The problem arises when the team members also have high overlap in their indirect relationships—with people who are not on the team. Insofar as such overlap is significant, the team members will be limited in the resources and information they can access. However, it is possible for an organization's founders to have good working relationships from their past experiences together but not to overlap greatly in their indirect relationships (perhaps because each worked in a different function or region of their parent organization).

Second, there is a subtle difference between the internal-density hypothesis and the external-range hypothesis as they relate to our strategy for testing social-capital hypotheses. In particular, while the external range hypothesis can be and has been applied to both individual and collective units of analysis, the internal-density hypothesis only applies to collective units. Thus, for the latter hypothesis the value of our approach lies in exploiting certain aspects of team organization (short lives, and overlap in membership across teams) to identify when internal density allows a team to achieve a level of performance beyond what they would achieve if the members had no prior relationships. And for the former hypothesis, the value of our approach lies in identifying a strategic research site for testing the hypothesis because it is difficult to test in other contexts (as reviewed earlier).

"Proof of Concept": The Social Capital of Project Teams at Malibu Research

We now turn to an empirical application that illustrates the approach we have developed. The empirical context provides us with a good opportunity to examine how much of a team's performance can be traced to unobserved individual differences and how much to the team's social capital. That is, the context provides us with a unique opportunity to apply the hedonic approach that we propose and therefore to examine the network exogeneity assumption.

Research Context

We present a concise summary of the data and analytic approach here and refer the reader to our prior work (Reagans, Zuckerman, and McEvily 2004; see Reagans and McEvily 2003) for more details. Briefly, the firm we call Malibu Research is a midwestern contract research and development firm that specializes in material sciences and undertakes projects for two types of clients: its parent organization and outside firms in its local market. Projects fall into six categories, for six basic types of services provided by Malibu: "scientific analyses" such as analyzing material properties or assessing product reliability; conceptualization, or analyzing the potential and feasibility for new product ideas; product and material development, which involves either developing a new product or assisting the client in developing a new product more efficiently; "process development," whereby Malibu helps the client to improve its process designs and flows; "manufacturing," which involves either performing material compounding for the client or assisting the client in manufacturing in-house or with a third firm; and "cost and quality initiatives," which includes an array of services whereby Malibu assists clients in improving the cost or quality of a product subsequent to its initial launch.

Data collection followed the procedures described for dealing with reverse causality and unobserved heterogeneity. First, since the projects are short-lived and network data were collected before the commencement of the projects whose performance we model, the challenge of reverse causality is minimized. In particular, surveys were completed in the summer of 2001 by 104 out of the 113 Malibu employees who had worked on project teams during a one-year period subsequent to the survey.[5] We then obtained detailed data on the several hundred projects that were initiated by the firm in the year subsequent to our survey. Thus, although the networks of team members may change once the team is constructed, and such networks may be shaped by the team's level of success in reaching its goal, the network structures we observe cannot be subject to such endogeneity because these networks antedate the team's formation. Insofar as a team's position in such networks affects its performance, this would imply a path-dependent process of network formation such that a team's network may be treated, at least in part, as exogenous.

The second key aspect of this data set is that, just as with the hypothetical teams in table 6.1, each individual participated in a unique set of projects but with significant overlap with others. As a result, we can apply the hedonic approach described earlier, whereby we calculate baseline expectations for a team's performance on the basis of the composition of the team, and then examine the extent to which the team's social capital explains residual differences in team performance. In particular, our baseline model expects a significant amount of variation in team performance to be explained by dummy variables, or "fixed effects," for each of the individuals (who worked on at least two projects) who make up the team.

Data and Methods

In the analysis that follows, our performance metric is project duration (see Hansen 1999). There are of course many ways of measuring team performance and it would be ideal to model multiple such measures. Yet project duration, which is the only metric available, is widely regarded at Malibu as a reliable indicator of team performance (see Reagans, Zuckerman, and McEvily 2004, 33–35). Indeed, although Malibu bills clients on a cost-plus basis and thus could be said to benefit from longer projects, the reputational costs from project delays loom large. As one of our main Malibu informants explained, "If you overstay your welcome, there's a perception that you don't deliver. Everybody wants it done yesterday. Deliver quickly and they will always invite you back." Thus, we model the amount of time until a project's completion starting with the day it was initiated as a function of network variables and a variety of control variables, including individual fixed effects and labor input.

As detailed by Reagans, Zuckerman, and McEvily (2004; see also Reagans and McEvily 2003), social network data were collected using a combination of sociometric and egocentric techniques (Wasserman and Faust 1994, 45–50). Each respondent was first presented with a roster composed of a random sample of fifteen potential contacts from among the set of coworkers who had billed hours to the same projects as the respondent in the prior year. Respondents were asked to eliminate the names of individuals with whom he or she did not "share knowledge" during that year and copy up to ten of the remaining names onto a contact list. Respondents copied a mean of nine names onto this list. Next, each respondent was asked two free-recall questions. The respondent was first asked to list the names of colleagues who had been a significant source of knowledge during the previous year and then was asked to list the names of colleagues for whom he or she had been a significant source of knowledge. A respondent could list up to five colleagues in response to each name-generator question, for a total of ten additional contacts. Respondents provided a mean of six additional names, with three unique names for each free-recall question. Reagans, Zuckerman, and McEvily (2004, 24–33) discuss the advantages and disadvantages of this network survey methodology. They show that the data do not appear to suffer from appreciable bias in relation to data collected from a purely sociometric instrument.

Internal Density and External Range

We measure internal density as the mean strength of ties between project members:

$$ND_k = \sum_{i=1}^{Nk} \sum_{j=1}^{Nk} \frac{z_{ij}}{\max(z_{iq})} \bigg/ N_k(N_k - 1),$$

where z_{iq} is the strength of the tie from team member i to member j, $\max(z_{iq})$ is the strongest of i's reported ties to anyone in the firm, N_k is the number of members in team k, and $N_k(N_k - 1)$ is the maximum number of ties among members of team k. Scaling by $\max(z_{iq})$ removes individual differences in the tendency to report high tie strength to others. Network density varies from zero (no relations between team members) to 1 (maximum-strength relations between all team members).

Our measure of external range is the reverse of network constraint:

$$ER_k = 1 - C_k,$$

where constraint is measured as in Burt (1992, chapter 2) and averaged over all team members:

$$C_k = \sum_{i=1}^{N_k} \sum_{j=1}^{N_e} \left(p_{ij} + \sum_{q=1}^{N} p_{iq} p_{qj} \right)^2 \Big/ N_k,$$

where N_e is the number of contacts external to the team. Constraint has two components. The first is the proportion of total tie strength that person i allocates to contact j directly:

$$p_{ij} = (z_{ij} + z_{ji}) \Big/ \sum_{q=1}^{N} (z_{iq} + z_{qi}).$$

The second component is the proportion of total tie strength i spends with contact j indirectly through mutual contacts q, where p_{iq} is the proportion of network time that person i allocates to contact q and p_{qj} is the proportion of network time that contact j allocates to contact q,

$$\sum_{q=1}^{N} p_{iq} p_{qj}.$$

In essence, the constraint measure is a concentration score akin to the familiar Herfindahl index. If none of i's contacts are connected with each other then the measure reduces to the square of the sum of the proportions of tie strength devoted to each contact j. Thus, constraint is decreasing as i spreads his tie strength among more contacts. The second component captures the possibility that some of these contacts may have strong ties with each other and thus make i's network more concentrated than is implied solely by inspecting her direct ties.[6] And the lower the mean constraint of a team, the higher is its external range.[7]

Control Variables

In addition to the social-capital variables, the models to be presented include seven control variables included in the prior analysis. Three such variables concern the allocation of labor hours by team members to current and past projects. First, although our analysis focuses on projects that were initiated after the administration of the network survey, projects prior to the network survey were used to define the sampling frame for formal contacts. Thus, it is important to identify the aspect of network structure that is due solely to the construction of the survey and the aspect that reflects "true" network patterns. To that end, we use data on the number of hours each person allocated to projects in the prior year to calculate the tendency for each pair of team members in the current year to have worked together in the prior year, which is the team members' shared prior-year experience:

$$PYE_k = \sum_{i=1}^{N_k} \sum_{j=1}^{N_k} (s_i + s_j) \, / \, (total_i + total_j) \Big/ N_k(N_k - 1),$$

where s_i is the number of hours that person i allocated to projects that included j, s_j is the number of hours that person j bills to the same projects, and $total_i$ and $total_j$ are total hours they each billed in the previous year. Using the same billing data, we calculate the tendency for project members to overlap in their billable hours on other, concurrent projects. The equation for team members' shared concurrent experience is identical to the equation for shared prior-year experience, except we consider only projects that are ongoing as of day d rather than those from the final year. Finally, we include the cumulative labor hours devoted to the project, which reflects the total resources dedicated to the project to date. This variable is logged to adjust for skewedness.

The remaining control variables measure aspects of the team's size and composition. Team size is simply the number of people on the team. We log this variable to adjust for skewedness. We also include two indicators of demographic diversity, function-based and tenure-based diversity. Function-based diversity is defined as

$$DV_k = 1 - \sum\nolimits_{c=1}^{C} P_c^2 ,$$

where C is the number of functional areas (six) and P_c is the proportion of team members from area c. Tenure-based diversity is measured as the average difference in tenure between project members,

$$CMD_k = \frac{1}{N_k(N_k - 1)} \sum_{i=1}^{N_k} \sum_{j=1}^{N_k} |t_i - t_j|, j \neq i,$$

where t_i and t_j are the tenure of person i and person j, respectively (Kendall and Stuart 1977, 48). We also include a measure of mean tenure, which is the average organizational tenure of project members. And as discussed above, we control for unobserved differences between teams stemming from their composition by including individual fixed effects.[8]

Results

In table 6.4, we present descriptive statistics and a correlation matrix for the variables used in the models in table 6.5. As in Reagans, Zuckerman, and McEvily (2004), we model the failure time (or time to completion) for the 1,518 projects initiated in the year subsequent to the administration of our survey, 785 of which were completed by the close of our observation window. The models are continuous-time models estimated using the streg procedure with the Stata statistical package. The error terms in the models are assumed to have a log-logistic distribution, though results are not sensitive to this assumption. For example, we get the same pattern of results if we assume a Weibull or lognormal distribution. Our models also include robust standard errors to account for clustering of the errors among the multiple observations for the same project.

To illustrate how much the different predictors contribute to team

Table 6.4 Descriptive Statistics and Correlation Matrix

Variable	Mean	Standard Deviation	1	2	3	4	5	6	7	8	9
1. Number of previous completions	.731	1.349									
2. Cumulative labor hours devoted to project[a]	3.744	1.872	.630								
3. Members' shared prior-year experience	.514	.080	.017	.036							
4. Members' shared concurrent experience	.032	.056	.376	.505	.213						
5. Team size[a]	1.557	.762	.535	.803	-.069	.282					
6. Function-based diversity	.493	.178	.295	.300	-.267	-.048	.293				
7. Tenure-based diversity	4.981	2.265	-.058	-.133	-.026	-.069	-.274	.159			
8. Mean tenure	5.941	3.295	-.181	-.272	-.045	-.209	-.115	-.097	-.377		
9. Internal density[a]	.186	.134	-.171	-.200	.380	-.050	-.126	-.392	-.164	.150	
10. External range[a]	.272	.030	.215	.313	.216	.148	.361	.034	-.151	.007	.383

Source: Reagans, Zuckerman, and McEvily 2004.
[a] Logged values.

Table 6.5   Log-Logistic Continuous Failure-Time Models of Project Duration with Robust Standard Errors[a]

Predictor	I Individual Dummies	II Controls	III Internal Density	IV External Range	V Network Structure
Constant	2.953* (.091)	1.938* (.341)	1.753* (.346)	2.934* (.400)	2.574* (.417)
Number of previous completions		.103* (.029)	.102* (.028)	.103* (.028)	.102* (.027)
Cumulative labor hours devoted to project		.010 (.039)	.012 (.039)	.021 (.039)	.020 (.039)
Team members' shared prior-year experience		.928* (.407)	1.847* (.528)	1.264* (.425)	1.978* (.529)
Team members' shared concurrent experience		.429 (.710)	.394 (.695)	.388 (.694)	.362 (.684)
Logged team size		.450* (.170)	.477* (.170)	.444* (.168)	.467* (.168)
Diversity					
Function based		.327 (.261)	.117 (.265)	.258 (.261)	.090 (.265)
Tenure based		.014 (.018)	.010 (.018)	.017 (.018)	.013 (.018)
Mean tenure		.006 (.009)	.004 (.009)	.007 (.009)	.005 (.009)
Network structure					
Logged internal density			−1.052* (.347)		−.889* (.348)
Logged external range				−4.572* (1.285)	−3.625* (1.255)
Model fit					
N of projects	1,518	1,518	1,518	1,518	1,518
N of completions	785	785	785	785	785
N of project days	10,554	10,554	10,554	10,554	10,554
Log likelihood	−980.32	−957.98	−951.62	−953.34	−948.85
pseudo R-square	.187	.206	.211	.209	.213

Source: Reagans, Zuckerman, and McEvily 2004.

[a] Robust standard errors are in parentheses.

* $p < .05$

performance, variables of interest are entered sequentially across table 6.5. Model 1 contains the individual fixed effects. Model 2 contains the control variables. The social-capital variables are entered individually in models 3 and 4. All of the variables are entered in model 5. As with the hypothetical teams in table 6.3, a large part of the reason that some teams outperform others is that the faster teams have members who typically finish faster (and thus have lower mean duration, which is captured in the fixed effect) than others. Note that the unobserved heterogeneity captured here is not due only to differences in the average skill levels of the teams. Another likely reason is that different types of projects (which vary in their typical duration) require different personnel. Thus, the fixed effects capture unobserved differences between teams due both to any advantage in human capital that one may have over another and to differences in the tasks that different teams are asked to perform. The question then is whether differences in social capital can explain residual differences in team performance beyond the hedonic baselines.[9]

The social-capital variables make significant contributions beyond the hedonic baselines. In model 5 we see that the coefficient for internal density is negative and significant. This reflects the idea that structural holes that are internal to a group or collectivity hinder effective collaboration. Also in model 5, we see that the coefficient for external range is negative and significant as well. Where internal holes are detrimental to performance, holes in the external network are beneficial. The results, therefore, provide support for the social-capital hypotheses. Moreover, by controlling for unobserved individual differences, we can conclude that the effects of the network variables are exogenous, which provides support for the premise of network exogeneity. At the same time, although social capital matters, it would be incorrect to say that team social capital is the factor that matters the most. The bottom row in table 6.5 contains a pseudo R-square and provides a sense for the "variance explained" by each kind of factor. The jump in variance explained occurs after the fixed effects are introduced. The scale, demographic, and social-capital variables contribute to the variance explained, but the vast majority of the variance explained is accounted for by the individual fixed effects. This is not surprising. There are a large number of fixed effects in the model, so the individual fixed effects should explain more variance. The social-capital effects indicate that our teams are clearly more than the sum of their individual parts, but the amount of variance explained by the individual fixed effects reminds us not to forget the human capital contributed by individual team members.

We have also conducted two sets of additional analyses to check the robustness of these results. First, we tested the possibility that unobserved individual differences are better captured by the amount that individuals contribute to a team. That is, instead of simply including the individual fixed effects and the total number of labor hours contributed to the project, it seems appropriate to control for the number of labor hours contributed by each individual team member. Indeed, hours contributed by more able or skilled individuals could have more of an effect on the likelihood that the project will be completed. There is no guarantee, however, that hours contributed by more able or knowledgeable individuals will have a positive effect on completion times. More able individuals could be assigned to more complex and difficult projects. When we replace the individual fixed effects and the total number of labor hours contributed to the project with the individual labor hour variables, the coefficient for internal density is $-.88$ ($p < .001$) and the coefficient for external range is -2.33 ($p < .05$).

A related issue concerns the possibility that team performance is driven by the presence of particular combinations of actors on a team. That is, as previously discussed, certain dyads may have complementary skills such that they make their teams more productive, quite apart from the social capital they bring to the team. This issue is particularly salient because, although we have assumed that pairs of individuals are randomly assigned to projects (and our Malibu informant assures us that teams are staffed solely on the basis of availability), it is possible that particular sets of people end up on the same teams because they are particularly productive when they work together (and are recognized as such by those with influence over team staffing). As discussed above, resolving this issue requires the inclusion of dyadic (or even higher order) fixed effects in our models.

Across the 785 projects, there are 2,877 distinct pairs of individuals. The vast majority of people work with each other on a small number of projects. On average, members of each pair worked with each other on approximately five projects and more than 90 percent of the individuals worked with each other on less than ten projects. There is, however, a small subset of individuals who did work with each other on a large number of projects. Models will not converge if we include all of the dyadic fixed effects in the duration equation and we are concerned with particular pairs of individuals who appear to be interdependent. Pairs of individuals who worked on twenty-three or more projects during the observation year are one standard deviation above the mean, so it seems unlikely that these two individuals are randomly assigned to those projects. When we replace the individual fixed effects with the dyadic fixed effects for team members who worked on twenty-three or more projects, the coefficient for internal density is $-.63$ ($p < .05$) and the coefficient for external range is -4.50 ($p < .001$). In other words, the coefficient for internal density is weaker but is still significant.

Summary and Discussion

To recap, we have introduced and validated a general-purpose research strategy for validating network exogeneity in naturally occurring human collectivities. Results from our study of Malibu Research project teams suggest that the hedonic approach should increase our confidence that observed network effects are truly causal. That is, we have seen evidence for substantial effects of a team's position in the organizational social network above and beyond a baseline hedonic expectation that is caused by variation in human-capital endowments.

This conclusion relates to the other contributions in this volume and the larger theme of network formation and decay on two interlocking levels. First, a concern with network dynamics puts a spotlight on the premise of network exogeneity. As network analysis has matured and as economists (and natural scientists) have joined sociologists and anthropologists in the study of networks, sensitivity has grown to issues of endogeneity. The working assumption that long guided network analysis, whereby the network is treated as a given and the observed associations with outcomes of interest as causal, cannot be taken on faith. Indeed, although there are certainly cases where networks are exogenously given (for example, Munshi 2001) and social experiments sometimes occur whereby networks are randomly assigned (for example, Karlan 2004; Rubineau 2007; Sacerdote 2001), these cases are rare. Moreover, most of the interesting network-based theories apply precisely to situations where the networks are at least partially endogenous. For instance, the network-based theories in economic sociology reviewed above apply almost exclusively to such classes of network structures. In many cases, the premise of network exogeneity can be defended in these cases with some mix of the two rationales presented above—that the observed networks are by-products of networks constructed in other arenas and thus are only partially endogenous to the arena under analysis; and that path-dependent processes render networks at least somewhat exogenous for processes within a restricted temporal time frame. The premise of network exogeneity can be defended in the abstract, but it is quite another matter to defend it in a given analysis. The hedonic approach developed in this chapter helps in this regard, by providing a tool for setting up a baseline expectation above which we may have greater confidence that the observed association between network position and performance reflects a causal relationship.

At the same time, it is worth reflecting on the limitations of this approach. The most obvious is that it applies only to cases of short-lived collectivities with unique but highly overlapping membership. We think that there are many instances of such collectivities—for example, academic collaborations, short-term project organizations such as films (Soda, Usai, and Zaheer 2004) and events such as conventions, professional service firms (for example, consulting, legal, accounting) and even organizations themselves, when viewed over a longer period of time. At the same time, this approach clearly cannot be applied to individuals. Thus, additional approaches are needed to help validate network exogeneity.

Another limitation relates to the thematic issue of this volume, whose theme is the formation and decay of economic networks.

Because we anticipate that networks change as a result of past and expected performance, our hedonic approach focuses on short-lived collectivities for which one may collect social-network data from a period that predates the existence of the collectivities. And insofar as we observe effects of network variables applied to the teams that eventually form, this reflects the importance of path-dependence in network formation. But note that although our results suggest the importance of such path dependence, we have had to "black-box" the nature and extent of path dependence and, more generally, the social networks that are formed subsequent to the formation of the team. The ideal data set would include social network data both from the period before the formation of the teams and throughout the teams' life spans. Such data would allow the analyst to answer key questions on network formation and decay. For instance, what is the degree of path dependence in the network? That is, to what extent are the networks that are enacted and used by team members in the course of a project shaped by prior networks or constructed in the course of the team's work? And, is team performance determined more by the preexisting exogenous networks or the networks that emerge endogenously? In particular, do teams pool the networks of different members, which would work to dampen path dependence by building new connections between people who were not previously tied, and do such new ties endure to become part of the individuals' networks? As sensitivity grows to issues of network formation and decay, and as our capacity to collect temporal network data grows, we hope and expect that significant progress will be made on these questions.

Notes

1.   There is already a substantial literature on the challenges of verifying a second type of hypothesis—that which expects social or spatial autocorrelation in the attitude or behavior of linked actors (see, for example, Frank and Fahrbach 1999; Leenders 1995; Mouw 2003; see also Manski 1993).

2.   The term "social capital" is notorious for being imprecise even while (or perhaps because) it has become very popular throughout the social sciences and popular discourse more generally. In this chapter we use

"social capital" as an umbrella term to cover a family of social network–based processes that have been hypothesized (primarily by sociologists) to explain differential success or performance.

3. This is a weaker criterion than that suggested by James A. Davis (1985), whose rule of thumb is that, "when estimating a direct effect of x_i on x_j, [one should] control all prior and intervening variables" (68). In this discussion we ignore variables that intervene between network position and performance because it is uncontroversial that social-network effects must operate through processes that are more proximate to performance. For example, structural autonomy is thought to raise the likelihood of success because such structural positions increase the information available to an actor and the control that she may exert over others (Burt 1992; but see Reagans and Zuckerman 2006). Similarly, status increases a firm's profitability because it reduces the costs of placing securities (Podolny 1993). Such hypotheses may be challenged not on the basis of assuming direct effects when the impact is in fact indirect, but in providing insufficient evidence for the posited intervening causal pathways. See Christopher Winship and David J. Harding (2005) for related discussion concerning the identification of age, period, and cohort effects through intervening mechanisms.

4. A study that attempts directly to control for an indicator of both past performance and expectations of future performance is Zuckerman's (1999) analysis of the impact of coverage mismatch on a firm's stock price.

5. This response rate of 92 percent compares extremely well with past research in this vein (for example, Burt 1992; Podolny and Baron 1997). See Reagans, Zuckerman, and McEvily (2004, 19) for more detail on the handling of missing data as well as how attrition and the arrival of new employees were handled in the analysis.

6. Our measure of external range is based on the tendency for contacts outside the team to be disconnected because such alters are more likely to provide access to nonredundant information (Burt 1992). Even if two contacts are disconnected, however, they may have very similar sets of ties to third parties—that is, they may be structurally equivalent—and therefore provide highly redundant information. Accordingly, we have reanalyzed the results presented here with an alternative measure of external range that considers the extent to which external contacts are both disconnected and structurally nonequivalent. This variable has an even more powerful effect on team performance than the conventional measure of range. We have chosen to present results based on direct ties because this measurement strategy is closest to past practice and a full discussion of the issue exceeds the scope of this chapter.

7. Taking the (inverse of the) mean constraint reflects a model whereby a team that is composed of members who each have ties to nonredundant actors beyond the team provide a wide array of information and resources to complement that accessed teammates. It is also interesting to consider an alternative model of aggregation, whereby the team pools the members' networks rather than pooling the information and resources. According to the latter model, a team that is composed of a set of individuals who each have low external range but who have ties to different people off the team could be considered to have high external range. Analysis using such an alternative measure generated weaker results than those presented below.

8. As discussed by Reagans, Zuckerman, and McEvily (2004), functional heterogeneity is also a useful control in this regard because it should reflect the complexity of the project. Reagans, Zuckerman, and McEvily (2004, 38) discuss additional models designed to address the issue of unobserved heterogeneity.

9. From the other control variables, we see that project scale seems important as well. Larger projects take longer to complete. It is not clear whether projects in trouble attract more labor input or whether larger teams find it more difficult to coordinate their behavior. We also see that demographic diversity (in terms of functional area and tenure) does not seem to have much of an effect on project performance. Reagans, Zuckerman, and McEvily (2004) describe how the effect for demographic diversity is mediated by the network variables.

References

Adler, Paul S., and Seok-Woo Kwon. 2000. "Social Capital: The Good, the Bad, and the Ugly." In *Knowledge and Social Capital: Foundations and Applications*, edited by E. Lesser. Boston, Mass.: Butterworth-Heineman.

Ahuja, Gautam. 2000. "Collaboration Networks, Structural Holes, and Innovation: A Longitudinal Study." *Administrative Science Quarterly* 45(3): 425–55.

Aldrich, Howard E., and Catherine Zimmer. 1986. "Entrepreneurship Through Social Networks." In *The Art and Science of Entrepreneurship*, edited by Donald L. Sexton and Raymond W. Smilor. Cambridge, Mass.: Ballinger.

Bae, Jonghoon, and Martin Gargiulo. 2003. "Local Action, Network Evolution, and Effective Alliance Strategies in the Telecommunications Industry." Working paper. Fontainebleau and Singapore: INSEAD.

Baum, Joel, and Christine Oliver. 1991. "Institutional Linkages and Organizational Mortality." *Administrative Science Quarterly*, 36(2): 187–218.

———. 1992. "Institutional Embeddedness and the Dynamics of Organizational Populations. *American Sociological Review*, 57(4): 540–59.

Benjamin, Beth A. and Joel M. Podolny. 1999. "Status, Quality, and Social Order in the California Wine Industry." *Administrative Science Quarterly* 44(3): 563–89.

Burt, Ronald S. 1980. "Autonomy in a Social Topology." *American Journal of Sociology* 85(4): 892–925.

———. 1982. *Toward a Structural Theory of Action: Network Models of Social Structure, Perception and Action.* New York: Academic Press.

———. 1992. *Structural Holes: The Social Structure of Competition.* Cambridge, Mass.: Harvard University Press.

———. 1997. "The Contingent Value of Social Capital." *Administrative Science Quarterly* 42(2): 339–65.

———. 2001. "Structural Holes Versus Network Closure as Social Capital." In *Social Capital: Theory and Research*, edited by Nan Lin, Karen S. Cook, and Ronald S. Burt. New York: Aldine de Gruyter.

Coleman, James S. 1988. "Social Capital in the Creation of Human Capital." *American Journal of Sociology* 94(Supplement): S95–S120.

Cook, Karen S., Richard M. Emerson, Mary R. Gillmore, and Toshio Yamagishi. 1983. "The Distribution of Power in Exchange Networks: Theory and Experimental Results." *American Journal of Sociology* 89(2): 275–305.

Cross, Rob, and Jonathan N. Cummings. 2004. "Tie and Network Correlates of Individual Performance in Knowledge-Intensive Work." *Academy of Management Journal* 47(6): 928–38.

Davis, James A. 1985. *The Logic of Causal Order.* Beverly Hills, Calif.: Sage.

Frank, Kenneth A., and Kyle Fahrbach. 1999. "Organizational Culture as a Complex System: Balance and Information in Models of Influence and Selection." *Organization Science* 10(3): 253–77.

Gabbay, Shaul M., and Ezra W. Zuckerman. 1998. "Social Capital and Opportunity in Corporate R&D: The Contingent Effect of Contact Density on Mobility Expectations." *Social Science Research* 27(2): 189–217.

Gould, Roger V. 2002. "The Origins of Status Hierarchies: A Formal Theory and Empirical Test." *American Journal of Sociology* 107(5): 1143–78.

Granovetter, Mark. 1973. "The Strength of Weak Ties." *American Journal of Sociology* 78(6): 1360–80.

———. 1974/1995. *Getting a Job.* 2nd edition. Chicago, Ill.: University of Chicago Press.

———. 1985. "Economic Action and Social Structure: The Problem of Embeddedness." *American Journal of Sociology* 91(3): 481–510.

Greene, William H. 1997. *Econometric Analysis.* 3rd edition. Upper Saddle River, N.J.: Prentice-Hall.

Griliches, Zvi. 1961. *Hedonic Price Indexes for Automobiles: An Economic Analysis of Quality Change*. The Price Statistics of the Federal Government. New York: Columbia University Press.

Hansen, Morten T. 1999. "The Search-Transfer Problem: The Role of Weak Ties in Sharing Knowledge Across Organization Subteams." *Administrative Science Quarterly* 44(1): 82–111.

Hanushek, Eric A., and John E. Jackson. 1977. *Statistical Methods for Social Scientists*. San Diego, Calif.: Academic Press.

Homans, George C. 1950. *The Human Group*. New York: Harcourt Brace.

Ingram, Paul, and Peter Roberts. 2000. "Friendships Among Competitors in the Sydney Hotel Industry." *American Journal of Sociology*, 106(2): 387–423

Karlan, Dean S. 2004. "Social Capital and Group Banking." Working paper. Princeton, N.J.: Princeton University, Research Program in Developmental Studies.

Kendall, Maurice, and Alan Stuart. 1977. *The Advanced Theory of Statistics*. 4th edition. Volume 1. New York: Macmillan.

Lawler, Edward J. 2001. "An Affect Theory of Social Exchange." *American Journal of Sociology* 107(2): 321–52.

Leenders, Roger Th. A. J. 1995. *Structure and Influence: Statistical Models for the Dynamics of Actor Attributes, Network Structure and Their Interdependence*. Amsterdam: Tesla Thesis Publishers.

Manski, Charles F. 1993. "Identification of Endogenous Social Effects: The Reflection Problem." *Review of Economic Studies* 60(3): 531–42.

McEvily, Bill, and Akbar Zaheer. 1999. "Bridging Ties: A Source of Firm Heterogeneity in Competitive Capabilities." *Strategic Management Journal* 20(12): 1133–56.

Merton, Robert K. 1987. "Three Fragments from a Sociologist's Notebooks." *Annual Review of Sociology* 13(1): 1–28.

Mouw, Ted. 2003. "Social Capital and Finding a Job: Do Contacts Matter?" *American Sociological Review* 68(6): 868–98.

Munshi, Kaivan. 2001. "The Identification of Network Effects: Mexican Migrants in the U.S. Labor Market." Unpublished paper (mimeographed). Providence, R.I.: Brown University.

Oh, Hongseok, Myung-Ho Chung, and Giuseppe Labianca. 2004. "Group Social Capital and Group Effectiveness: The Role of Informal Socializing Ties." *Academy of Management Journal* 47(6): 860–76.

Podolny, Joel M. 1993. "A Status-Based Model of Market Competition." *American Journal of Sociology* 98(4): 829–72.

———. 2005. *Status Signals: A Sociological Study of Market Competition*. Princeton, N.J.: Princeton University Press.

Podolny, Joel M., and James N. Baron. 1997. "Resources and Relationships:

Social Networks and Mobility in the Workplace." *American Sociological Review* 62(5): 673–93.

Portes, Alejandro, and Julia Sensenbrenner. 1993. "Embeddedness and Immigration: Notes on the Social Determinants of Economic-Action." *American Journal of Sociology* 98(6): 1320–50.

Powell, Walter W., Kenneth W. Koput, and Laurel Smith-Doerr. 1996. "Interorganizational Collaboration and the Locus of Innovation: Networks of Learning in Biotechnology." *Administrative Science Quarterly* 41(1): 116–45.

Reagans, Ray, and Bill McEvily. 2003. "Network Structure and Knowledge Transfer: The Effects of Cohesion and Range." *Administrative Science Quarterly* 48(2): 240–67.

Reagans, Ray, and Ezra W. Zuckerman. 2001. "Networks, Diversity and Productivity: The Social Capital of R&D Teams." *Organization Science* 12(4): 502–18.

———. 2006. "Why Knowledge Does Not Equal Power: The Network Redundancy Trade-Off." Unpublished manuscript. Pittsburgh, Pa.: Carnegie Mellon University, Tepper School of Business.

Reagans, Ray, Ezra W. Zuckerman, and Bill McEvily. 2004. "How to Make the Team: Social Networks vs. Demography as Criteria for Designing Effective Teams." *Administrative Science Quarterly* 49(1): 101–33.

Rosen, Sherwin. 1974. "Hedonic Prices and Implicit Markets: Product Differentiation in Pure Competition." *Journal of Political Economy* 82(1): 34–55.

Rubineau, Brian. 2007. "Gendering Engineering: Professional Identity Formation and Peer Effects." Working paper. Cambridge, Mass.: MIT, Sloan School of Management.

Sacerdote, Bruce. 2001. "Peer Effects with Random Assignment: Results for Dartmouth Roommates." *Quarterly Journal of Economics* 116(2): 681–704.

Sgourev, Stoyan V., and Ezra W. Zuckerman. 2006. "Breaking Up Is Hard to Do: Irrational Overcommitment in an Industry Peer Network." Working paper. Cambridge, Mass.: MIT, Sloan School of Management.

Singh, Jitendra V., David J. Tucker, and Robert J. House. 1986. "Organizational Legitimacy and the Liability of Newness." *Administrative Science Quarterly* 31(2): 171–93.

Soda, Giuseppe, Alessandro Usai, and Akbar Zaheer. 2004. "Network Memory: The Influence of Past and Current Networks on Performance." *Academy of Management Journal* 47(6): 893–906.

Sørensen, Aage B. 1977. "The Structure of Inequality and the Process of Attainment." *American Sociological Review* 42(6): 965–78.

Stuart, Toby E., Ha Hoang, and Ralph C. Hybels. 1999. "Interorganizational

Endorsements and the Performance of Entrepreneurial Ventures." *Administrative Science Quarterly* 44(2): 315–49.

Uzzi, Brian. 1996. "The Sources and Consequences of Embeddedness for Economic Performance of Organizations." *American Sociological Review* 61(4): 674–98.

———. 1997. "Social Structure and Competition in Interfirm Networks: The Paradox of Embeddedness." *Administrative Science Quarterly* 42(1): 35–67.

Wasserman, Stanley, and Katherine Faust. 1994. *Social Network Analysis*. Cambridge: Cambridge University Press.

Willer, David. 1999. *Network Exchange Theory*. Westport, Conn.: Praeger.

Winship, Christopher, and David J. Harding. 2005. "A General Strategy for the Identification of Age, Period, Cohort Models: A Mechanism Based Approach." Unpublished manuscript. Cambridge, Mass.: Harvard University, Department of Sociology.

Winship, Christopher, and Stephen L. Morgan. 1999. "The Estimation of Causal Effects from Observational Data." *Annual Review of Sociology* 25(1): 659–706.

Zuckerman, Ezra W. 1999. "The Categorical Imperative: Securities Analysts and the Illegitimacy Discount." *American Journal of Sociology* 104(5): 1398–1438.

———. 2000. "Focusing the Corporate Product: Securities Analysts and De-Diversification." *Administrative Science Quarterly* 45(3): 591–619.

———. 2003. Review: On *Networks and Markets* by Rauch and Casella, eds. *Journal of Economic Literature* 41(2): 545–65.

Zuckerman, Ezra W., Tai-Young Kim, Kalinda Ukanwa, and James von Rittman. 2003. "Robust Identities or Non-Entities? Typecasting in the Feature Film Labor Market." *American Journal of Sociology* 108(5): 1018–75.

Chapter 7

Network Decay in Traditional Economies

Kaivan Munshi and Mark Rosenzweig

Community-based networks serve many roles in a traditional economy. In India, the setting of this study, rural caste networks have provided mutual insurance and credit to their members for centuries. More recently, these networks have been transplanted to the city, where they provide jobs to migrants drawn from the same caste.

Economists have increasingly recognized that networks, and nonmarket institutions more generally, can play an important role in facilitating economic activity when markets function imperfectly. It is commonly thought, therefore, that modernization inevitably then leads to the destruction of networks, but this is not always the case. First, economic growth can occur without altering the problematic markets in which networks play a role. The persistence of some market imperfections in developing economies thus provides one explanation for the resilience of networks. An alternative but related explanation for this resilience, which we will elaborate on, is based on the idea that communities often put restrictions on network exit in place to preserve the integrity of these institutions. Thus, an individual who chooses to exit a mutual insurance arrangement might have to deal with the loss of insurance as well as with the social sanctions that accompany defection from the network.

Despite their remarkable resilience, in some cases traditional networks break down when the environment is sufficiently altered. This occurs when the returns to participation in the economic activity for which networks are helpful are eroded. Thus it is an empirical question whether economic development leads to the decay of traditional institutions, and to predict what happens to traditional networks requires a deeper understanding of how the networks operate and why individuals do or do not exit them. In this chapter we describe the relationship between economic growth and the integrity of networks in two separate contexts: Bombay city and in rural India. In both cases we describe the traditional structure of the network, the exogenous economic change that may have threatened its viability, and the resulting change in network integrity. This description of the institutions' dynamics also allow us to identify those individuals who would have been the first to exit. In the applications that we consider it is the most able individuals or the wealthiest individuals who exit, leaving the most vulnerable individuals behind in the traditional arrangement.

— The characterization of network decay in this chapter draws on both the sociology and the economics traditions. As in the sociological literature on networks, individuals are born into or embedded in a caste network. This allows us to focus on network exit, treating entry or the initial state of the network as exogenously determined. However, following the economics literature, we treat individuals as distinct from the ties they maintain with the network. The individual's decision to maintain the ties he or she is born with depends on the returns from participation in the network versus the individual's outside options, which in turn depend on his or her characteristics and the state of the world. Network decay in our framework is thus determined by initial conditions (the sociological view), yet at the same time shaped by individual incentives (the economic view).

This melding of economics and sociology is also evident in our characterization of social sanctions and the formation of group (caste) identity as mechanisms through which exit from the caste network is constrained. Sociologists posit that networks exogenously inform and shape preferences that are themselves constituent elements of identity, blurring the lines between individuals and their ties to the network. By contrast, we view such restrictions as being endogenously determined as a self-interested group-response to the negative externality that is associated with individual exit from the network.

How do we measure exit from the network? Although the caste system may originally have formed for other reasons, networks in India today are typically organized around the subcaste, or *jati*. The fundamental marriage rule in Hindu society is that no individual can marry outside the *jati*. Marriage ties thus link all the members of the *jati*, either directly or indirectly, improving information flows and ensuring that members of the network do not renege on their obligations. An individual who has married outside the *jati* cannot be punished as effectively by the network when he reneges on his obligations and will consequently be excluded from the collective arrangement in equilibrium (see Greif 1993 for a formal characterization of this result). Out-marriage is consequently a convenient and accurate measure of network exit. The stability of caste networks up until recent times, according to this measure, is readily apparent from our data: among the older-generation parents of the young sampled respondents in our Bombay survey, only 3.7 percent were married to someone outside their *jati*; in rural areas in the 1970s the out-marriage rate among the newly married was only 4 percent.

Although community networks are often established in multiple locations, geographical proximity is another important determinant of network stability. An individual who lives and works far away from his home location in a setting in which there are few members of his or her subcaste is clearly at greater risk of reneging on his obligations. He will consequently be excluded from the collective arrangement in equilibrium, as already described; thus, the increase in the propensity of network members to migrate is the second indicator of individual exit that we consider in this analysis.[1]

The first example of network response to economic change that we consider is associated with the economic and financial liberalization of the Indian economy in the 1990s. This restructuring of the economy led to a substantial increase in relative wages in the commercial and the corporate sectors of the urban economy. The traditional caste-based networks in the city were concentrated in blue-collar jobs—in the mills and factories and on the docks. Not surprisingly, the 1990s witnessed a migration out of these jobs, and this was accompanied by exit from the networks that supported them, as evidenced by the schooling choices that parents made for their children.

Bombay is the commercial capital of India. Schooling in Bombay can be either in English or Marathi, the local language. Marathi schooling effectively channels the child into blue-collar jobs, whereas more expensive English-language schooling substantially increases the probability that the child will obtain a coveted white-collar job in the future. Kaivan Munshi and Mark Rosenzweig (2006) show that beginning in the late 1980s, the returns to being schooled in English rose substantially and that the proportion of children sent to English-language schools increased over the course of the 1990s, implying a substantial future decline in the traditional job networks.

The simple model of job networks that we lay out tells us which children might be the first to exit the traditional occupation. We assume that the wage in the networked blue-collar jobs depends on the proportion of the caste that is engaged in those jobs and is independent of the individual's ability. In contrast, white-collar wages depend on the individual's ability alone. Within any caste there consequently exists an ability threshold above which individuals choose the white-collar occupation. English schooling maps one-for-one into these occupations, implying that all individuals above the ability threshold will be schooled in English. The increase in white-collar wages in the 1990s would have been associated with an accompanying decline in the ability threshold across all *jatis*, with a corresponding increase in the proportion of children schooled in English who will ultimately exit the network.

Consistent with this discussion, we later verify that English-language schooling is indeed associated with higher ability, as measured by observable characteristics such as parental education. And consistent with the accompanying prediction that English schooling is associated with network exit, we verify that children schooled in English are more likely to marry outside their *jati* and to live and work outside their home state of Maharashtra, of which Bombay is the capital.

The second example of the relationship between network integrity and economic growth that we consider is in rural areas of India in which the Green Revolution was a principal source of economic gains. New high-yielding varieties (HYVs) of wheat and rice were introduced throughout the developing world in the 1960s. Certain areas of rural India were better suited to the early HYVs than others and so were quicker to benefit from the new technology. Although the development of new hybrid varieties over time made this superior technology available throughout the country and led to higher wages and incomes in most rural areas, Munshi and Rosenzweig (2005) present evidence that some areas got an early start and that this resulted in rising wealth inequality. *Jatis* typically span a wide area, and the uneven introduction of the new grain varieties led to increasing wealth inequality within *jatis*. We are interested in studying the effect, over time, of this increase in inequality, propelled by the advances in agricultural technology, on the integrity of traditional rural caste networks.

In a subsistence economy of the sort that was historically in place in rural India, the single most important role of the network was to assist households in maintaining their levels of consumption in the face of the adverse shocks to incomes that are the hallmark of an agricultural economy. One popular mechanism through which consumption can be made less volatile is a mutual insurance arrangement: an individual who receives a positive income shock in a given time period will transfer resources to one or more members of the network who received a negative shock in that period. Given that there is limited assurance that the recipients will reciprocate when fortunes are reversed, transfers flow in the opposite direction for some periods in the future even when all network members are experiencing good times. Such quasi-loans, originating within the *jati*, are the predominant mechanism for reducing consumption variability in our representative sample of rural Indian households—more important than pure gifts and transfers, or bank and money-lender credit.

When wealth is distributed uniformly within the *jati*, this arrangement is relatively easy to implement because loans flow with roughly equal probability in both directions between individuals. Implementation is more difficult when some individuals become wealthier than others, for example, by receiving positive shocks relatively often. These individuals end up being net lenders in the mutual insurance arrangement, and unless the compensatory transfers that flow back to them increase in magnitude they will end up subsidizing the network. We argue that thresholds on individual consumption that are important in low-income settings place natural restrictions on the compensatory transfers that can flow to the wealthy members of the network. Consequently, an exogenous increase in wealth inequality within the *jati* could threaten the integrity of the network.

When an individual is deciding whether to marry inside or outside the network, he or she will trade off the benefits of network participation with the benefits from marrying on the "open market" and matching with a partner on individual attributes such as wealth and ability. Because wealthier individuals do better on the open marriage market, an exogenous increase in wealth inequality without a corresponding increase in compensatory transfers will reinforce their natural propensity to exit the network. Consistent with this view, we find that individuals who are relatively wealthy within their *jati* are significantly more likely to marry outside. Although an increase in an individual's relative wealth within the *jati* should increase the person's propensity to migrate, an increase in absolute wealth could work in the opposite direction. We show that the latter effect dominates, and hence, evidence of network exit in the rural application will rely on the relationship between wealth and out-marriage.

These patterns of network exit in both urban and in rural India indicate that the most vulnerable individuals remain in the traditional arrangement following a period of economic change. This is not to imply that these networks will necessarily collapse; it depends on the setting. In the urban setting the service provided by the labor-market networks has grown less useful over time, with the decline in the manufacturing sector. Given the dramatic exit of individuals from traditional occupations through English-language schooling, this suggests that the urban networks may soon cease to be viable. The rural networks, in contrast, continue to serve their core function of providing mutual insurance, and despite some exit by individuals at the top of the wealth distribution we expect that these networks will remain stable in the face of economic development in the future. The Green Revolution raised crop yields and average incomes but it did not reduce the volatility of agricultural incomes and thus did not diminish the need for social arrangements that provided households with insurance against consumption shortfalls.

In this chapter we discuss first the exit from the urban caste-based networks, in response to the globalization of the Indian economy in the 1990s; then the exit from the rural caste networks associated with the Indian Green Revolution; and we conclude with a discussion of the welfare implications of these patterns of network exit.

Exit from Urban Networks

Labor-market networks organized at the level of the subcaste, or *jati*, have found jobs for their male members for over a hundred years in Bombay (even though the urban occupations most often did not correspond to the traditional caste occupations). Consequently, it is not surprising that particular castes came to occupy particular niches in the Bombay labor market.

In both developed and in developing economies, blue-collar jobs often are acquired through referrals rather than by competitive processes, perhaps because it is more difficult to assess an individual worker's ability in those jobs than in white-collar jobs (see, for example, Rees 1966 for evidence from the U.S. labor market).[2] In our sample of students in Bombay, 68 percent of the fathers engaged in working-class jobs reported that they obtained their first job by a referral from a member of the *jati*. In contrast, only 44 percent of fathers in white-collar occupations entered those occupations through a referral. *Jatis* whose members did get access to relatively stable blue-collar jobs tended to guard those jobs, passing them down from one generation to the next. As a consequence of this, historical occupation patterns organized by caste under the British persisted long after independence, in 1947. Only with the economic and financial liberalization of the 1990s have these patterns started to change.

The school system in Bombay, as elsewhere in India, allows the student to choose between instruction in English and the local language; in Bombay this is Marathi. Schooling in Marathi essentially restricts the child to a blue-collar job, whereas more expensive English schooling enhances future opportunities in the white-collar sector. Although the parents of the children schooled in the 1990s were locked into their occupations when the economic restructuring occurred, we can assess the response to the new opportunities by studying whether parents enrolled their children in English or Marathi schools.

We assume that the wage that a child will receive in a blue-collar job over his working life depends on the proportion of his *jati* that was employed in that occupation in the preceding generation. The implicit assumption here is that established workers provide job referrals (as in Munshi 2003) and that returns in the heavily networked blue-collar jobs are independent of individual ability but depend on the overall quantity of the workers in the network. In a moment we will see that an increase in quantity maps into an increase in average quality in equilibrium, providing one justification for the positive relationship between the blue-collar wage and network size that we have specified. A larger network is also better positioned to find jobs for its members in a labor market characterized by a positive level of unemployment. In contrast, we assume that returns in the alternative white-collar occupations are determined by the individual's ability, which can be observed by the hiring firm.

Now suppose that the highest-ability individual within a *jati* always chooses the white-collar occupation, and the lowest-ability individual prefers the blue-collar occupation. In this case there exists a cutoff ability level such that all individuals above the cutoff choose the white-collar occupation and all individuals below the cutoff choose the blue-collar occupation. The level of this cutoff will in general be increasing in the proportion of the *jati* that was engaged in blue-collar jobs in the preceding generation, because this determines the wage received in such jobs. By a similar reasoning, the cutoff will be decreasing in the returns to ability in the white-collar occupation.

This network-based description of the labor market provides a simple explanation for the persistence in the occupational distribution across generations that is described by Munshi and Rosenzweig (2006). Even if the ability distribution is the same across *jatis*, a *jati* that was (randomly) disproportionately represented in the blue-collar occupation historically would be associated with a higher ability cutoff and, hence, a relatively high proportion of individuals in the same occupation in subsequent generations. Munshi and Rosenzweig treat ability as a discrete variable and show that the occupational distribution could be replicated across multiple generations, under reasonable conditions, even as the returns to ability in the white-collar occupation grow. There is a cost to the network when an individual exits from the traditional occupation and so we would expect castes to have imposed explicit punishments and made attempts to develop a strong sense of community identity among their members to discourage such exit.

However, the ability cutoff will ultimately shift down as the returns to ability grow sufficiently large. And it is evident from the structure of the model that it is the relatively high-ability individuals within a *jati* who will be the first to shift out of the traditional occupation. Once such an individual has chosen English-language schooling and the white-collar occupation that follows it, he benefits little from the network. This lowers the cost to out-marriage; since high-ability individuals do relatively well on the open marriage market in any case, we expect that individuals schooled in English will be unambiguously more likely to marry outside the *jati*.

We expect that individuals schooled in Marathi should also be more likely to live and work in Maharashtra state, where Marathi is spoken. Once again there are two reinforcing effects that generate this relationship: Marathi schooling is associated with inferior English-language skills, making it less likely that the individual will find a job outside the state, and individuals schooled in Marathi lean more on the *jati* network when looking for a job in Bombay and so have more to lose by migrating.

We use marriage and migration to measure exit from the *jati* network. The individual attribute that is seen to directly determine these outcomes is the language of schooling—English versus Marathi—and not the individual's ability. The effect of individual ability on marriage and migration will depend on the historical occupational distribution within the *jati* (the level of networking), which determines the ability cutoff as described earlier, and hence the individual's decision to exit. English-language schooling in contrast is directly associated with exit from the network and so its effect on marriage and migration is not *jati*-specific.

Our empirical analysis is based on a survey, conducted in 2001 and 2002, of 4,900 households in the Maharashtrian community residing in Bombay's Dadar area. The household survey was based on a stratified random sample of students who entered first grade in twenty-eight of the twenty-nine schools in Dadar over a twenty-year period, 1982 to 2001. The parents of the randomly selected students were interviewed at their homes. Detailed information was collected on the schooling, occupation, and incomes of the parents and the grandparents of the selected students. Information on the students' and their siblings' subsequent education and labor-market outcomes and their marriage patterns (where relevant) was also collected.

Munshi and Rosenzweig (2006) show that returns to schooling in English among the parent generation in the Bombay sample rose substantially over the period 1980 to 2000 for both men and women, while returns to years of schooling remained constant. They also document that enrollment rates of children in all castes shifted significantly in the 1990s from Marathi to English-language schools. Children from a particular subcaste with more-educated parents were more likely to enroll in English-language schools, consistent with the hypothesis that the more able exit first. Moreover, girls showed a greater propensity to enroll in English-language schools over time than boys, particularly in castes heavily represented in blue-collar jobs, reflecting the fact that men, not women, tend to benefit from caste-based job networks in Bombay.

The students sampled in the survey range in age from six to twenty-five years old; most of them are too young for us to study

Table 7.1   Comparison of Siblings, by Language of Instruction (Standard Errors in Parentheses)

	Siblings' Outcomes and Characteristics	
	Marathi Schooling	English Schooling
Resides in Maharashtra	0.97	0.88*
	(0.004)	(0.02)
Married outside the jati	0.09	0.34*
	(0.01)	(0.06)
Education	11.64	13.99*
	(0.07)	(0.13)
Father's education	8.83	13.10*
	(0.07)	(0.18)
Mother's education	6.73	11.83*
	(0.09)	(0.23)
Household income	2.45	6.04*
	(0.08)	(0.50)
Number of observations	1,864	303

Source: 2001 survey of school children in Bombay.
Note: Sample restricted to siblings aged twenty to fifty and households for which incomes are available. Education is measured in years and 1995 monthly household income is measured in 1980 rupees.
* denotes rejection of the equality of means at the 5 percent level.

marriage and migration outcomes. Instead, we examine the effect of the language of instruction on these outcomes for their siblings aged twenty to fifty. There are 2,167 of them in the data set, of whom 14 percent attended English-language schools. Table 7.1 compares marriage, migration, and individual attributes for siblings educated in English and Marathi. It can be seen that a large proportion of the siblings reside in Maharashtra, but those educated in English are over 9 percent less likely to reside in the home state. The difference in the probability of out-marriage by schooling type is even more dramatic: 34 percent of the siblings schooled in English married outside the *jati*, compared with only 9 percent of those schooled in Marathi.

The differences in out-migration and out-marriage rates by medium of instruction are consistent with our view that the En-

Table 7.2   Determinants of the Choice of English Versus Marathi
Schooling Among Siblings Aged Twenty to Fifty

Dependent Variable	English Schooling	
	Jati Dummies[b]	Estimates Without Jati Fixed Effects
Age	−0.003	−0.001
	(0.001)[a]	(0.002)
Boy	0.051	0.052
	(0.014)	(0.014)
Father's education (years)	0.023	0.026
	(0.004)	(0.003)
Mother's education (years)	0.012	0.015
	(0.003)	(0.003)
1995 household income (1980 rupees)	0.005	0.009
	(0.003)	(0.004)
R-squared	0.268	0.223
Number of observations	2,231	2,231

Source: 2001 survey of school children in Bombay.
[a] Standard errors in parentheses are clustered at the level of the household.
[b] The regression includes a full set of jati dummies.

glish-schooled are more likely to exit the network. But siblings schooled in English have higher education and are endowed with greater parental schooling and household incomes. Education and income are important correlates of preschool skill or ability, so these comparisons imply that siblings schooled in English are likely to also have greater ability (as implied by the model). The higher migration and marriage rates of those who attended English-language schools may therefore merely reflect the superior backgrounds of those schooled in English. The regressions that follow will subject the comparison of means by language of instruction just described to greater scrutiny.

Table 7.2 reports regression estimates of the determinants of the choice of English versus Marathi schooling for the siblings. The regressors include the sibling's age, sex, parental schooling, and household income. The upper castes gained access to professional and administrative jobs during the colonial period, while the blue-collar jobs in the mills, the factories, and the docks were captured by particular low-caste *jatis*. Because blue-collar jobs require less schooling, low-caste parents might have invested less in their children's human capital over many generations. These historical cross-caste patterns could explain differences in schooling choices that are made in the current generation, so table 7.2, column 1, includes a full set of *jati* dummies to control for one potential aspect of individual heterogeneity.

We find that within *jatis*, older cohorts are less likely to be schooled in English, consistent with the economic changes over time described above. Men and women historically participated in distinct labor markets in Bombay, and continue to do so, which might explain the observation that boys are much more likely to be schooled in English in our sample of siblings. More years of schooling, for both fathers and mothers, significantly increases the likelihood that the child will be schooled in English. The effect of greater household income goes in the same direction, but is insignificant at the 5 percent level. In general, attributes associated with individual ability have a positive effect on English schooling, consistent with the findings for the sampled children in Munshi and Rosenzweig (2006).

Table 7.2, column 2, reports estimates without *jati* fixed effects. Munshi and Rosenzweig show that parental schooling and household income together account for most of the variation in ability across *jatis*, for the sampled children based on a different set of education outcomes. Consistent with their result, we find that the estimates in columns 1 and 2 are very similar, across all the regression coefficients.

Table 7.3 reports estimates of the effects of English schooling on migration and marriage for the siblings of the sampled children, aged twenty to fifty. Columns 1 and 2 report estimates with a specification that includes age, sex, and a full set of *jati* dummies, but no parental or household controls. Higher individual ability could be reflected in both the language of instruction and the years of schooling, and so we include the latter variable as an additional regressor to emphasize the important link between the language of instruc-

Table 7.3   The Effect of English Schooling on Residence and Marriage
(Standard Errors in Parentheses Are Clustered at the Household Level)

Dependent Variable	In-Residence	Out-Marriage[a]	In-Residence	Out-Marriage	In-Residence	Out-Marriage
	1	2	3	4	5	6
English schooling	-0.059	0.135	-0.048	0.143	-0.046	0.157
	(0.019)	(0.059)	(0.020)	(0.064)	(0.019)	(0.064)
Age	-0.005	-0.006	-0.005	-0.006	-0.005	-0.001
	(0.001)	(0.003)	(0.001)	(0.003)	(0.001)	(0.003)
Boy	0.011	0.006	0.006	0.034	0.006	0.021
	(0.008)	(0.028)	(0.008)	(0.031)	(0.008)	(0.032)
Education (in years)	-0.005	0.005	-0.004	0.001	-0.005	0.003
	(0.001)	(0.005)	(0.002)	(0.005)	(0.002)	(0.004)
Father's education (in years)	—	—	-0.0004	-0.003	-0.002	0.001
			(0.002)	(0.005)	(0.002)	(0.005)
Mother's education (in years)	—	—	0.0003	0.003	-0.001	0.005
			(0.001)	(0.004)	(0.001)	(0.004)
1995 household income (1980 rupees)	—	—	-0.005	0.007	-0.006	0.010
			(0.003)	(0.008)	(0.003)	(0.007)
Jati fixed effects	Yes	Yes	Yes	Yes	No	No
R-squared	0.069	0.086	0.079	0.108	0.070	0.075
Number of observations	2,447	766	2,167	661	2,167	661

Source: 2001 survey of school children in Bombay.

Note: In-residence is a binary variable that takes the value 1 if the sibling resides inside Maharastra, zero otherwise. Out-residence is a binary variable that takes the value 1 if the sibling resides outside Maharashtra, zero otherwise.

[a] Out-marriage is a binary variable that takes the value 1 if the sibling marries outside the jati, zero otherwise.

tion and network exit, independent of educational attainment, that is implied by the model. As expected, English schooling lowers the probability that the sibling continues to reside in Maharashtra. The point estimate indicates that an English-schooled person is 6.2 percent less likely to stay in the home state than his or her Marathi-schooled counterpart. English schooling also substantially increases the probability of marriage outside the *jati*, by 15.4 percent. An increase in years of schooling has qualitatively the same effects on these outcomes, but the effects are relatively small (the coefficient is only significant in the migration regression)—a difference in ten years of schooling would be required to equal the effect of going to an English-language school on out-migration and the effect of English schooling on out-marriage is equivalent to a difference of more than twenty years of schooling!

Columns 3 and 4 repeat this exercise, with parental schooling and household income included as additional controls. Although these variables had a strong effect on the language of instruction in table 7.2, they have an insignificant effect on migration and marriage once the language of instruction is included as a regressor. This result emphasizes one important insight from the model, which is that English-language schooling rather than individual ability directly reflects exit from the network. In contrast with the weak effects that we obtain for the parental controls and household income, the coefficient on English schooling continues to be significant at the 5 percent level and is very similar to what is observed in columns 1 and 2.

Finally, columns 5 and 6 include all the regressors from the previous specification but drop the *jati* dummies. We saw earlier that the additional controls had no role to play once the language of schooling was included as a regressor. Because the *jati* dummies are only included as additional controls (for heterogeneity across castes), we expect that their exclusion should have no effect on the estimated coefficients in the marriage and migration regressions either. The coefficients on parental education and household income remain insignificant in columns 5 and 6, while the English schooling coefficient is similar to the estimates obtained in columns 1 to 4, as expected.

Exit from Rural Networks

A mutual insurance arrangement is perhaps the simplest mechanism that can be employed to smooth consumption in traditional economies. In rural India, networks organized at the level of the *jati* have smoothed consumption for centuries. To better understand this arrangement, consider a setup with two individuals and two payoffs: high (H) and low (L). Assume that the individuals are equally wealthy, in the sense that they are equally likely to receive the high payoff. Assume also that the payoffs they receive in any period are independent. With a perfect insurance arrangement, the risk-averse individuals will receive $(H + L)/2$ in any period in which their payoffs differ.

When individuals cannot have any assurance that individuals will reciprocate (no commitment), as analyzed by Stephen Coate and Martin Ravallion (1993), the incentive to deviate from the mutual insurance arrangement is greatest when the individual receives the H payoff in a given period and his partner receives L. Assuming that both individuals will no longer receive any aid once either deviates, the individual with the high payoff will weigh the current gain from deviation $(H - L)/2$ against the future loss in insurance. Social sanctions help deter such deviations, but it will often be the case that only partial insurance will be sustainable.

The partial insurance arrangement without commitment essentially describes a series of reciprocal gifts or transfers, with value strictly less than $(H - L)/2$, that flow back and forth (with equal probability) between the two partners. Ethan Ligon, Jonathan P. Thomas, and Tim Worrall (2002) describe how a higher level of insurance can be sustained with limited commitment: in that case the individual who receives H in a given period t and makes a transfer (loan) to his partner who received L will receive compensatory transfers in return that maintain the same ratio of marginal utilities as in period t (or as close as possible to that ratio) in all subsequent periods, as long as both individuals receive the same payoff (L,L, or H,H). With partial insurance, the lender maintains a higher level of consumption than the borrower in period t, which implies that transfers will flow in the opposite direction in subsequent periods until unequal payoffs are once again obtained (H,L or L,H), at which point the process starts afresh.

The arrangement that we have just described allows a higher level of mutual insurance to be sustained because the individual who receives H in period t and makes a transfer to his partner expects to receive compensatory transfers in the future in addition to the future benefits of the mutual insurance arrangement over autarky, reducing his incentive to default on his obligation. Mutual insurance with limited commitment can be characterized as a series of quasi-loans connecting members of the network, and caste loans are indeed more important (in terms of total value) than gifts or transfers in our rural Indian sample.

This type of insurance arrangement is relatively easy to implement when both individuals obtain the high state with equal probability, because loans will flow in both directions with equal probability as well. Implementability is more of a challenge when wealth inequality grows within the network, for example, when the two individuals have different probabilities of attaining the high state, because one individual will now be a net lender. Under the limited-commitment arrangement described above, the individual in the lending state does better than he would have without commitment, because the quasi-loans compensate him to some extent, but the implementability condition still binds when he is a lender; the subsidy that he provides his partner when he is in the lending state is just offset by the future gains from insurance. Holding fixed the level of transfers in the lending and borrowing states, an increase in the probability of being a lender must lead to a violation of the implementability constraint.

One solution to this problem is to reduce the level of transfers when the wealthy individual is the lender and increase the level when he is the borrower; this effectively implies that the wealthy individual makes small, high-interest loans more frequently, occasionally receiving a large, low-interest loan in return. This also implies that the less wealthy individual will be pushed below his previous minimum consumption level (in the L,L state), following the receipt of a loan. If we assume that there is a consumption floor that might arise due to nutrition constraints on survival (Gersovitz 1983; Atkeson and Ogaki 1996) or due to community norms, then an increase in wealth inequality increases the probability that the constraint associated with this consumption threshold will be binding. Such constraints on consumption inequality could prevent the constrained-efficient limited-commitment insurance arrangement from being sustained.

Previous research on the relationship between wealth inequality and network participation, for example, that of Abhijit Banerjee and Andrew Newman (1998), suggests that in some cases the wealthiest members of the network might have the greatest propensity to exit, whereas in other cases the least wealthy might be most likely to choose to leave. In general, the exit decision will depend on the payoff from participation in the network compared to the outside options that are available. If restrictions on transfers are in place, perhaps because a consumption threshold is reached by the less wealthy members of the network, then wealthier individuals will end up subsidizing the rest of the network. These individuals are also better positioned to access alternative sources of insurance and credit, reinforcing our prediction that an increase in wealth inequality could lead to the disintegration of this traditional institution, with the wealthiest individuals being unambiguously the first to exit.

Our empirical analysis of exit from rural networks makes use of a panel survey of rural Indian households covering the period 1982 through 1999. The baseline survey is the 1982 Rural Economic Development Survey (REDS) carried out by the National Council of Applied Economic Research from 1981 to 1982 in 259 villages in sixteen states (the major states except Assam). The sample of 4,979 households is meant to be representative of all rural Indian households in those states. The survey obtained comprehensive information on agricultural and nonagricultural production as well as on assets and flows of incomes, including loans. An important feature of the data is that they include information for the loans obtained by the sample households in the survey year or still outstanding in that year, with respect to loan source, purpose, interest rate, and collateral requirement.

Munshi and Rosenzweig (2005) show, using the 1982 round of

the survey, that caste loans are a preferred source for consumption smoothing. Caste loans account for 12 percent of all loans by value, roughly equal in importance to loans from money lenders, but they account for 43 percent of all loans received for contingencies such as illness or marriage and 23 percent of all consumption loans. Caste loans also have lower interest rates than either bank loans or loans from money lenders. On average (the rates are weighted by loan amounts), loans provided by caste members have interest rates that are four percentage points lower than those of bank loans (10.7 percent versus 14.9 percent). Both rates are lower than those for loans from money lenders (17.0 percent). Along the same lines, 35 percent of all caste loans are zero-interest loans, versus 0.3 percent for bank loans and 3.0 percent for loans from money lenders. Furthermore, in 1982, 43 percent of bank loans required some collateral, whereas 16 percent of caste loans (and 19 percent of money-lender loans) had a collateral requirement.

If the lower costs of caste loans reflect superior information within the community and the ability of caste networks to enforce repayment; then the differences in loan terms by source demonstrate that there are costs associated with exit from the network. Nevertheless, the integrity of this traditional institution might still be threatened if the subsidy to the less wealthy members (tax on wealthy members) of the network grows sufficiently large, as discussed earlier.

Historically, members of the same *jati* were engaged in the same occupation and had comparable permanent incomes. *Jatis* did, however, span fairly large geographical areas, which allowed them to smooth income shocks. The relatively egalitarian wealth distribution within *jatis* had persisted for centuries in rural India when the technological change associated with the Green Revolution unexpectedly threatened the viability of the traditional networks. High-yielding grain varieties of wheat and rice were introduced in India in the late 1960s. These dwarf varieties have a greater grain-to-stalk ratio than the traditional varieties, resulting in tremendous increases in agricultural yields. However, only a limited area was suitable for cultivation of the early HYVs. Subsequent generations of HYVs were adapted to diverse growing conditions, and by the 1980s,

HYVs were developed that were suitable for cultivation in most of the country. Although the production technology was the same at any subsequent point in time, spatial differences in the timing of HYV adoption across the country gave rise to persistent differences in the level of accumulated assets, and hence permanent income. Because *jatis* were widely dispersed geographically, this process of sequential technology adoption gave rise to substantial wealth inequality within *jatis*. In fact, inequality within *jatis* rose more than inequality within villages over the period from 1982 to 1999.

Munshi and Rosenzweig (2005) exploit the relationship between the timing of HYV adoption and wealth inequality within the *jati* in their instrumental-variables analysis of the effect of inequality on loans, savings, migration, and out-marriage. As noted, there was little spatial variation in the agricultural production technology by 1980. However, areas that were the first to receive the HYVs were clearly distinct geographically from areas that subsequently adopted the new technology, and they could in principle be different along other dimensions that directly determine investment and marriage choices. The current analysis of network exit uses a single cross-section, 1982, and so we will include variables that are associated with the timing of HYV adoption as controls.

Although the base-line survey in 1982 did not collect detailed subcaste information, this deficiency was remedied in the 1999 follow-up survey. It is thus possible to identify *jati* membership for all households in the set of 1982 villages (excluding the state of Jammu and Kashmir) in which at least one member still remained in the village in 1999. The 1999 survey also collected information on the marriages of all immediate relatives (sons, daughters, sisters, brothers) of the heads of households, including the caste membership of spouses. This information makes possible an assessment of the determinants of network exit, as measured by out-marriage. The 1999 survey also obtained information on the location of all immediate family members of the household heads as well as information on the date of out-migration for those who left the village.

As in the urban application, the two outcomes that we use to measure network exit are migration and out-marriage. Migration accompanies marriage for most women in rural areas of India. Indeed, the practice of patrilocal exogamy is seen as facilitating risk sharing given

Table 7.4   Comparison of Households, by Wealth
(Standard Errors in Parentheses)

Variables	Household Outcomes and Characteristics[a]	
	Low Wealth[b] (1)	High Wealth (2)
Proportion of migrants	0.06	0.06
	(0.01)	(0.01)
Proportion that married less outside the jati	0.04	0.06
	(0.01)	(0.01)
Education of household head	2.08	2.31[c]
	(0.05)	(0.05)
Age of household head	51.78	53.77[c]
	(0.34)	(0.38)

Source: 1982 Rural Economic Development survey (REDs).
[a] Sample restricted to households belonging to jatis with more than ten observations and age of household head greater than thirty-five.
[b] Wealth cutoff separating low and high categories is the median in each jati.
[c] Denotes rejection of the equality of means at the 5 percent level.

the spatial covariance of agricultural risks (Rosenzweig and Stark 1989). Women move into the households of their husbands, who typically remain in their village of birth. Thus, we measure network exit as the migration of men. In particular, we measure migration by the proportion of adult males aged twenty to thirty in 1982 who left the village in the ten years prior to the 1982 survey. Roughly 6 percent of adult males migrated outside the village. We measure out-marriage as the proportion of all marriages among the immediate relatives of the household head that took place between 1972 and 1982 in which the spouse belonged to a different *jati*.

Table 7.4 divides the sample into low-wealth and high-wealth households, using median wealth within the *jati* in 1982 as the cutoff and reports in the first two columns rates of out-migration and out-marriage. We see that male out-migration is independent of household wealth. However, there is 50 percent more out-marriage among the wealthier households, consistent with our model of network exit, but the difference in means is not significantly different from zero at the 5 percent level.

We noted previously that areas that adopted HYVs early could be different on other dimensions, which could independently determine marriage and migration patterns. For example, the early wheat varieties were adopted throughout the northern plains, where wheat was grown traditionally, whereas the adoption of HYV rice varieties, in south India, where rice was the traditional crop, was a slower process that required more technological fine tuning. Migration and marriage patterns could very well be different in north and south India, which is why we control for the timing of HYV adoption in the regressions that follow. By a similar line of reasoning, households with different education levels or demographic structures will also display different propensities to migrate or marry outside the *jati*. Indeed, there is a vast literature suggesting that education and migration are positively associated. Rows 3 and 4 in table 7.4 report statistics for two important household variables, education and age, which we will include as controls in regressions estimating the determinants of migration and out-marriage. Education levels of the household heads are extremely low in rural India, just above two years in 1982, but even these low levels are significantly related to household wealth. Household heads in wealthier households are also, not surprisingly, significantly older than the heads of households below the cutoff, emphasizing the importance of including these controls.

Table 7.5 reports estimates of the relationships between household wealth and migration and out-marriage. As discussed, geographical variables that are associated with the timing of HYV adoption as well as the education and age of the household head are included in these regressions. The specification in table 7.5, columns 1 and 2, includes, in addition, a full set of *jati* dummies, to study the effect of variation in household wealth within the *jati* on marriage and migration. Recall from our model of mutual insurance that relative wealth within the *jati* is what matters for network exit. We see that, as predicted, an increase in relative wealth does increase the likelihood of out-marriage (the estimated coefficient just misses being significant at the 5 percent level). The point estimate indicates that for every thousand-rupee increase in relative wealth there is a 2 percent increase in the probability of out-marriage. Increases in

Table 7.5   The Effect of Wealth on Migration and Marriage
(Standard Errors Clustered at the Level of the State Are in Parentheses)

Dependent Variable	Migration (1)	Out-Marriage (2)	Migration (3)	Out-Marriage (4)
Wealth × 10[7]	−2.91	8.16	−5.31	9.34
	(3.21)	(4.15)	(2.65)	(6.77)
Age of household head[a]	0.0001	−0.001	0.0002	−0.0006
	(0.0005)	(0.0006)	(0.0005)	(0.0005)
Education of household head	0.013	−0.007	0.014	−0.007
	(0.005)	(0.004)	(0.004)	(0.003)
Jati fixed effects	Yes	Yes	No	No
R-squared	0.026	0.200	0.019	0.014
Number of observations	1,375	886	1,375	886

Source: 1982 Rural Economic Development Survey (REDS).
Note: Additional controls include a binary variable that measures maximum yield in the village and indicators for whether the village is an Intensive Agricultural Development Program (IADP, IAADP) village, and whether any HYV was grown in 1970.
[a] Sample restricted to households belonging to jatis with more than ten observations and age of household head greater than thirty-five.

relative wealth within the *jati*, however, weakly lower the propensity to migrate.

This last observation, which runs counter to the predictions of our framework, is not entirely surprising. Wealthy households in rural India are predominantly households that own highly productive and large landholdings. Out-migrants from such households have high opportunity costs to out-migration to the extent that out-migration entails the loss of returns from land. This absolute wealth effect could confound the positive effect of an increase in relative wealth on migration that is implied by our theory of network exit. To assess this, in column 3 we report regression estimates in which *jati* fixed effects are omitted.

Our theory specifies that an increase in household wealth, conditional on *jati* wealth, increases the propensity to migrate. The *jati* wealth term, which has a negative coefficient in the migration regression, since households in wealthier networks are less likely to migrate, is subsumed in the *jati* fixed effects in column 1. When the fixed effects are excluded, this term appears in the residual of the migration regression. Because household wealth and *jati* wealth are positively correlated, this implies that the coefficient on household wealth will be biased downward, becoming even more negative than it was before. As expected, the column 3 negative-wealth coefficient is larger in absolute magnitude than the estimate obtained with *jati* fixed effects, and significant at the 5 percent level.

Conclusion

There is now a fairly large body of empirical work that documents the important role that nonmarket institutions in general and community-based networks in particular play in developing economies (Rosenzweig 1988, Townsend 1994, and Udry 1994 are early contributions to this literature). However, the transformation of these institutions in the face of economic development is less well understood. Our analysis of caste networks in rural and urban India during a period of substantial economic change indicates that it is the wealthiest and most able individuals who tend to leave this important traditional institution but that network decay is not an inevitable feature of economic development.

Nancy Luke and Munshi (2006) find a similar pattern of selective entry into kin networks in urban Kenya. Marriage in Kenya, as elsewhere in sub-Saharan Africa, is exogamous in the sense that the man must find a partner outside his clan. Each individual is consequently born into a network organized around his father's family and then, when he marries, acquires a new network, organized around his wife's family. Kin and affine networks serve a particularly important role in urban Africa, helping their members find jobs and providing other forms of support. Controlling for selective entry into the marriage institution, Luke and Munshi find that marital status does indeed have a causal effect on labor-market outcomes; everything else equal, married men are more likely to be employed and have higher incomes than single men. Their analysis also indicates that it is the low-ability men, who would otherwise—without the help of their wife's network—fare worse in the labor market, who are more likely to be married.

Why are high-ability individuals of any given age less likely to be married in urban Africa? Luke and Munshi argue that high-ability individuals end up providing jobs, accommodation, and financial support for the other members of their network, while receiving few benefits in return. We saw in India that wealthy and able individuals were the first to exit the caste networks. In urban Africa, the most able individuals who would also have ended up subsidizing the other members of their network similarly defer entry into these networks through marriage.

It should in principle be possible to compensate more able or wealthy individuals for the services they provide. Instead, we consistently observe a pattern in which the better-off subsidize the worse-off, which encourages the former to either leave or not participate in the network. One explanation for this inability to implement sufficient transfers within the network to reduce defection or encourage entry is based on a minimum consumption threshold, as discussed earlier. Another explanation is based on the idea that collective institutions of this sort require frequent social interactions among their members to function efficiently. Only then will information flow smoothly and individual obligations be enforced. But such frequent interactions require fairly uniform consumption patterns within the community, which restricts the extent to which wealthy or able individuals can be compensated.

The implication of the exit that we document in this paper is that the traditional caste networks, which have remained firmly in place for centuries, could ultimately break down in the face of economic development. The contrast between the rates of exit from Indian urban and rural networks, however, suggests that the speed of network decay depends on the characteristics of the growth process. In urban areas, liberalization led to increased demand for workers in jobs unrelated to traditional networks, thereby substantially eroding the value of network services. In rural areas, however, the growth in seed productivity did not significantly change the need for insurance against the vagaries of agriculture, and thus the value of the fundamental services of rural networks was not challenged. Rural caste erosion resulted only from shifts in wealth positions that accompanied rural growth and consequently rates of exit did not appreciably accelerate. Nevertheless, in both settings, individuals with higher incomes, owing to ability or wealth, were the first to exit, leading to lower-quality services for the remaining members. Until market institutions emerge to substitute for these traditional institutions, the most vulnerable members of the community could face a substantial loss in welfare. Policies that promote economic development need to take account of the potentially substantial costs that could result from the disintegration of traditional economic arrangements.

Acknowledgments

The authors gratefully acknowledge support for their research from the Mellon Foundation, through the University of Pennsylvania and the National Science Foundation.

Notes

1. In rural areas of India, almost all women migrate out of their birth village when they marry, but to a household within their caste. Men typically stay in their birth village, and it is the out-migration of men in rural areas that signals departure from the network.
2. By ability we mean productivity at work that is related to human capital before the child attends school. Ability thus depends on the resources of a child's household, including household income and the human capital of the parents.

References

Atkeson, Andrew, and M. Ogaki. 1996. "Wealth Varying Intertemporal Elasticities of Substitution: Evidence from Panel and Aggregate Data." *Journal of Monetary Economics.* 38(3): 507–34.

Banerjee, Abhijit, and Andrew Newman. 1998. "Information, the Dual Economy, and Development." *Review of Economic Studies.* 65(4): 631–53.

Coate, Stephen, and Martin Ravallion. 1993. "Reciprocity Without Commitment: Characterization and Performance of Informal Insurance Arrangements." *Journal of Development Economics* 40(1): 1–24.

Gersovitz, Mark. 1983. "Savings and Nutrition at Low Incomes." *Journal of Political Economy* 91(5): 841–55.

Greif, Avner. 1993. "Contract Enforceability and Economic Institutions in

Early Trade: The Maghribi Traders' Coalition." *American Economic Review* 83(3): 525–48.

Ligon, Ethan, Jonathan P. Thomas, and Tim Worrall. 2002. "Informal Insurance Arrangements with Limited Commitment: Theory and Evidence from Village Economies." *Review of Economic Studies* 69(1): 209–44.

Luke, Nancy, and Kaivan Munshi. 2006. "New Roles for Marriage in Urban Africa: Kinship Networks and the Labor Market in Kenya." *Review of Economics and Statistics* 88(2): 264–82.

Munshi, Kaivan. 2003. "Networks in the Modern Economy: Mexican Migrants in the U.S. Labor Market." *Quarterly Journal of Economics* 118(2): 549–97.

Munshi, Kaivan, and Mark Rosenzweig. 2005. "Why Is Mobility in India so Low? Social Insurance, Inequality, and Growth." BREAD working paper 092. Cambridge, Mass.: Harvard University, Bureau for Research and Economic Analysis of Development.

———. 2006. "Traditional Institutions Meet the Modern World: Caste, Gender and Schooling Choice in a Globalizing Economy." *American Economic Review* 96(4): 1225–52.

Rees, Albert. 1966. "Information Networks in Labor Markets." *American Economic Review* 56(1/2): 559–66.

Rosenzweig, Mark. 1988. "Risk, Implicit Contracts and the Family in Rural Areas of Low-Income Countries." *Economic Journal* 98(393): 1148–70.

Rosenzweig, Mark, and Oded Stark. 1989. "Consumption Smoothing, Migration and Marriage: Evidence from Rural India." *Journal of Political Economy* 97(4): 905–26.

Townsend, Robert. 1994. "Risk and Insurance in Village India." *Econometrica* 62(3): 171–84.

Udry, Christopher. 1994. "Risk and Insurance in a Rural Credit Market: An Empirical Investigation in Northern Nigeria." *Review of Economic Studies* 61(3): 495–526.

Chapter 8

Clusters and Bridges in Networks of Entrepreneurs

James E. Rauch and Joel Watson

The predominant sociological approach to formation of economic networks focuses on past interaction: people get to know and trust each other, especially in social settings ("embeddedness"), and are then able to share information and do business together. Economists argue instead that actors strategically choose to invest in certain relationships on the basis of forward-looking incentives. To oversimplify the two positions: in economics you choose your network whereas in sociology your network chooses you.

In this chapter we take a step toward merging these two approaches. We do not attempt to do so at the most general level, focusing instead on a specific class of actors: entrepreneurs. In this way we hope to show how merging the economic and sociological approaches can yield new predictions and policy recommendations in a concrete empirical setting.

Our model of network formation is guided by the desire to match two common features of economic networks identified by sociologists. The first feature is what we call a "cluster and bridge" network structure, in which groups of densely tied agents (clusters) are connected by sparse ties (bridges), as opposed to a structure characterized by either completely isolated groups or a uniform density of ties among all agents.[1] A cluster and bridge network structure arises in many economic settings from a combination of exogenous and endogenous forces that produce densely tied groups within a larger whole: divisions within a large firm, industries within an economy, metropolitan areas within a country. A second common feature of economic networks is higher rewards to agents whose ties span clusters than to agents whose ties are confined within one cluster. Evidence has accumulated in diverse settings that agents with bridge ties perform better than agents with cluster ties (see Burt 2000 for a survey): firms that bridge clusters in interfirm networks show higher profits; managers who bridge clusters in intrafirm networks receive higher pay and more rapid promotions.[2] This may be due to opportunities for arbitrage ("brokerage") across clusters of differences in information or resources, or it could reflect selection of the most able agents into bridging positions. In our model economy a combination of gains from trade and selection will be at work.

We will be specifically concerned with clusters that form among entrepreneurs who spin off from a common "parent firm." Having already worked together, such entrepreneurs know each other's capabilities and needs and are thus at least weakly tied at "birth."[3] It is thus relatively easy for them to form partnerships with each other or to do business with each other as independent firms.

It is widely recognized that spin-offs, or "entrepreneurial spawning," are a major source of entrepreneurship. Amar Bhide (2000, 94) reports that 71 percent of the firms in the Inc. 500 (a list of young, fast-growing firms) were founded by entrepreneurs who "replicated or modified an idea encountered through previous employment." This process has been especially well studied in the high-tech, venture-capital context, where the classic example is the spin-offs from Fairchild Semiconductor in Silicon Valley (Braun and Macdonald 1982). Paul Gompers, Josh Lerner, and David Scharfstein (2003, 3) explain the fertility of this process as follows: "Working in such firms exposes would-be entrepreneurs to a network of suppliers of labor, goods, and capital, as well as a network of customers. Because starting a new venture requires suppliers and customers to make relationship-specific investments before it is guaranteed that the venture will get off the ground, networks can be particularly useful in alleviating this chicken-and-egg problem." They report that the share of U.S. venture-capital-backed entrepreneurs in the period from 1986 to 1999 who previously worked for publicly traded firms is around 45 percent.

There is no need to invoke a high-tech, venture-capital-backed environment to explain entrepreneurial spawning, however. It is also generated by a more mundane process of "client-based entrepreneurship" (Rauch and Watson 2003), in which employees try to wrest the value of client relationships from their employers by setting up their own firms and taking their clients with them. This can occur in any industry in which client relationships are important, including manufacturing, business services, and personal services. According to the 1992 Economic Census of the United States (U.S. Census Bureau 1997, 86), 45.1 percent of nonminority male business owners "previously worked for a business whose goods/services were similar to those provided by the [current] business."

In our model economy, workers leaving their firms to become entrepreneurs may take the relatively easy avenue of forming partnerships with their former colleagues, or might at greater cost seek partnerships with unknown workers leaving other firms to become entrepreneurs. Those who succeed in the latter endeavor form bridges, whereas those who do not form clusters. Specifically, we assume that a cluster partnership serves as the fallback option when deciding whether to accept a potential bridge partnership. Selection then ensures that accepted bridge partnerships will be of higher quality and thus perform better on average than cluster partnerships, and the extent to which this is true will increase with the average of the quality of potential bridge partnerships relative to cluster partnerships, representing the potential for gains from trade.

Entrepreneurs tend to form their firms in the communities in which they live. A cluster consisting of entrepreneurs who spun off from a common parent firm will therefore tend to be geographically localized. This tendency allows us to link our model of entrepreneurial network formation to the literature on "border effects" in interregional and international trade. This literature began with a paper by John McCallum (1995) that found that Canadian provinces traded more than twenty times as much with other Canadian provinces as with U.S. states of comparable economic size and distance away. Border effects were subsequently found for jurisdictional borders that impose no apparent cost on trade. In particular, Holger C.

Wolf (2000) found much higher trade within U.S. states than across U.S. states than could be explained by relative economic size and distance. Our model economy displays community-border effects because cluster partnerships are formed only within communities whereas bridge partnerships are formed both within and across communities.

We investigate two types of policies that affect network formation. One type of policy targets effort expended to form bridge partnerships and is analogous to programs that subsidize the search for international trading partners (see Rauch 1996; Rauch and Watson 2004). The other type of policy is enforcement of employment contracts that restrict the ability of workers to form firms that compete with their former employers and thus discourage formation of cluster partnerships (see Rauch and Watson 2003).

We present our model economy in the next section of this chapter. In the following section we analyze this model economy; then we extend it so we can address additional issues. The last section summarizes what we have accomplished in light of the goals set forth in this introduction.

A Model Economy and Its Underlying Network Structure

Here we will describe a hypothetical or model economy. One purpose of this exercise is to show how a simple, empirically observed mechanism of firm formation can generate a cluster and bridge network structure. The fact that our model economy is logically consistent enables us to do even more. First, we can observe how changes in features of the economic environment affect key outcome variables and use these results to make some new, testable empirical predictions. Second, we can ask how government actions affect the total income generated by the model economy and therefore draw implications for policy.

The model economy and its analysis can be presented in mathematical language, but we will keep this entirely in the background, with some loss of precision but considerable gain in intuitive understanding. Unlike Rachel Kranton and Deborah Minehart, and Ronald S. Burt (chapters 3 and 5, respectively, in this volume), we will not keep track of individual network links. Instead we will focus on two aggregate features of the model economy: its wage level and its distribution of firm sizes. These in turn will be determined by the level of effort expended to form bridge partnerships, which yields the aggregate division of partnerships into bridge and cluster types. Bridge and cluster partnerships are the underlying network structure of the model economy. We will also be concerned with the "bridge premium" and the border effect, which summarize important features of this structure.

In our model economy there exist two generations of agents in every period, young and old. The young agents are workers and the old agents are entrepreneurs. In each successive period, the old agents die, the young agents become the new entrepreneurs, and a new generation of young workers is born.

Workers are employed by firms. Each firm is made up of two entrepreneurs who have formed a partnership. The quality of the partnership or the size of the firm depends on how well the partners are matched. Partners who are better matched hire more workers and produce more output.

Every firm produces the same type of output and thus we assume that no firm has the ability to influence the market price. Similarly, firms take the wage rate of labor as given. It follows that the only choice variable for each firm is how much labor to hire, and it chooses this amount to maximize profits. The higher the wage rate, the less labor each firm hires. In the aggregate, the wage rate adjusts so that the total amount of labor demanded by all firms equals the total amount of labor supplied by workers.

We assume that the amount of labor supplied is simply fixed by the number of young workers born in each period. The number of firms (partnerships) equals half the number of entrepreneurs, which is determined by the number of workers born each preceding period. The key determinant of the wage rate in any period will therefore be the quality of firm partnerships, because this determines how many workers firms want to hire for any given wage. We now discuss how the distribution of this quality across firms is obtained.

At the end of a given period, when young agents employed as workers in existing firms are about to become old, they engage in a matching process culminating in the formation of the firms that they will manage in the next period. An agent can match with someone in the same existing firm (a cluster match) or with someone who is currently working in a different firm (a bridge match).

The matching process proceeds as follows. First, each young agent expends effort at some personal cost to search for a match with someone in a different firm. We allow for the possibility that his effort is subsidized by the government, and the rate of this subsidy will be one of the key policy variables in our analysis. In an international context, this subsidy could be interpreted as support for participation in international trade missions or trade shows, or as favorable tax treatment for foreign direct investment. The probability that an agent will find a match in another firm increases with both his own effort and the effort being made by his potential partners. When two potential partners from different firms actually find each other, the quality of their match is random and is drawn from a fixed distribution of qualities for bridge matches. Knowing this quality level, the agent and his potential partner then decide whether to form a firm.

If an agent fails to form a partnership with someone from another firm (either because he does not obtain a bridge match or because he does not consummate such a match), then this agent freely obtains a cluster match with someone from his current firm (who also failed to form a bridge partnership). The quality of the cluster match is always the same. This lack of randomness reflects the idea that within a firm agents already know each other and know whom to approach and what they are getting. After all matches are consummated, firms hire labor and engage in production.

The part of firm output that is not paid out as wages accrues to the firm partners as profits. How do the partners share the profits of the firm? Note that when they form a bridge partnership their outside options are to find partners within their own firms, and when they form cluster partnerships their outside options are zero. In either case, the two partners are in symmetrical positions, so it is natural to assume that each receives half of the profits.[4] Total profits scale up in proportion to firm size, that is, in proportion to match quality. It follows that potential partners who draw a match quality

Figure 8.1   Determination of Search Effort, Distribution of Firm Sizes, and Wage Rate in the Model Economy

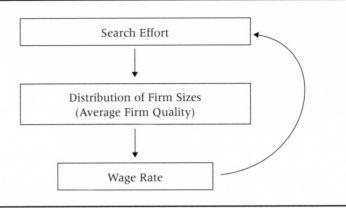

Source: Authors' configuration.

from the bridge distribution will form a bridge firm if and only if this quality is at least as great as the cluster-match quality.

We can understand how our model economy works with the aid of figure 8.1, which shows how the amount of effort each agent will spend in his search for a bridge partnership is determined. Reading from top to bottom, the distribution of firm-match qualities or sizes is determined by the search effort of each agent: the greater the search effort, the more bridge matches are formed and the higher average firm quality is. The wage rate depends on the distribution of firm sizes because this is what determines the aggregate demand for labor in the economy. To complete the circle, note that the incentive of each agent to search is the prospect of finding a better match than he could in his own firm, given the existence of potentially complementary information, resources, and skills across firms. This incentive in turn depends on the wage rate: the lower the wage rate, the greater the extent to which better match quality translates into higher profits.[5]

An equilibrium for our model economy consists of a wage rate that equates aggregate demand for labor to supply, a distribution of firm sizes that generates that aggregate demand at the equilibrium wage rate, and a search effort that generates this distribution of firm sizes and equates the incentive for search to its cost. To see that an equilibrium exists, and to see why there is only one equilibrium, consider what happens if each agent were, hypothetically, to choose a very low level of search effort. In this case very few bridge matches will be formed and average firm quality will be low. Demand for labor will then be low and so will the wage rate. This low wage rate, however, yields a high return to search effort, implying that the original choice of low search effort was not an equilibrium level. As search effort is increased, the distribution of firm qualities improves and the wage rate increases, reducing the return to search effort, so eventually the incentive for search and its cost are brought to equality.

The underlying network structure of our model economy is shown in figure 8.2. Agents within a shaded circle are all weakly tied to each other by virtue of having previously worked together in the same "parent firm." Some of these agents have formed partnerships (new firms) with their former colleagues; these strong ties are denoted by dotted lines and labeled "cluster ties." The rest of these agents have formed partnerships with entrepreneurs from different parent firms; these strong ties are denoted by dashed lines and labeled "bridge ties." Some bridge ties are formed within the agents' own community and some are formed between communities, where communities are denoted by large circles.

Figure 8.2 reflects our assumption that entrepreneurs who spin off from a given parent firm remain in their original community. In the representative cluster shown in detail, two-thirds of the agents have formed partnerships with their former colleagues and one-third have formed bridge ties. Since bridge ties are the result of random matching, they are formed in proportion to the sizes of the communities: community α contains half of all entrepreneurs and thus receives half of all bridge ties, community β contains one-third of all entrepreneurs and receives one-third of all bridge ties, and community γ receives the remaining one-sixth of all bridge ties.

Two empirically observable features of this underlying network structure have received considerable attention in the literature. The first could be called a bridge premium: the excess of the return to an agent with a bridge tie over the return to an agent with a cluster tie.

Figure 8.2   Underlying Network Structure

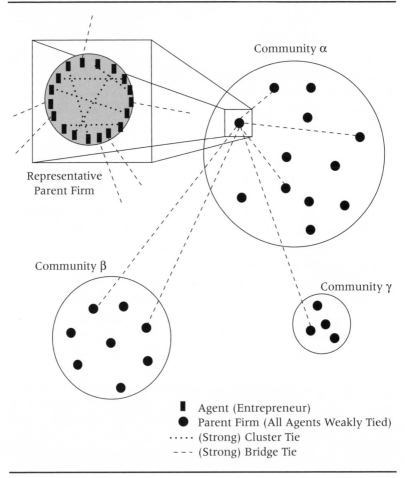

Source: Authors' configuration.

The second is the border effect: the excess of observed trade within a community above what would be predicted if intracommunity trade were determined in the same way as intercommunity trade. We now analyze these two features of the underlying network structure of our model economy.

Subsidies, Distributions of Match Qualities, Bridge Premia, and Border Effects

Absent any government subsidy to effort for building bridge partnerships, we can see that the equilibrium search effort supplied in our model economy will be less than the level that would maximize aggregate output (net of effort). The reason is that agents do not take account of the fact that their own search effort makes the efforts of others more productive. It follows that a small subsidy to search effort to build bridge partnerships must increase aggregate output, and that there exists a positive optimal subsidy that maximizes aggregate output.[6] Most governments provide subsidies to formation of international bridge partnerships by sponsoring international trade missions and trade shows (Rauch 1996). Our analysis suggests that these subsidies raise world output, provided that international bridge partnerships are not systematically less productive than domestic bridge partnerships.

We can also analyze the impacts of changes in the distribution of qualities for bridge matches. An improvement in the bridge distribution of match quality (technically, a first-order stochastic dominant shift) implies an increase in the "gains from trade." Therefore agents will increase the effort they make to search for bridge partners, which will improve the size distribution of firms (also in the sense of first-order stochastic dominance), and thus increase the equilibrium wage. Note that increased variability of bridge-match quality (technically, a second-order stochastic dominant shift) can have the same effect as an increase in average bridge-match quality: intuitively, increased variability intensifies the selection effect for bridge-partnership formation. In contrast, improved match quality in cluster partnerships leads to less effort to form bridge partnerships. This has an ambiguous effect on the distribution of firm sizes, because the size of firms formed through cluster partnerships increases but fewer larger firms are formed through bridge partnerships. Since improved cluster-match quality has an ambiguous effect on the distribution of firm sizes, it also has an ambiguous effect on the level of wages.

As we noted, the cutoff match quality for a bridge partnership is the match quality of a cluster partnership. Thus, it must be that a firm formed from a bridge partnership generates a profit that is higher than that achieved by a firm formed from a cluster partnership. We define the bridge premium as the ratio of the observed average return to agents in bridge partnerships to the observed average return to agents in cluster partnerships. It follows that the bridge premium is a function only of the (constant) cluster-match quality and the distribution of bridge-match qualities.

The community-border effect for measured trade arises in our model because trade across communities is generated by random matching of agents forming bridge partnerships, whereas trade within a community is generated by the sum of cluster partnerships and random matching of agents forming bridge partnerships. Hence there is "excess trade" within a community beyond what would be predicted by random matching. The border effect measures this excess trade relative to predicted trade and thus varies directly with the value of cluster partnerships relative to bridge partnerships.[7] This will be a function of the cluster-match quality and the distribution of bridge-match qualities, like the bridge premium, and of the search effort, through its effect on the probability of finding a potential bridge partner.[8]

We can now see how the bridge premium and border effect vary as the characteristics of our model economy change. First, an increase in the rate of subsidy leaves the bridge premium unchanged and reduces the border effect. The increased subsidy induces greater search effort, which raises the probability of finding a potential bridge partner. This does not change the quality of realized bridge partnerships relative to cluster partnerships, but it increases the proportion of agents who form partnerships across communities and therefore reduces the border effect. Second, an improvement in the bridge distribution of match quality (technically, a first-order stochastic dominant shift) will increase the bridge premium and decrease the border effect. Again, greater variability in bridge-match quality (technically, a second-order stochastic dominant shift) can have the same effects. The first effect follows from the definition of the bridge premium, whereas the second effect follows because the induced increase in effort to form bridge partnerships combines with their greater productivity to reduce the share of trade accounted for by cluster partnerships and therefore the border effect. Finally, improved match quality in cluster partnerships tends to decrease the bridge premium and certainly increases the border effect. The requirement for the first effect is that average bridge-match quality increases less than proportionately with an increase in the quality of the fallback cluster match, and the second effect follows from the fact that with greater incentive to form cluster partnerships, the share of trade taking place within a community will increase and therefore so will measured border effects.

Noncompete Covenants and Similar Restrictive Employment Contracts

One of the goals of this chapter is to gain insight into policies that can affect network formation. So far, the only policy we have analyzed is a subsidy to effort to form bridge partnerships. The closest corresponding real-world policy is government sponsorship of international trade missions and trade shows. In some countries similar activities are sponsored at the regional level, but it is doubtful whether effort to form intracommunity bridge partnerships could even be observed by government, let alone subsidized. It might, however, be possible to achieve a similar effect by discouraging formation of cluster partnerships. In this section we will analyze the impact of one such policy, enforcement of covenants not to compete and similar restrictive employment contracts.

Entrepreneurs who spin off from a parent firm may capitalize on technological knowledge or client relationships developed while working for their former employer, or they may simply go into direct competition with their former employer. All of these outcomes are more likely when an agent forms his new firm in partnership with a former colleague from the same parent firm than when he forms his new firm with a partner from a different parent firm, since the former colleagues are more likely to stay in an identical line of business or one very closely related to that of their common former employer.[9] Restrictive employment covenants such as noncompete agreements, nonsolicitation agreements, or restrictions on use of intellectual property developed within the firm will therefore tend to discourage cluster partnerships relative to bridge partnerships.[10]

We can incorporate restrictive employment covenants into our model economy in the following simple way. We assume that all workers have to sign restrictive employment contracts when hired, and that these contracts are enforced with probability p. A worker who leaves at the end of a period to form a cluster partnership causes a reduction (tax) T in the profits of his former employer (so the employer loses $2T$ for each cluster partnership formed by his former employees). If the former employer sues successfully to block formation of the new firm, each worker in the partnership must buy out his contract by paying his former employer T. In contrast, a worker who leaves at the end of a period to form a bridge partnership leaves the profits of his former employer unchanged.

Under these assumptions, on average a worker-turned-entrepreneur loses pT from a cluster partnership relative to the situation in which he did not have to sign a restrictive employment contract. This will affect both his decision whether to accept a bridge partnership rather than a cluster partnership and his decision regarding the effort he will make to find a bridge partnership. Specifically, an entrepreneur is willing to accept a lower-quality bridge partnership now that a cluster partnership is a worse alternative, and will expend more effort to find a potential bridge partner for the same reason. The impact of restrictive employment covenants on the distribution of firm sizes (qualities) is therefore ambiguous. Since the distribution of firm sizes determines the demand for labor, the effect of restrictive employment covenants on the wage rate is also ambiguous.[11]

The enforcement probability p is the government's policy instrument.[12] Starting from a subsidy to search of zero, the impact on aggregate output (net of effort) of increasing p from zero is clearly positive, since it both causes agents to internalize the cost T when deciding whether to accept a bridge partnership and induces them to increase search effort in the same way as would a positive subsidy. However, it may be that if we were to enrich our model economy we would find that the cost T to the worker's former employer is not a cost to society as a whole—for example, it could be offset by a benefit to a client that the worker took from his employer. In this case, the positive effect on aggregate output of increasing p from zero through its impact on effort is offset by a negative effect through its impact on the cutoff match quality for bridge partnerships. A necessary (but not sufficient) condition for aggregate output to increase is that the distribution of firm sizes improves (again, in the sense of first-order stochastic dominance), which will be reflected in an increase in the wage rate.[13]

The predicted effects of variation in the enforcement probability p on the bridge premium and border effect are more straightforward to analyze than is the impact on aggregate output. Since the cutoff match quality for bridge partnerships falls as p increases, the bridge premium (gross of pT) unambiguously decreases. The border effect decreases unambiguously for the same reason: more bridge partnerships and fewer cluster partnerships are formed. In principle these predictions could be tested using data for U.S. states, which differ widely in their policies regarding enforcement of noncompete and nonsolicitation covenants. In fact, the data needed to estimate border effects for U.S. states have already been collected (see Wolf 2000).

Extending the Model Economy: Phased Formation of Partnerships

In addition to border effects, an interesting feature of intercommunity trade revealed by the data is the predictive power of past trade for current trade, even in the presence of explanatory variables (specifically, community-pair fixed effects) that capture the influence of all contemporary determinants of trade (for example, Moenius 2004). It has been argued that this predictive power is at the root of the continued influence of past colonial relationships on current international trade (Eichengreen and Irwin 1998). Some have hypothesized that this influence of past trade on current trade reflects network effects, where networks formed in the past continue to have an impact on trade in the present (Anderson and Smith 2003). This is not a feature of our model economy, since we assume that networks dissolve at the end of every period and are recreated from scratch in the next period. However, if we modify our model economy to allow for the possibility that some entrepreneurs form their partnerships before others, we may find that it is useful for analyzing this phenomenon.

Let us divide all agents into groups 1 and 2. There are two rounds of entrepreneurial matching. Group 1 agents match first. Since the outcomes of their matches are unaffected by the actions of group 2 agents, their matching process is identical to what we already described. Group 2 agents match second. As before, firms hire labor and engage in production after all matches have been consummated. We relax our assumption that all agents within a parent firm are weakly tied to each other, and suppose that some group 2 agents are lucky enough to be weakly tied to group 1 agents who formed bridge partnerships and some are not. We will call these group 2 agents "well connected" and "poorly connected" and label their shares in group 2 population a and $1 - a$, respectively. The well-connected share of group 2 agents, a, will increase with the ratio of group 1 to group 2 agents and with the share of group 1 agents that form bridge partnerships. We assume that a well-connected group 2 agent has a higher probability of meeting a potential bridge match for a given level of effort. For example, a well-connected group 2 agent may learn from a group 1 colleague which trade show to attend to meet potential matches from the parent firm (cluster) from which the colleague's match was drawn. This and other plausible motivations for our assumption suggest that a well-connected group 2 agent will seek to meet agents from particular parent firms, specifically those from which the partners of their group 1 former colleagues originally came. However, this behavior will have no consequences for the pattern of trade at the community level, which at this point will not display dependence of current trade on past trade.

Clearly there will be more bridge matches and a higher value of trade per agent for group 2 than for group 1, provided $a > 0$. The border effect will be lower for group 2 than for group 1, but otherwise the pattern of trade will be unaffected. For any given parent firm, well-connected group 2 agents will on average realize higher incomes than will poorly connected group 2 agents. A survey would therefore show that, among agents who pursued their entrepreneurial ventures later, those whose intrafirm networks were "better" in the sense that the members of the network had been luckier in forming bridge partnerships will have been more successful on average, all else equal. (This is a clear example of the kind of situation discussed in this volume by Toby E. Stuart, chapter 4, and by Ray E. Reagans, Ezra W. Zuckerman, and Bill McEvily, chapter 6, in which features of an agent's network that are beyond his control—exogenous features—influence his measurable economic outcomes.) Finally, we should note that the argument for a subsidy to search effort will be strengthened, because not only is there an external effect of the average effort of any group on the productivity of each individual's effort but there is also an external effect through a of the effort of group 1 agents on the productivity of effort of group 2 agents.

The reason that the pattern of intracommunity trade in our extended model shows no dependence of current trade on past trade is that the determinants of this pattern do not change between the first and second phases of partnership formation, so if these determinants are used to predict current trade then past trade will have no additional explanatory power.[14] We will therefore study the following simple scenario. Divide all communities into non-overlapping groups separated from each other by trade barriers or internally unified by preferential trading agreements. Intercommunity trade therefore takes place only within each of these community groups. Between round 1 and round 2, all barriers to trade between communities are removed or all preferential trading agreements between communities are eliminated. Poorly connected agents now match randomly among all communities, but well-connected agents follow the pattern of trade established in round 1, effectively behaving as though the trade barriers or preferential trading agreements still exist.

Figure 8.3 illustrates our scenario using four equal-size communities with equal population shares for groups 1 and 2 and $a = 1/2$ (recall that a is determined by the equilibrium of our extended model economy). During the first round of matching, all intercommunity partnerships are formed between entrepreneurs from communities α and β or between entrepreneurs from communities γ and δ. Between

Figure 8.3   Trade Barrier Eliminated Between First and Second Round of
              Partnership Formation

Intercommunity Trade from First
Round of Partnership Formation

Intercommunity Trade from Second
Round of Partnership Formation

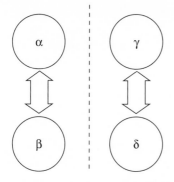

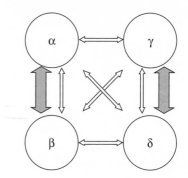

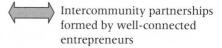

Intercommunity partnerships
formed by poorly connected
entrepreneurs

Intercommunity partnerships
formed by well-connected
entrepreneurs

Source: Authors' configuration.

the first and second rounds of matching, the trade barrier between
the two groups of communities is removed (for example, a bridge is
built across a river that had divided them) or preferential trading
agreements within each group of communities are eliminated (for
example, colonial relationships are terminated). Poorly connected
agents now match randomly among the four communities, so there
are six intercommunity trading relationships instead of two. Since
there are half as many poorly connected agents matching in round 2
as total agents matching in round 1, the value of trade between any
two communities generated by poorly connected agents is one-sixth
of the round 1 value $(1/6 = (1/2)(2/6))$. To this must be added the

trade generated by well-connected agents between communities α and β and between communities γ and δ. This will be somewhat more than half of the round 1 value because well-connected agents have a higher probability of finding bridge matches.[15]

In addition to helping to interpret the effect of past trade on current trade, our extended model economy allows us to predict that denser intrafirm networks will generate a larger impact of past trade on current trade by increasing the proportion of agents who are well connected. If surveys can establish a regularity such as inverse variation of intrafirm network density with firm size (which seems plausible but hardly obvious), then countries whose exports are dominated by small- to medium-sized firms (Italy and Taiwan, for instance) can be predicted to show greater impacts of past exports on current exports than countries whose exports are dominated by large firms (Korea, the United States).

Extending the Model Economy: Postmatching Production

Here we will sketch another extension that takes us further afield from the basic model economy described in the preceding section. We will suppose that, after all the new firms hire labor and generate output, they engage in an additional round of production before dissolving as their workers become the next generation of entrepreneurs. This additional round of production allows for exchange across firms and therefore exploitation of additional interfirm complementarities. As the result of formation of bridge partnerships, it should now be possible for a firm from a given cluster (parent firm) to interact with a firm from any other cluster through a series of weak ties. Nevertheless, survey evidence indicates that information transmission decays rapidly after one or two links (see, for example, Friedkin 1983), and it is in accord with common experience to limit referral-based exchange to those no more than two links away ("our friend recommended me to you"). If we make this assumption, it follows that all firms belonging to clusters between which at least one bridge partnership exists can interact, if all agents within a parent firm are weakly tied to each other. It also follows that if no bridge partnership exists between two clusters, firms formed from cluster partnerships cannot interact across the two clusters.[16]

If we maintain this two-link limitation on interfirm exchange, the complementarities exploitable by a given cluster firm are limited by the number of clusters to which its cluster is connected through bridge partnerships. In principle, we could test for the existence of such "cluster connectivity effects": firms formed from cluster partnerships whose clusters have more connections to other clusters should be involved in more productive exchanges and hence have higher sales and profits, all else equal. These effects should be present even after controlling for cluster size.

As in the previous extension, externalities are generated by bridge partnerships. Specifically, complementarities in production across clusters are realized by firms formed through cluster partnerships through the links established by bridge partnerships. These are analogous to the benefits generated for well-connected group 2 entrepreneurs by group 1 entrepreneurs who form bridge partnerships. Again, there is an argument for subsidizing the formation of bridge partnerships.

Finally, we should note the possibility that the benefits from connectivity may appear at a global level rather than at, or in addition to, the cluster level. This could occur if complementarities in production could be realized through more than two links. In this case, it is tempting to think in terms of the classic "small-world" phenomenon (Watts and Strogatz 1998), where formation of a sufficient number of bridge partnerships could drastically reduce the smallest number of links needed to connect any two firms. For this phenomenon to be of economic importance in our model, it would need to be the case that the efficiency with which production complementarities can be realized diminishes with the number of links used, yet does not become too small for more than two links.

Conclusions

We set out to meld the economic and sociological approaches to network formation in a specific real-world context. In our model economy the impact of past interaction emphasized by sociologists was captured by weak ties among colleagues of the same parent firm, and the forward-looking decisions to form links emphasized by economists were captured by effort to find potential business partners from other parent firms and decisions to form these partnerships only if they are superior to partnerships with known colleagues. The result of this process is that partnerships within any parent firm are much more dense than across any pair of parent firms, since an entrepreneur has an equal chance of meeting up with a potential partner from any other parent firm of given size but his fall-back option is always the colleagues from his own parent. A graph of the network links for our model economy therefore has a cluster and bridge structure, as we saw in figure 8.2, with a cluster existing among the colleagues from each parent firm.

The sociological literature finds that agents whose links span clusters are more successful than agents whose links remain within clusters, but it is usually unclear whether this is true because of selection (better agents form bridges) or because bridges make agents more productive. In our model economy it is true for both reasons: potential bridge partnerships may be no more productive than cluster partnerships on average but they are more variable, allowing entrepreneurs to select the more productive bridge partnerships because they are more profitable than cluster partnerships. Nevertheless, in this basic story there is no exogenous effect of network structure on agent success in that only links that entrepreneurs choose to form have any impact on their profits. Put differently, all agents are in a symmetrical position with regard to network links prior to their search for business partners, so one cannot predict their success on the basis of differences in network structure.

This limitation is surmounted when we extend the model economy to allow for two rounds of partnership formation. In this extended model economy, agents who search for partners in the second round will do better if linked to entrepreneurs who found bridge partnerships in the first round. Being linked to these fortunate entrepreneurs is itself a matter of chance, and thus constitutes an exogenous impact of network structure on agent success. Only then does network structure have a causal force in our model economy similar to the kind found, for example, by Reagans, Zuckerman, and McEvily in chapter 6 of this volume.

Our model economy also generates predictions regarding the observed pattern of inter- and intracommunity exchange. In particular, given the assumption that cluster partnerships form within a community (because both partners live in the same community by virtue of working for the same parent firm) whereas bridge partnerships may form within or across communities, intracommunity exchange is predicted to be greater than would be generated by random matching of partners. This prediction is consistent with "border effects" that are found in observed trade, where the amount of trade drops off sharply when trade within to trade across communities is compared, controlling for determinants of trade such as community sizes and distance between trading partners.

When extended to two rounds of partnership formation, the model economy predicts that agents who search for partners in the second round, and who are linked to entrepreneurs who found bridge partnerships in the first round, will imitate the patterns of bridge-partnership formation established in the first round. This behavior will create a tendency for patterns of intercommunity exchange to persist over time, even if other determinants of intercommunity exchange change, and is therefore consistent with the observed impact of past trade on current trade.

The major policy implication of our model economy is that formation of bridge partnerships relative to cluster partnerships should be encouraged, for two reasons. First, when agents search for bridge partnerships they do not take account of the fact that their own search makes the search of others more productive (because others are looking for them), and therefore do not devote enough effort to finding potential bridge partners. Second, agents choose their effort level on the basis of the profit they expect from bridge partnerships relative to cluster partnerships, but their decision ignores the additional output for workers (wages) that is generated by the bridge partnerships that are actually selected.

This analysis helps us to evaluate a real-world policy regarding entrepreneurship: restrictive employment covenants that prohibit employees from competing with their former employers after they have left a parent firm. Such a policy tends to discourage cluster partnerships, since firms that result from such partnerships are more likely to be in the parent's line of business and market area. Enforcement of restrictive employment covenants should therefore increase intercommunity exchange and reduce observed border effects in trade. It is possible, however, that it overcorrects the problem of insufficient effort to find bridge partners, because agents will now accept bridge partnerships whose quality is too low relative to cluster partnerships.

An important area for improvement of our analysis is network decay, which takes place in a very artificial way in our model economy: the entire network vanishes as the old generation of entrepreneurs dies and a new generation of workers-turned-entrepreneurs takes its place. As a result of this assumption, networks in our model economy cannot evolve over time. Capturing richer network dynamics such as those described by Ronald Burt in chapter 5 of this volume and by Kaivan Munshi and Mark Rosenzweig in chapter 7 of this volume could be a fruitful next step.

Acknowledgments

We thank Jennifer Poole for excellent research assistance. Earlier drafts of this chapter were presented at the Research Institute of Industrial Economics conference "Networks: Theory and Applications" in Vaxholm, Sweden; to the MacArthur Foundation Working Group on Social Interactions; at the Kennedy School of Government; and at George Mason University. James Rauch thanks the Institute of Financial Economics at the American University of Beirut for its support during his work on this draft.

Notes

1. The much more abstract network formation model of Matthew O. Jackson and Brian W. Rogers (2005) is similarly motivated. Their "islands" play the same role as our "parent firms."
2. Insofar as exporting connotes a bridge tie, additional supporting evidence is provided by consistent findings that exporting firms are larger and have higher productivity than nonexporting firms. Marcel

Fafchamps, Said El Hamine, and Albert Zeufack (2003) list the relevant references, and also report that Moroccan exporting firms were typically exporters at start-up or very soon thereafter. This is consistent with our model below, in which firms are born through the formation of either bridge ties or cluster ties.

3.   For a definition of "weak ties" along these lines see Rauch (2001, 1179).

4.   This is the outcome if we apply the Nash bargaining solution with equal bargaining weights.

5.   Each agent searches with a fixed expectation of the search intensity of his potential partners. In our model economy, all agents are in a symmetrical position and they exert the same level of search effort in equilibrium.

6.   We implicitly assume that a method of taxation is available to finance this subsidy that does not itself create "distortions" in the economy that more than offset the benefit of the subsidy.

7.   Real-world data used to estimate border effects measure trade in physical commodities, simply because this is observed relatively easily. To use our model economy to make predictions about real-world border effects, it must be that the process of partnership formation we are studying generates observed trade in physical commodities. Elsewhere (Rauch and Watson 2003) we have argued that spin-off entrepreneurship, even more than entrepreneurship in general, is more common in business services than in manufacturing. Nevertheless, it is plausible that a business service firm such as a consultancy that has partners in two communities will tend to generate shipments between those communities, by linking across the two communities clients involved in goods production or distribution or by finding sales opportunities for such clients across the two communities.

8.   In our model economy the probability of forming a bridge partnership within a community increases with its size but the probability of forming a cluster partnership is invariant to community size. Border effects therefore vary inversely with community size. If we were to "estimate" the border effect using the "data" generated by our model economy, we would have to adjust for the share of agents in each community in the total population of agents. This procedure is in agreement with James E. Anderson and Eric van Wincoop (2003), who show that estimating border effects by applying the standard equation based on random matching to trade data will yield values that vary inversely with community size.

9.   Indeed, one could argue that more bridge partnerships are likely to be associated not only with smaller "border effects" but also with more

trade across industries ("interindustry trade") relative to within industries ("intra-industry trade").

10. Strictly speaking, in our model economy the spin-off firms do not begin to operate until the parent firms have ceased to exist: only one generation of firms operates in any given period. It would seem that this precludes competition between the spin-off firms and the parent firms. One way to allow them to compete would be to suppose that parent firms serve clients that survive into the next period. If the new cluster firms are formed by "stealing" the clients of the parent firms, agents can prevent their current employer from realizing the profit from a client despite the fact that they do not serve the client until the next period.

11. Actually, unless $p = 1$, the demand for labor is also influenced by the risk to the employer that he will lose T if a worker he hires leaves to form a cluster partnership. We can avoid complicating the model in this way if we assume (unrealistically) that the average loss to the employer is deducted from each worker's pay when he is hired. In effect, this is a "lump-sum tax" on labor.

12. The government loses this policy instrument if employers and workers do not choose to negotiate restrictive employment contracts. Rauch and Watson (2003) present evidence that they do, and show why they will want to negotiate such contracts in the case in which the workers-turned-entrepreneurs take clients away from their former employers: a noncompete or nonsolicitation covenant increases the bargaining power of the employer and worker vis-à-vis the client when the separation of the worker from his employer is negotiated.

13. This condition is not sufficient because more effort has been expended, which could cause output net of effort to decline.

14. If these determinants (that is, community sizes), are omitted, past trade predicts current trade perfectly since there is no reason for agents, be they well connected or poorly connected, to behave differently in round 2 than in round 1.

15. We can see from this example that the smaller the size of any group of communities that were preferentially linked in the past relative to the total size of all communities, the greater will be the ratio of "excess" trade between any two formerly linked communities to trade predicted by the standard determinants. This point has been missed by, for example, the literature estimating the impact of past colonial relationships on current bilateral trade. Correct estimation requires an adjustment along the lines of the adjustment for border effect estimation discussed in note 8.

16. The situation for firms formed from bridge partnerships is less clear. It

could be argued that these firms can interact with any firms not only from their own two clusters but from any cluster connected by a bridge partnership to either of their own two clusters.

References

Anderson, James E., and Eric van Wincoop. 2003. "Gravity with Gravitas: A Solution to the Border Puzzle." *American Economic Review* 93(March): 170–92.

Anderson, Michael A., and Stephen L. S. Smith. 2003. "How Does History Matter? Hysteresis in Canadian Trade." Working paper. Lexington, Va.: Washington and Lee University.

Bhide, Amar. 2000. *The Origin and Evolution of New Businesses*. New York: Oxford University Press.

Braun, Ernest, and Stuart Macdonald. 1982. *Revolution in Miniature: The History and Impact of Semiconductor Electronics Re-Explored in an Updated and Revised Second Edition*. New York: Cambridge University Press.

Burt, Ronald S. 2000. "The Network Structure of Social Capital." In *Research in Organizational Behavior*, volume 22, edited by Robert I. Sutton and Barry M. Staw. Greenwich, Conn.: JAI Press.

Eichengreen, Barry, and Douglas A. Irwin. 1998. "The Role of History in Bilateral Trade Flows." In *The Regionalization of the World Economy*, edited by Jeffrey A. Frankel. Chicago, Ill.: University of Chicago Press.

Fafchamps, Marcel, Said El Hamine, and Albert Zeufack. 2003. "Manufacturing Exports and Market-Specific Knowledge." Working paper. Oxford: Oxford University.

Friedkin, Noah E. 1983. "Horizons of Observability and Limits of Informal Control in Organizations." *Social Forces* 62(1): 54–77.

Gompers, Paul, Josh Lerner, and David Scharfstein. 2003. "Entrepreneurial Spawning: Public Corporations and the Genesis of New Ventures, 1986–1999." NBER working paper no. 9816. Cambridge, Mass.: National Bureau of Economic Research (July).

Jackson, Matthew O., and Brian W. Rogers. 2005. "The Economics of Small Worlds." *Journal of the European Economic Association* 3(April–May): 617–27.

McCallum, John. 1995. "National Borders Matter: Canada-U.S. Regional Trade Patterns." *American Economic Review* 85(June): 615–23.

Moenius, Johannes. 2004. "Information Versus Product Adaptation: The Role of Standards in Trade." Working paper. Evanston, Ill.: Northwestern University.

Rauch, James E. 1996. "Trade and Search: Social Capital, Sogo Shosha, and Spillovers." NBER working paper no. 5618. Washington: National Bureau of Economic Research (June).

———. 2001. "Business and Social Networks in International Trade." *Journal of Economic Literature* 39(December): 1177–1203.

Rauch, James E., and Joel Watson. 2003. "Are There Too Many Entrepreneurs? A Model of Client-Based Entrepreneurship." Working paper. San Diego, Calif.: University of California.

———. 2004. "Network Intermediaries in International Trade." *Journal of Economics and Management Strategy* 13(Spring): 69–93.

U.S. Census Bureau. 1997. *1992 Economic Census: Characteristics of Business Owners.* Washington: Government Printing Office.

Watts, Duncan J., and Steven H. Strogatz. 1998. "Collective Dynamics of 'Small-World' Networks." *Nature* 393(June 4): 440–42.

Wolf, Holger C. 2000. "Intranational Home Bias in Trade." *Review of Economics and Statistics* 82(4): 555–63.

INDEX

Boldface numbers refer to figures and tables